In Lady Liberty's Shadow

In Lady Liberty's Shadow

The Politics of Race and Immigration in New Jersey

11/30/17

Dearest Kris,

Hoping the book offers you new insights & inspiration!

Best,

Robyn Rodriguez

ROBYN MAGALIT RODRIGUEZ

Rutgers University Press

New Brunswick, Camden, and Newark, New Jersey, and London

978-0-8135-7009-9
978-0-8135-7008-2
978-0-8135-7010-5
978-0-8135-7371-7

Cataloging-in-Publication data is available from the Library of Congress.

A British Cataloging-in-Publication record for this book is available from the British Library.

∞ The paper used in this publication meets the requirements of the American National Standard for Information Sciences—Permanence of Paper for Printed Library Materials, ANSI Z39.48–1992.

www.rutgersuniversitypress.org

Manufactured in the United States of America

For migrants everywhere

Makibaka, huwag matakot (Struggle, don't be afraid)

Contents

Preface and Acknowledgments

I think of this book as my love letter to New Jersey, particularly immigrant New Jersey. It comes out of my work as an immigrant rights and antiracism scholar-activist and thus from a deep place of identification with and affection for the people I worked with, people who have made the state their home and yet are treated like outsiders. Even though there is much that I am critical about, I came to love a lot about New Jersey in the time that I lived and worked there. I loved its incredible diversity. Although I am an immigration scholar and a native Californian who grew up in what some scholars call a "majority-minority ethnoburb" like many of the communities I would get to know during my time on the East Coast, my home state simply does not possess the same degree of diversity that New Jersey does. People who identify as black or African American in New Jersey are just as likely to be recent immigrants from Africa or the Caribbean as they are to be people with long roots in the United States. People I thought of as white could be fluent in any number of Western and Eastern European languages and identify more as immigrants than as Americans. Not only could I easily find the cuisines of my childhood hometown of Union City, California (namely Filipino, Mexican, and Vietnamese food), but I also found myself discovering new tastes and cultural traditions I had not yet been exposed to. I got to know Coptic Egyptians and Russian Jews, Cypriots and Kenyans, and even a mixed-race Dominican Saudi Arabian.

Encountering such wonderfully amazing diversity, I was taken aback and rather disappointed by the fact that the state is so deeply segregated. My newly adopted town, Highland Park, a charming borough where many Rutgers faculty and graduate students live, has been lauded for its diversity.[1] Many of its residents are quite self-congratulatory about the diversity of the town, yet I quickly learned that it is a town divided. A mere two square miles and everyone (unless completely in denial) knows exactly where the white and black (or nonwhite) parts of town are. For the most part, you know that the north side is the "better," white area. The south side is okay, as long as you don't go farther than South Sixth Street. The "Triangle," along with the blocks from South Seventh and higher, pretty much constitutes the "ghetto": black, brown, working class, and immigrant. We lived on South Seventh by choice. I wanted my biracial, Filipino and South African son to live with people he could share a connection with. While one of my son's (white) friend's parents (they are immigrants from Russia) refused to let him come over because we lived in the "bad" part of town (it helped later, of course, when they learned I was a university professor), we loved where we lived. Our neighbors included a second-generation Costa Rican couple, an elderly African American couple with roots in the South, an immigrant family from Sierra Leone, and a "mixed" family: the wife was Puerto Rican and her husband Jewish. I think most of us lived on South Seventh because we were invested in diversity and we made active efforts to connect with one another despite the fact that the rest of our town lived very different and very separate lives. Maybe it's not totally coincidental that one of the most outspoken African American civil rights activists in the town's recent history, Vicky White, lived on our street.

My students told me similar stories about their towns. Although many of them came from a vast array of ethnic and racial backgrounds, they lived highly segregated lives. They knew very little about people whose ethnic or racial background they did not share or even about the towns neighboring the ones where they grew up. Those who lived in communities like the one I grew up in seemed to have far more cloistered existences than my own. Nearly all of my high school friends married or were partnered to people of a different racial/ethnic background. With few exceptions, that did not seem to be the case for the young New Jerseyans I met in my classes.

This book emerged, in part, out of my desire to gain understanding of the dynamics of race and immigration in my newly adopted state so that I could better connect with and teach my students. In order to get "insider" perspectives, I organized my undergraduate courses around the themes that now organize this book. I gave my students assignments that would help me better understand where they were coming from even as I was trying to get them to apply ideas we discussed in class to their everyday lives. I asked students to get census data on their communities and to research how immigration was being discussed and debated in their towns. In many cases, their work became data for this book. My undergraduates also assisted me in recruiting their friends and family members to participate as respondents for this project. Alongside the research that students in my classes conducted, through Rutgers's Aresty Research Center I recruited undergraduate research assistants who grew up in municipalities where some of the most heated and raucous debates about immigration were taking place (and that are the municipalities of focus in this book). I drew from their local knowledge to gain on-the-ground perspectives about those debates.

More important, this book is motivated by my work as a scholar-activist. In late 2005, I joined the faculty of Rutgers University as an assistant professor in the Department of Sociology. Having worked as an immigrant rights and antiracism activist for many years prior to moving to New Jersey, I was anxious to get involved in social justice work in my new state. I joined the New Jersey Civil Rights Defense Committee (NJCRDC), which works to end the detention of immigrants in New Jersey's county jails. Their campaign at the time was particularly focused on the Passaic County jail. Immigrant detainees wrote numerous letters to the group detailing the horrific conditions they faced. I assisted the NJCRDC in preparing a "shadow report" that we hoped would be read alongside and against the Department of Homeland Security's Office of Inspector General's report on immigrant detainee abuse in New Jersey's county jails, including but not limited to Passaic. Our report put the voices of immigrant detainees front and center. The county sheriff, Jerry Speziale, would later be the subject of federal investigation for abuses meted out to immigrant detainees under his watch. My involvement with the NJCRDC, however, would expose me to immigrant rights issues throughout the state, not just those in detention. Among the issues that intrigued and incited me most was the spate of anti-immigrant local ordinances targeting undocumented Latino immigrants being introduced, both successfully and unsuccessfully, in white communities around the state. These anti-immigrant local ordinances are a key focus of this book. My involvement in the immigrant rights movement in

New Jersey offers me a unique lens into the local politics of race and immigration as they play out in the state. I had the opportunity to get a close-up view of the ways immigrants as well as immigrant rights' activists define and redefine belonging in the face of forces exclusion. I've tried to do my best to do justice to the people whose lives I discuss in this book, and I've tried to write this book in a manner that is accessible to them as well as to my past, present, and future students.

In some ways, my motivation for writing this book has also been to serve as a counterpoint to conservative pundits who seem to dominate the immigration debate. In particular, I imagined my book as a direct response to Michelle Malkin's positions on immigration. Malkin is often featured in conservative news outlet Fox News's forums on immigration based on her books, in which she essentially calls for an end to Muslim immigration (a proposal reprised by Donald Trump recently) and even tries to justify Muslim immigrants' mass incarceration. She and I are polar opposites. Although we share an ethnic background—we are both Filipino American—our similarities end there. Unfortunately, we live in a society where people of color who are in the public eye are often treated as spokespeople for their entire race or ethnic group. I don't want people to think that Malkin speaks for all Filipinos. Of course, I don't either, however at least I can offer this book as an alternative perspective to hers. I don't know whether my book will get as wide a readership as she did (at least one of her books was a *New York Times* best seller) and I don't have direct access to major media outlets as she does, but I hope that people who do pick up this book come away from it not simply being more informed about immigration but moved to fight for just and humane immigration policy in their communities and at the national and global levels.

My research agenda has always been about unpacking structures of power within the context of neoliberal globalization. Specifically, I've always been interested in understanding the processes by which migrants are defined as belonging or not belonging in both the countries to which they move and their countries of origin. I've always wanted to understand how states, often in collusion with the global corporate elite (the so-called one percent), do the work of what one scholar calls "savage sorting," and most of all, I've always been committed to lifting up the inspirational examples of how people individually and collectively resist these processes.[2]

I have too many people to thank. All of the students who were enrolled in my race and immigration courses (after six years of teaching at Rutgers

University, they number in the hundreds if not thousands) have all, in their own ways, shaped my understandings in this book; however, I have to give special shout-outs to the ones who worked closely with me while I was researching this book in New Jersey, including Amanda Cannella, Elizabeth Dabbagh, Han Fang, Samantha Galarza, Lauren Krukowski, Michele Lam, Amytza Maskati, and Nismah Sarmast. I am deeply grateful for their wonderful insight and their commitment to this project. Thanks, too, to my graduate student Carolina Alonso, who takes some of the ideas that I only tentatively approach here and runs with them in ways I could have never anticipated. I'd like to think that our books will one day be read as companion pieces. To the members of the New Jersey Civil Rights Defense Committee, particularly Flavia Alaya and Marion Munk: you both have inspired me in ways few others have. You are my role models. You've taught me that radicalism is truly not something that dies with youth but is a fire that burns enduringly. I only hope in the years to come to have the same sort of energy and enthusiasm you have. I thank my former colleagues at Rutgers, including my colleagues at the Institute for Research on Women, the Eagleton Institute of Politics Immigration Group, and the Department of American Studies who read very early versions of my work. Zaire Dinzey Flores, Ulla Berg, Carlos Decena, Allan Isaac, Rick Lee, Ethel Brooks: your friendship is much valued and your company sorely missed. At UC Davis, I want to extend a special thanks to Trisha Barua, whose work on a different project proved to be just as crucial to this one. I appreciate, too, the work done by my undergraduate students, Miggy Cruz, Anna Lam, Niba Nirmal, Jessica Page, Eric Thai, and Johnny Wong, whose interest in my courses sparked their interest in my research. Thanks to my editor, Leslie Mitchner, for believing in this project and giving me the time and space to write when life took me through numerous ups and downs over the last few years. Thanks to my family, particularly Amado Canham, Joshua Vang, and Ezio Vang. This book is complete because of you. You inspire and support me in so many ways.

In Lady Liberty's Shadow

1

The Politics of Race and Immigration in the "Garden State"

New Jersey, USA

There is no icon more recognizable and most associated with the United States than the Statue of Liberty. If she represents a specific narrative about the country, it is that America is a nation of immigrants. An excerpt from Emma Lazarus's poem "The New Colossus," inscribed at Lady Liberty's base, is just as famous as the statue itself: "Give me your tired, your poor, Your huddled masses yearning to breathe free." Not far from the Liberty Island, where the Statue stands, was the site of one of the greatest flows of immigrants from Europe to the United States in the early twentieth century: Ellis Island. Between 1892 and 1954 more than twelve million people passed through it.[1]

The Statue of Liberty has long been associated with New York City and is among the top tourist sites for people visiting the Big Apple, yet what I came to learn only when I moved to New Jersey was this: the fastest and best way to get to the Statue of Liberty is not from New York. Both Ellis Island and Liberty Island are just a few hundred yards away from Jersey City, New Jersey. The two states battled for the right to claim Ellis Island

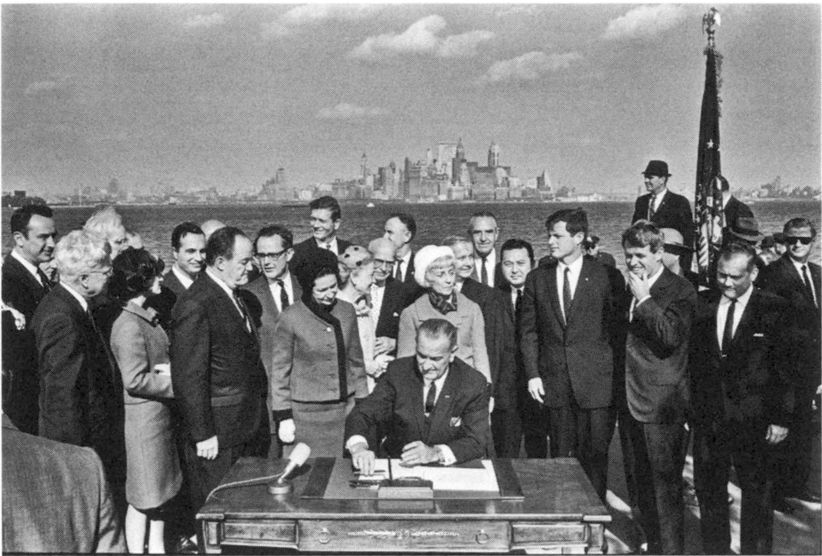

PHOTO 1. Signing of 1965 Immigration Act by President Lyndon Johnson at the base of the Statue of Liberty (http://www.migrationpolicy.org/sites/default/files/source_images/FE-1965Act-2015.jpg)

and thus to claim a central place in the grand American story of immigration. Perhaps surprising to most people, New Jersey eventually won.[2]

Though outsiders malign it, one-time residents deny being associated with it, and television shows like *The Sopranos, Boardwalk Empire, The Real Housewives of New Jersey*, or *The Jersey Shore* may further tarnish its image, New Jersey has long been the state where immigrants have started off their lives in pursuit of the American Dream—the dream of upward mobility; the dream of a "social order in which each man and each woman shall be able to attain to the fullest stature of which they are innately capable, and be recognized by others for what they are, regardless of the fortuitous circumstances of birth or position."[3] For most immigrants, if not most Americans, the American Dream is the dream of owning a house in the suburbs. That's the reason why paying close attention to how immigration is debated in the state's suburban municipalities allows us to better understand conflicts related to the issue on a national scale. New Jersey is important. What happens in that state matters for the rest of the country.

New Jersey was a first stop for a good majority of immigrants at the turn of the twentieth century. The Central Railroad of New Jersey Terminal served 70 percent of the immigrants processed at Ellis Island.[4] Now that most people get to the United States by plane, immigrants enter through the Newark Liberty International Airport instead. The state continues to offer immigrants their first taste of America. One can literally get a proverbial slice of apple pie at any one of the numerous diners that line its intricate and somewhat complicated network of highways.

According to the U.S. Census, not only do many new immigrants enter the United States through New Jersey, it is a place where they eventually settle. Since 1990, it has been one of the ten states with the greatest percentage of foreign-born residents. In 1990, 12.5 percent of the total U.S. foreign-born population made New Jersey home, putting it in fifth place of all fifty states. According to the Pew Center, as of 2012 New Jersey's overall ranking went up, and it became the state with the third highest foreign-born population with 21 percent of the total foreign-born population residing there compared to New York (ranked number two) at 22.7 percent and California (ranked number one) at 27 percent. These numbers are made more significant by the fact that since 1990, the number of immigrants in the state increased five times as much as the native-born population.[5] Today, one in five (a total of 1,900,000) New Jerseyans is foreign-born.[6]

New Jersey is diverse both racially and ethnically and has an exceptionally diverse pool of immigrants. It continues to attract European immigrants. In fact, 20 percent of the state's foreign-born population is European compared to the rest of the country (13 percent). It also attracts immigrants from throughout Africa.[7] As for Latinos and Asians, the two groups that are most associated with post-1965 immigration, they are also quite diverse.[8] The Latino population is made up of people from the Caribbean as well as south of the border. Indeed, the Dominican Republic counts as one of the top three immigrant-sending countries to the state. The Asian population, meanwhile, is composed of people from throughout the continent, with India and the Philippines being the top two Asian immigrant-sending countries.[9] The Latino and Asian populations are so numerous that today more than one in four New Jerseyans is either Latino or Asian.[10] According to the U.S. Bureau of the Census, Population Estimates Program, 19.3 percent of the New Jersey population in 2014 was Latino (compared with the United States as a whole at 17.4 percent). Asians, meanwhile, made up 9.4 percent (5.4 percent of the total U.S. population is Asian).

In terms of legal status, about half of New Jersey's immigrant population is naturalized citizens. The other half of the immigrant population is mostly made up of legal permanent residents.[11] The state is also home to a sizable undocumented immigrant population. New Jersey counts as one of the top six states that undocumented immigrants (mostly Mexican) call home. California, Texas, Florida, New York, and Illinois along with New Jersey are home to 60 percent of the total undocumented population.[12] New Jersey is also home to a large native-born, second-generation immigrant population.[13]

Paradoxically, some of the most anti-immigrant policies in the United States are being introduced in this diverse state so central to immigration history. What sets New Jersey apart is that these policies are being introduced at the municipal level, generally in the state's suburbs. Local ordinances to prohibit the settlement and facilitate the expulsion of undocumented immigrants have been introduced and in many cases passed across the state. These ordinances, for example, try to limit immigrants' opportunities to rent houses or apartments or lease businesses in different towns by requiring that they provide proof of legal residency in the United States to prospective landlords. Even long-term legal immigrants find themselves dealing with a range of restrictions on their lives. Despite the fact that one of the immigration stories we learn in elementary school is that the Pilgrims sailed from England to the New World to escape religious persecution, there are places in New Jersey where immigrants can't engage in their religious practices. In some towns, even when anti-immigrant local ordinances aren't being passed, politicians and local residents make it difficult for immigrants to live their lives. They try to prohibit the children of those suspected of being undocumented from attending local public schools (though these children have the constitutional right to do so). They even prevent immigrants from playing the sports they enjoy like soccer or cricket. Just when they thought they had achieved the American Dream in their suburban homes, immigrants instead experience an American nightmare. The paradox of anti-immigrant local politics in a historically immigrant state like New Jersey is what I try to understand in this book. How can we make sense of it? The answer lies partly in the changing dynamics of immigration policy and politics nationally after 9/11, but perhaps more significantly, it lies in the dynamic that predates 9/11: the suburban character of the state.

Anti-Immigrant Local Ordinances Nationally

Before I go through an extended discussion of immigration politics in New Jersey, I think it is important to put New Jersey in context. The subnational (that is, state, county, and municipal) introduction of anti-immigrant policies is actually a national trend, and it has spread in the years since 9/11. The federal government is responsible for regulating the exit and entry of foreign nationals and determining how long they can stay and whether they are eligible to settle permanently and become American citizens. However, subnational governmental units are increasingly trying to limit the settlement and facilitate the expulsion of immigrants from their borders.

With the passage of the especially draconian SB1070 in Arizona in 2010, scholars, journalists, and activists have begun to pay closer attention to state-level anti-immigrant laws. The state of Arizona made national headlines and elicited a heated national debate when its governor, Janet Brewer, signed a law that gave Arizona law enforcement personnel broad powers to detain anyone they suspected of being an undocumented immigrant. Supporters praised the state for taking a bold step toward more stringent immigration enforcement in the face of what they consider the federal government's failure to adequately secure the nation's borders. Opponents of the law, meanwhile, were outraged by what they believed to be legal sanction for racial profiling.[14] At this writing, provisions of the law, which opponents fear have a discriminatory effect on Latinos and other immigrants of color, have been affirmed by the courts.[15] According to one report, two years after SB1070 was passed, 164 "copy cat" bills were passed by state legislatures.[16] Immigrant rights activists claimed that Donald Trump's bid for the Republican presidential nomination inspired more state legislatures to introduce anti-immigrant laws in 2016.[17]

Although the data is not easy to come by, numerous experts, from scholars to journalists to activists, have attempted to document the introduction of anti-immigrant ordinances at the county or municipal level. Most of the recent research indicates that from 2000 to 2009 more than two hundred communities attempted to introduce anti-immigrant ordinances.[18] One study finds that between May 2006 and September 2007, a mere sixteen-month period, more than one hundred cities and counties in thirty states deliberated on anti-immigrant local ordinances. Some of these ordinances are explicitly anti-immigrant. In Farmer's Branch, Texas, for instance, the city council passed an ordinance that requires landlords to verify renters' legal status and prohibits them from renting property to those without legal authorization to reside in the United States.[19] Other ordinances, however, do not specifically target immigrants but disproportionately affect them. In fact, these ordinances may already be on the books but are more stringently enforced by communities that want to get rid of their immigrant populations. Political science professor Monica Varsanyi finds, for example, that some communities use public space and land-use ordinances to prohibit Latino day laborers from seeking employment.[20] Policies that limit immigrants' children from getting an adequate education by eliminating ESL (English as a second language) resources or that make English the official language of a locality can also be considered "back door" mechanisms for excluding immigrants from particular communities.[21] These policies may not target immigrants outright but are meant to keep immigrants out.

This is a national phenomenon, but there are clear geographic patterns of where and what type of immigration-related local ordinances are being introduced and passed across the country. Research by geographers tracked the spatial distribution of immigration-related local ordinances (a total of 370 in their study). It found that of the municipalities introducing anti-immigrant ordinances, 90 percent are located in the South (namely in the states of Alabama, Georgia, South Carolina, and North Carolina). This statistic contrasts dramatically from the statistic on municipalities in the West. The geographers note, "in some metropolitan regions, such as the San Francisco Bay Area, the majority of local policy responses are pro-immigration in nature, with cities such as San Francisco, Oakland, Richmond, Berkeley, and Santa Cruz all implementing inclusive policies."[22] Meanwhile, 57 percent and 74 percent of municipalities in the Midwest and the Northeast respectively have passed anti-immigrant ordinances.[23]

Immigration Enforcement after 9/11

Politicians and community members in areas where anti-immigrant ordinances are being introduced and in some cases implemented often frame their arguments in support of such policies as being a response to the federal government's failure to effectively enforce immigration law. Yet most scholars agree that the rise in anti-immigrant ordinances is in fact due to the *expansion* of the federal government's immigration enforcement efforts, especially after 9/11.

Since the destruction of New York's Twin Towers on September 11, 2011, the geography of and authority for immigration enforcement has dramatically changed in the United States. It has increasingly been characterized by interiorization and localization.[24] On one hand, immigration enforcement is not just geographically focused on the U.S.-Mexican border but is increasingly focused on the country's interior. On the other hand, even while greater numbers of federal immigration enforcement agents are working both at and within United States borders, state, county, and municipal police are also becoming increasingly involved in immigration enforcement. Immigration enforcement has become the key focus of the Department of Homeland Security (DHS), as over half of its budget is devoted to immigration law enforcement as well as border control.[25] Immigration enforcement agents can also rely on the resources of county and local police in their efforts. Consequently, undocumented immigrants are being apprehended, detained, and deported at an alarming rate throughout the United States. Immigrant detention is considered "the fastest-growing incarceration system in the United States."[26] Meanwhile, the current number of deportations is unprecedented in U.S. history, reaching a record high of 438,421 in 2013 during the Obama administration.[27] Around the time I started doing more focused research for this book in 2006–2007, New Jersey was home to an estimated 600,000 undocumented immigrants.[28] During this time, DHS's Immigration and Customs Enforcement (ICE) reported that it had deported a record number of people. In 2007 it had deported 3,339 people from the state, the following year in 2008, it had deported 4,194 people.[29]

The expansion and intensification of enforcement efforts is connected to increasingly dominant understandings of immigration and immigrants since 9/11. Immigration enforcement has become more "securitized," meaning that immigrants are not only thought of as economic, cultural, or social threats (that is, that they take away our jobs, they don't assimilate, or they are criminals) but as national security threats (they are potential terrorists).[30] The very renaming of the agency tasked with implementing immigration and citizenship law from the Immigration and Naturalization Service (INS) to the Department of Homeland Security (DHS) is suggestive of the securitization of immigration. What has emerged is what Nicholas De Genova calls the "Homeland Security State."[31] Immigration enforcement has become an "utterly decisive site in the ostensible War on Terror."[32] Arabs and Muslims were the target of specific forms of racial profiling by the DHS in the immediate aftermath of 9/11.[33] However, the Homeland Security State that has arisen since that time has ultimately targeted all non-white immigrants of a wide range of ethnic and religious backgrounds.

Enhanced enforcement apparatuses have disproportionately targeted Latino immigrant men.[34]

Federal authorities can draw on more locally based (state, county, and municipal) resources in their enforcement efforts. State, county, and municipal police involvement in immigration enforcement has emboldened state, county, and municipal governments to go a step further and take immigration matters into their own hands by introducing anti-immigrant policies. These policies cannot expel immigrants from the United States (that is something only the federal government can do), but they can certainly ensure that immigrants are effectively expelled from specific communities. Anti-immigrant ordinances forcibly displace immigrants by making it impossible for them to settle down and plant roots for their families. Even in places where neither formal nor informal (what Varsanyi calls "back door") anti-immigrant local ordinances are being introduced and passed, immigrants live in fear being apprehended, detained, and ultimately deported since local law enforcement officers are proactively turning undocumented (and sometimes legal) immigrants over to the feds. Moreover, there are armed militias of citizens like the Minute Men Project, who have taken it upon themselves to do the work of immigration enforcement.[35]

Although 9/11 was especially important in precipitating the consolidation of the Homeland Security State and the intensification of immigration enforcement through interiorization and localization, its origins can be traced to the immigration reform law of 1996, the Illegal Immigration Reform and Immigrant Responsibility Act (IIRIRA). IIRIRA expanded the criminal provisions of immigration law. For instance, the law increased the number of "aggravated felonies" for which all immigrants, both undocumented and legal, could be deported. When committed by immigrants, criminal misdemeanors like perjury, forgery, nonviolent theft, or drug offenses are considered "aggravated felonies." Immigrants convicted of such crimes are often subject to lengthy periods of detention after serving their sentences and are then removed from the United States. Even immigration violations have come to be defined as criminal offenses. Foreigners who overstay their visas or people who attempt to enter the United States without documentation, for example, are subject to both detention and deportation.

IIRIRA led to a convergence of the criminal justice system with immigration law. Consequently, federal immigration agents and local police began to cooperate more closely in the enforcement of immigration law.[36] Furthermore, IIRIRA created the 287(g) program, which enabled local police to be trained and certified as federal immigration enforcement agents.[37] The 287(g) program was created in 1996, but it wasn't until 9/11 and the laws that were passed in its wake that the 287(g) could really pick up steam. Since 9/11, formal federal-local cooperation related to immigration enforcement through the 287(g) has expanded. Informal cooperation has increased too. As I will discuss later in this book, several communities in New Jersey applied to the 287(g) program even though law enforcement in those places was already taking the initiative to work in close partnership with local ICE agents.

The proliferation of anti-immigrant local ordinances is a consequence of both pre- and post-9/11 immigration reforms. Scholars have identified other factors that can explain their increase since the mid-2000s, however. According to scholars from a range of disciplines, local ordinances tend to be introduced in communities where there is a greater than average increase in the immigrant population locally. Even though the overall population of Latinos and immigrants in these places may actually be quite small, the rate of the Latino and immigrant population's growth is higher than the national average. Indeed, these communities may not have high unemployment rates even though nativists who live in them might argue that immigrants "take away jobs."[38] Some political scientists are less convinced that demographic change is the best explanation for why anti-immigrant or what can also be described as restrictionist local ordinances are being passed. They attribute the trend instead to the partisan composition of a community (that is, the numbers of Republicans versus Democrats) and the extent to which immigration has been politicized locally. Municipalities in Republican areas are nearly twice and likely to introduce anti-immigrant local ordinances than those in Democratic areas.[39]

What is happening in New Jersey, however, can't be fully understood through these explanations. New Jersey is a northern state. It is racially diverse and it has long been an immigrant gateway for people from all around the world. Yet, anti-immigrant ordinances are being passed in different communities. At the same time, Republicans and Democrats alike champion these ordinances. So why is it happening here? I argue that anti-immigrant local ordinances are also a consequence of the history, economy, political structure, and most importantly the culture of suburbs where, not coincidentally, most anti-immigrant local ordinances are being passed.[40]

The suburb has long been imagined as the place where the "American way of life" or what many think of as the American Dream is lived out. To own a house in the suburbs is to have made it in America, since upward social mobility is an important hallmark of living out the dream. To be a suburbanite is, in many ways, to be truly, authentically "American." In other words, suburban living marks the achievement of American cultural citizenship in the popular imagination.[41] And the popular imagination is an incredibly powerful social fact. The suburban imaginary of the "home with the white picket fence" is an image that deeply shapes people's identities and aspirations in our country. Social scientists Caroline Brettell and Faith Nibbs argue that the passage of anti-immigrant local ordinances "is at its core a reflection of a debate about and anxiety over American identity—how it is defined and how it is changing."[42] Although they make this argument based on their research in Farmers Branch, a Texas suburb they studied, I believe it's just as applicable to the suburbs of New Jersey. At the heart of American identity or the "American way of life" is a middle-class lifestyle characterized by home ownership. I believe suburban citizens support anti-immigrant ordinances because they think immigrants threaten their lifestyles. This fear is one they experience in profoundly deep ways. It is a fear they feel most acutely not at work, not at school, but *at home*. Suburbanites draw on whatever tools are at their disposal to safeguard the borders of their communities, and among the main tools they use is their municipal government.

Because it is both an immigrant state and a suburban state, there is probably no place better than New Jersey that can help us make sense of anti-immigrant local ordinances nationally. It must be underscored, moreover, that the logic of antiblackness has perniciously and persistently shaped local, particularly suburban, institutions and imaginaries in the United States. State and nonstate actors have played a critical role in ensuring that suburbs stay and are imagined as white. The tools that have long been used to keep blacks out of the suburbs are being used to keep immigrants out today. This is a point that I believe has often been missed in other analyses of anti-immigrant suburban policies and politics. In the next section, I provide a history of the suburb starting from the mid-twentieth century, when mass suburbanization first took place. I then turn to an examination of how neoliberal reforms since the 1980s and into the twenty-first century have shaped suburban structures and institutions nationally. I end with an examination of suburban imaginaries. Throughout the section I am especially attentive to the antiblack logics that shape suburban formation and the ways they inform policies targeting immigrants of color.

History of the Suburb

New Jersey is known as the Garden State and I think it most aptly describes New Jersey's highly suburban character.[43] Long before the Turnpike was built and most people in New Jersey would identify their communities based on which exit they live off of (I was an Exit 9 for a few years myself), the state has served as a suburb for New York City as well as Philadelphia. It was often described as a "barrel tapped at both ends." As new forms of transport developed linking New York and Philadelphia to New Jersey, new suburbs cropped up throughout the state. With the development and expansion of the ferry system into and out of New York in the decades preceding the Civil War, suburban development and expansion followed. Brooklyn may have been New York City's first "ferry suburb," but parts of New Jersey followed soon after.[44] New Yorkers crossed the Hudson River by ferry to Hoboken and Jersey City.[45] Residents of the City of Brotherly Love (Philadelphia) would cross to Camden, New Jersey.[46] As rail transport expanded, so too did the possibility of commuting, and new suburbs proliferated. Jersey City was not only a hub for ferries, but by the mid-nineteenth century it was on a major railroad route to the suburbs.[47] When automobile transport outpaced other forms of transportation, it further facilitated the growth of New Jersey's suburbs. These suburbs, just like the cars that connected them to the cities, were increasingly accessible to a broader swath of society rather than just the elites. As cars helped facilitate physical mobility within the state, they could mean upward social mobility for New Jerseyans.[48]

New Jersey has been an important site for suburban experimentation for the nation for a very long time. It is in New Jersey where the templates for different versions of suburban life were originally constructed. Llewellyn Park, New Jersey, was one of several experiments in suburban design during the mid-nineteenth century. According to the historian Kenneth Jackson, it was among the developments to "set the sociological and architectural pattern for hundreds of communities that developed in the twentieth century."[49] The suburban community of Short Hills, New Jersey, also defined the "spatial script" of future suburbs. "[O]rder/efficiency, daily exposure to

34 W THE PHILADELPHIA INQUIRER, SUNDAY MORNING, JULY 13, 1958

A DIRECT LINE TO AD-TAKER—RITTENHOUSE 6-5000

NEW JERSEY REAL ESTATE FOR SALE

House A: Price $11,990, Down Payment $400, Monthly Carrying Charge $87

House B: Price $12,490, Down Payment $400, Monthly Carrying Charge $90

House C: Price $14,490, Down Payment $600, Monthly Carrying Charge $100

THIS IS LEVITTOWN, NEW JERSEY

FOREWORD—Just as the first was good, and the second better, the third Levittown will be the best of all. Located just 30 minutes from City Hall in Philadelphia, 20 minutes from Trenton or Camden, right on U. S. 130 just 2 miles south of Burlington, this newest of the world's most famous communities offers the utmost in suburban living.

No advertisement can be a substitute for seeing with one's own eyes. And so all this can do is give a few facts and figures to supplement a personal visit.

THE COMMUNITY—Different from any of the others. Levittown is really a collection of self-contained residential parks. Center of each park's cultural and social activities is the school, with its swimming pool (for adults as well as children), its recreational facilities, and its community hall.

Instead of one vast community house for all of Levittown, there is a smaller one for *each* neighborhood. Even roads have a meaning all their own. Each begins with the initial letter of the neighborhood. For instance, in Somerset Park each road name begins with an S; in Buckingham Park with a B; etc.

Houses of worship of all denominations are located throughout the community. Land has been donated by the builders to all major faiths for sufficiently sized structures as well as adequate off-street parking.

THE HOUSES—Three distinctly different houses are now being exhibited. In this advertisement you will see prices, terms, and pictures, but you should see the actual houses themselves, furnished charmingly by Hardwick & Magee of Philadelphia, under the expert direction of Alice D. Kenny, Interior Decorator.

These three houses are being intermingled side by side rather than being built in separate groups. In other words, no longer do we have a section of "A" houses, another of "B" houses, and a third of "C" houses. Instead we are building all types in the same neighborhood to provide greater variety and a more pleasing appearance.

Plots are a 65 by 100 minimum, although a great many are larger. There is no extra charge for larger plots but obviously they must go on a first-come-first-served basis. Corners are at least 80 by 100 and are priced $500 additional. A few locations—particularly suited for doctors, dentists, or professional people—are priced higher.

SCHOOLS AND SWIMMING POOLS—Plans call for schools, swimming pools, playgrounds, athletic fields, etc., serving all the separate neighborhoods of Levittown. Right at the very start construction of these facilities is being timed for completion with the houses.

The first school, in Somerset Park, is scheduled for use this Fall. This school, as well as a great many others, is being built by us at our expense and will be donated to the community. The eventual savings in school taxes should be enormous. This is one community that, unlike almost every other place in the United States, will be practically debt-free as far as its school system is concerned.

The same applies to the swimming pool, which will be ready next summer and all the other pools we expect to build. These are not privately owned facilities; they will all be owned by the municipality.

SHOPPING—A large regional shopping center is in the course of construction. At this writing Sears, Roebuck & Co., and Food Fair have already agreed to operate huge stores. Plans call for a bank, post office, another department store, drug stores, and dozens of others of all kinds.

Architecturally, we think this center will be the most beautiful of its kind in the country. Special consultants have been engaged on lighting, landscaping, parking, etc. We know you'll like it.

As the community grows, a small neighborhood shopping center or two will be built in the interior of Levittown.

A separate company has been especially created to do this work, and it leaves us free to concentrate on building the finest homes for the money that the industry knows.

SOME EXTRAS FOR NOTHING—Every house includes a General Electric refrigerator, automatic washer, electric range and oven, screens for all windows, and complete landscaping. In addition, the "C" house includes a General Electric dryer.

Total settlement charges are only $10, and even that is included in the down payments shown above.

THE LEVITTOWN EXHIBIT—On Route 130 there are six display houses plus the Levittown Exhibit Building. Not only can you see the houses themselves, but you can see the component parts that are included in them as well as a display of additional optional equipment. Courteous representatives are on hand to answer your questions and to clarify any points that you may raise. This Exhibit and the display houses are open every day until 9 P.M.

***Our Exhibit Building and six exhibit houses*—priced from $11,990 to $13,990—are open seven days a week until 9 P. M. Drive over and take a look. You're always welcome.**

Levitt and Sons
INCORPORATED
Route 130 · Levittown, New Jersey · Phone TRiangle 7-1100

TO LEVITTOWN, NEW JERSEY

From Philadelphia: Cross Benjamin Franklin Bridge and continue on Admiral Wilson Boulevard to Route 130. Turn left (north) on Route 130, thirteen miles to Exhibit.

From South Philadelphia: Cross Walt Whitman Bridge and drive north on Route 130 to Airport Circle. Continue on Route 130, thirteen miles to Exhibit.

From North Philadelphia: Cross Tacony-Palmyra Bridge to Route 130. Turn left (north) on Route 130, eight miles to Exhibit.

From Camden: Drive out Admiral Wilson Boulevard to Airport Circle. Turn north on Route 130, thirteen miles to Exhibit.

From Ft. Dix and McGuire Air Force Base: Take any road to Burlington and Route 130. Turn left (south) on Route 130, three miles to Exhibit.

PHOTO 2. Levittown brochure (http://philadelphiaencyclopedia.org/wp-content/uploads/2015/11/LevittownNJadvert.png) nature's beauty and goodness, use of technology to improve the resident's quality of life, aesthetic quality, and the values of individuality, family, and community" constituted the ethos of idealized suburban life.[50] Another model of suburban life that emerged in New Jersey was the country club of the late nineteenth and early twentieth centuries. "Country clubs represented a new method of making spacious fields and restful shade available to the city resident while adding a few social amenities to suburban life."[51] The country club would soon become a central feature to some suburban communities to the extent that in places like Morristown, New Jersey, membership in the country club was a requirement for residence in particular areas of town. By the mid-twentieth century the state became perhaps the most significant site for post–World War II suburban development, best exemplified by the construction of Levittowns in the 1950s. Levittown in New Jersey, like its counterparts in New York and Pennsylvania, offered the opportunity for home ownership not just to middle-class families, but, perhaps more important, it offered ownership of affordable homes to the working class. The postwar United States was experiencing a massive housing shortage. In addition, the parents of what became the "baby boom" generation demanded space.

The federal government played a crucial role in forming the suburbs both before and after World War II. In the wake of the economic collapse of 1929, one of President Franklin D. Roosevelt's New Deal initiatives was the rebuilding of the construction industry with the signing of the National Housing Act of 1934 and the setting up of the Federal Housing Administration (FHA) as a result of the act. The act established a public housing program as well as stimulated private housing development, particularly a market for moderately priced housing, through a program offering low-interest, long-term mortgages. Banks that offered mortgages in compliance with the FHA's terms were offered protection against losses on defaults. It was in New Jersey's Pompton Plains that the first FHA-insured mortgage for a house was approved.[52]

In the immediate post–World War II period, the suburbs would become accessible to more Americans as members of the working class could now become homeowners. In addition to FHA mortgages, the Veterans Administration (VA) created a veteran's mortgage guarantee program in 1944 for returning soldiers.[53] Consequently, the postwar period was a time when suburbs in the United States, including New Jersey, would experience accelerated growth. Mortgage programs like those offered through the FHA and VA made the dream of home ownership a very real possibility for a much broader swath of the American public, especially as suburban developers like William Levitt, the mastermind of Levittown, created homes targeted at working-class families. Levitt famously stated, "No man who own his own house and lot is a communist . . . he has much to do."[54] Indeed, suburbanization and the domestic prosperity that mass home ownership signified were important weapons in the Cold War ideological arsenal. They proved that American-style capitalism, an economic system fueled by a suburban lifestyle and a consumer culture, were superior to Soviet communism. Urban planning professor Robert A. Beauregard contends that it was in during the Cold War that American national identity came to be fundamentally defined as suburban.[55] Ironically, the federal government heavily subsidized business interests and other private sector actors. Groups like the National Association of Real Estate Boards lobbied for mortgage loan insurance from the FHA and the VA as well as tax relief for homeowners, which they were subsequently given.[56] These programs supported the growth of tract-home suburbs like Levittown.

If the federal government, along with real estate developers, realtors, bankers, and other interests, helped more and more Americans in the immediate postwar period to achieve the American Dream of home ownership, it was helping only white Americans. Indeed, Roosevelt's New Deal was in essence a form of affirmative action for whites.[57] State and business entities were the chief architects in ensuring that the suburbs would be white. As American Studies scholar George Lipsitz puts it, "By channeling loans away from older innercity neighborhoods and toward white home buyers moving into segregated suburbs, the FHA and private lenders after World War II aided and abetted segregation in U.S. residential neighborhoods."[58] The suburbs were always a respite from the city, particularly for the economically privileged, who could enjoy a higher standard of living away from the social ills associated with the poor.[59] After World War II, the state and the private sector played a crucial role in producing and reproducing racial as well as class segregation. They helped to ensure that suburbs were not just middle-class (or aspiring-to-middle-class working-class) spaces but "white spaces."[60] For example, statistics from 1950 based on mortgaged properties in the New York–Northeastern New Jersey Metropolitan Area indicate that of 449,458 mortgaged properties where the owner's race was reported, "nonwhites" owned only 1.7 percent of them.[61] The state and private sector facilitated "white flight" from different cities in the northern United States to the suburbs. For every black arrival in different urban localities, there were two white departures.[62] While the FHA (and its private sector partners) fostered the growth of white suburbs in the postwar period, black urban communities were completely left out. For example, in 1966, neither Camden, New Jersey, nor Paterson, New Jersey, received FHA funds.[63] Suburban spaces were constructed outside and against the cities like Camden, Paterson, Newark, and other New Jersey cities that had become populated more and more by blacks as part of the "Great Migration" of six million African Americans from the rural South to urban centers in the North and beyond. Although many probably believed that they were leaving Jim Crow behind when they moved north, this was not the case.

Suburbs became the site for the consolidation of a white identity. By benefiting from and participating in the exclusion of African Americans from the suburbs, white ethnics could share common cause and develop a greater sense of solidarity and unity across their differences.[64] This is in sharp contrast to the fractiousness and division that characterized relations between European immigrants and their descendants at the turn of the twentieth century. For example, novelist Henry James's observations of immigrants as they disembarked at Ellis Island were marked by anxieties about southern Europeans' difference from their Anglo predecessors.[65] At the same time, the suburb is the site where the "wages of whiteness" are to be enjoyed, that is, where the status and privilege associated with whiteness are concentrated.[66] Of course, although the corporate (generally white) elite has always been the real profiteer when it comes to the expansion of suburbs, suburban lifestyles allow previously marginalized and working-class whites to feel as if they are doing well because they have the "security of knowing that there would always be a group below them, that there was a floor below which they could not fall."[67]

The FHA and the private sector facilitated black exclusion through restrictive racial covenants.[68] These covenants justified racial segregation on the notion that nonwhite groups, particularly African Americans, would spoil the character of a neighborhood and their presence would result in decreased property values. The FHA would extend loans to prospective white homeowners in areas where racial covenants were in place. This was true in places like Levittown.[69] Not only did restrictive racial covenants define who could and could not reside in specific neighborhoods, covenants firmly linked "white racial status with property."[70] In other words, to be white also meant being a property owner. Until 1948, when the Supreme Court ruled against them, racially restrictive covenants were considered constitutionally sound because it was believed that they were private contracts. Property owners could do as they please with their property, including not selling to specific racialized groups.[71]

Racial covenants, significantly, have a history that predates their use by the FHA during the height of suburbanization. They appeared in the late nineteenth century and though they generally targeted blacks, they were also applied against other "nonwhite" immigrant groups including the Chinese, Japanese, and Mexicans.[72] Also, covenant campaigns were initially launched in cities.[73] They were passed in many northern cities in the 1920s in response to demographic changes resulting from the influx of African American migrants from the South, labor market competition, and demands for housing that at times ignited interracial violence. Racially restrictive covenants were an institutional response thought to contain racial tensions.[74]

The American Dream that suburban life is supposed to represent rests on a specific racialized social and spatial order. In other words, the very idea that so centrally organizes how people in the United States think about themselves and the lives they aspire to is at its very core an exclusive one. The suburb is a highly racialized space. It is, as sociologist James W. Loewen describes it, "all-white on purpose."[75] The formation of the suburbs is done through various kinds of racialized spatial practices. These practices ultimately delimit how different racialized groups can and cannot enjoy the privileges and opportunities of citizenship in the spaces—the communities—where they live. As George Lipsitz argues, "People of different races in the United States are relegated to different physical locations by housing and lending discrimination, by school district boundaries, by policing practices, by zoning regulations, and by the design of transit systems."[76] While the federal government has played a crucial role racializing suburban space, municipal governments, as this quotation suggests, are equally involved in the process. School district boundaries, policing practices, zoning regulation, transit design, and other policies are racialized spatial practices that are generally determined by local governments.

Perhaps one of the most significant ways the suburbs have been able to secure racial exclusion is through the process of municipal incorporation. In the nineteenth century, well before the advent of mass suburbanization in the post–World War II period, states were giving suburbs much leeway in terms of initiating municipal incorporation, thereby giving them a great degree of autonomy in shaping community life. Incorporation could, among other benefits, ensure that public services could be delivered exclusively to suburban residents.[77] In 1800 New Jersey was largely incorporated, but the state government allowed township fragments to split off from other areas to escape increasing taxes or social ills so that the state would not have to address those issues itself.[78] By the early twentieth century, Bergen County was the site of fifty municipal governments. These suburban municipalities formed to preserve local schools and thereby avert "consolidation with school districts with weaker tax bases."[79] By the end of the 1920s, through master plans and zoning policies, suburbs could protect themselves from the "infiltration" of low-income urban workers (presumably African Americans and white ethnic immigrants).[80] In other words, municipal incorporation became a mechanism by which suburban citizens could safeguard their rights and privileges. The crucial point here is that the early history of the suburbs in New Jersey is premised on an escape from the city, a degree of exclusivity, and the enjoyment of the rights and privileges of citizenship maintained by municipal governments.

New Jersey has an unusually large number of municipalities.[81] In fact, it has more local governments per square mile than all the states of the union.[82] New Jersey's system of "home rule" (that is, the dominance of municipal governance) has remained a consistently important aspect of suburban life. Hence, once racial covenants were ultimately made illegal, local governments had other policy mechanisms at hand to keep African Americans out of their communities. Although these policies deployed race-neutral language, they had the same sort of effect as racially restrictive covenants before them: to exclude blacks. Exclusionary zoning practices have been "the chief weapon in the suburban arsenal and has effectively rebuffed invasion by unwanted peoples and uses."[83] One way that municipalities use zoning policies to exclude "unwanted peoples" is by raising the minimum lot size requirements for prospective real estate developers. In the sixteen New Jersey counties where new suburban developments were being built in 1966, for example, a majority of land was zoned for lots of a minimum of one acre. Moreover, municipalities were imposing minimum square footage requirements for the houses being built on those lots. Not surprisingly, because the houses and the lots they sit on were large, people who could only afford a small house on a small lot were completely shut out.[84]

Exclusionary zoning policies did not go uncontested. In the early 1970s, long-time black residents of Mount Laurel, New Jersey, requested that their local government support low-income housing initiatives that would allow them to become homeowners. They were met, however, with an emphatic rejection from municipal leaders. Mount Laurel's mayor, Bill Haines, refused to support plans that might threaten his own vision of making Mount Laurel a rich, white community with little room for poor blacks. If they could not live in the town, then they would simply have to move out. According to David Kirp, John Dwyer, and Larry Rosenthal, the "power of law would be used not to promote the idea of community but instead to enshrine exclusivity by walling out the poor."[85] Zoning laws, in other words, could operate as figurative walls defining the boundaries and borders of a community. Though the New Jersey Supreme Court ultimately sided with Mount Laurel's African American plaintiffs in deeming the municipal government's laws a violation of the state constitution, after numerous judicial and legislative battles, exclusionary zoning practices remain virtually unchanged.[86] If zoning policies "wall out" poor African Americans, as I will discuss in the next chapter, other sets of municipal ordinances "wall out" working-class immigrants of color.

While various municipal policies in the suburbs kept blacks out, municipal policies in cities locked them into only the poorest parts. For example, in Camden, the city closest to Mount Laurel, "redlining" practices, that is, discriminatory zoning practices that demarcate the areas where banks would not lend to prospective buyers, limited blacks' ability to purchase homes in the "better" parts of town. Not being able to buy homes in those areas of the city contributed to racial segregation and therefore limited access to good schools, which only perpetuated limited social mobility among African Americans.[87]

If the process of suburbanization accelerated in the post–World War II years, it was hastened by the race rebellions in Newark and other cities in New Jersey in the late 1960s and early 1970s. In the years leading up to the 1967 Newark rebellion, historian Brad Tuttle argues, the city "stood out for the extraordinary speed, depth, and viciousness of its decline."[88] It is important to emphasize, however, that suburbanization is what ultimately produced the conditions of severe decline in urban centers that African Americans were contesting. Processes of suburbanization accelerated deindustrialization and blight in urban areas at the same time that it confined poor blacks to the worst parts of cities, thus resulting in the growing disenfranchisement and disenchantment of African Americans.

Notably, race "riots" were not confined to cities in the state of New Jersey but took place even in suburban communities, which led whites to flee these suburbs for others.[89] Historians Thomas J. Sugrue and Andrew P. Goodman, citing the Kerner Report, note that uprisings took place in several small cities and suburbs in New Jersey, including Plainfield, Rahway, Livingston, Elizabeth, East Orange, Paterson, Englewood, Irvington, Jersey City, and Montclair in the late 1960s.[90] Their case study of black uprisings in Plainfield offers a close look at the ways the politics of exclusion in and from the suburbs gave rise to growing discontent among the African American community there. 1960s Plainfield was promoted by its boosters as a prosperous "bedroom community." The so-called "Queen City," with its upscale downtown area, had become a regional shopping hub. Though predominantly white, Plainfield had a sizable African American community. In fact, by 1960 African Americans made up 40 percent of the population. In part, its presence was a response to wealthy suburbanites' demand for service labor. However, the African American presence in Plainfield was also due to the town's diverse economic base, which included a small-industrial core. Yet exclusions from access to affordable housing and decent schools as well as tense relations with the police made it difficult for Plainfield African Americans to live the suburban lifestyles of their white counterparts. As the industrial decline that hit bigger cities like Newark took its toll, the plight of the community in suburbs like Plainfield would only worsen. When Plainfield's municipal government failed to address concerns raised by reform-minded organizations like the National Association for the Advancement of Colored People (NAACP), Plainfield's African American youth drew inspiration from the Black Power movement and took more militant measures to capture the attention of local officials. Tensions between local black youth and local police exploded into a violent confrontation in the summer of 1967. Though focused on Plainfield, Sugrue and Goodman make it very clear that Plainfield was not an isolated case. For the purposes of my study, their examination of Plainfield is illustrative of the sorts of struggles around race and membership that have long plagued the suburbs in New Jersey and beyond and that continue to this day.

Exclusion from the suburbs and confinement to the poorest parts of cities is not simply about being excluded from the opportunity to buy a home. To be excluded from the suburbs and from home ownership has huge impacts for people's economic well-being. The wealth people can amass from buying a home in the suburbs has impacts for themselves and for the generations that follow them. Wealth, according to sociology and anthropology professor Heather Beth Johnson, "often originates from family financial assistance, gifts, or inheritance and becomes a way to create opportunities, shape life experiences and ensure the future. Family wealth can propel a family's mobility, access important resources for the next generation and cultivate a sense of security."[91] Intergenerational transfers of wealth, moreover, allow "parents the capacity to provide stable home ownership, safer neighborhood experiences, better educational experiences and more expansive opportunities for their children."[92] Whites have been able to amass wealth and therefore secure their economic and overall well-being because they have been able to buy homes in the suburbs. Being shut out of the suburbs, therefore, has made it impossible for most blacks and to some extent most people of color to amass wealth and the privileges that come with it. Access to the suburbs, even if one is not a homeowner, affords many opportunities that are simply not available in cities. Perhaps the most important of these is the opportunity to secure a good education.

Educational access has long been at the core of citizenship struggles in the United States. When integration became the political solution to educational inequalities due to racial segregation, suburbanites fought aggressively and sometimes viciously to maintain their racialized and classed privilege whether it was to violently resist school integration though busing or by instituting home-rule and other kinds of policies that would keep educational resources local. The landmark 1954 Supreme Court case *Brown v. Board of Education* was supposed to have signaled the end of school segregation, but it didn't. On one hand, desegregation efforts were often resisted. On the other hand, racialized segregation secured through the economic and political structure of the suburbs has allowed racialized inequities in public education to persist.[93] Whites have had the privilege of moving to suburbs for better schools in ways that blacks have not. Indeed, suburban homeownership is seen as having earned people the right to better schools.[94] For many decades in New Jersey, home rule ensured that public schools derived their budgets primarily from local property tax dollars.[95] Hence, better schools were located in richer, white communities.[96] Research by the Civil Rights Project at UCLA (CRP) and the Institute on Education Law and Policy at Rutgers University-Newark (IELP) published in 2013 finds that this continues to be the case. According to their findings, "the racial and socioeconomic divide in New Jersey public education continues to grow unabated. While the CRP report documents the jump from 1989 to 2010 in the number of "apartheid" schools in New Jersey, the IELP study shows that extreme isolation of poor students of color is concentrated in mostly urban areas."[97] Indeed, several studies based on both survey and qualitative research find that white families often avoid schools that are integrated or have significant numbers of students of color. As Heather Beth Johnson puts it, "Survey research confirms that white families often purposefully and conscientiously avoid residential areas with integrated or minority-populated schools."[98] Even if white families do not necessarily try to avoid diverse school districts, they "genuinely saw whiter neighborhoods as offering better schools for their children."[99]

As if their municipal governments were not enough, suburban citizens play an active role in ensuring that suburbs stay white. One of the ways they can do so is through homeowners associations. Indeed, homeowners associations, which often govern neighborhood life in master planned and gated communities, sometimes take on the role of local governments (for example, trash collection, provision of recreation space, security) and give suburbs a kind of "small town" feel.[100] Historically, however, homeowners associations have been responsible for ensuring the exclusion of blacks through, among other tactics, boycotting realtors who did not demonstrate a firm commitment to segregation.[101] With the preservation of property values being their top priority, homeowners associations can introduce restrictive covenants, even if they do not explicitly exclude specific racial or ethnic groups, by strictly defining their communities' socioeconomic composition and in so doing produce all- or nearly all-white populations.[102] I did not necessarily find homeowners associations to be behind the anti-immigrant local ordinances in the cases I study in New Jersey, nevertheless is it important to map out the various ways that suburban citizens in the United States can and do play a role in keeping suburbs segregated.

Gated communities, which are numerous in New Jersey, perhaps most starkly exemplify the racial and class exclusivity that generally characterizes suburban life in America. While it may be argued that the "fortress mentality" residents in these communities have is unique, I think their desire to live behind physical walls is not much different from the desires of other suburban residents who construct virtual walls around their communities. In her ethnographic study of residents in gated communities, anthropologist Setha Low finds that when asked how they feel about where they live, residents answer that they feel "secure." This sense of security and comfort is at once psychological, physical, and social. This latter point is important. According to Low, living in a gated community "provides a haven in a socially and culturally diverse world, offering a protected setting for their upper-middle class," and I would add white, "lifestyle."[103] Even when a community is not actually fully enclosed by walls and secured by guards, gates and fences are frequently used as a decorative feature in many New Jersey housing developments. This may suggest a desire on the part of developers (one homeowners may also have) to demarcate a community as "exclusive" in any number of senses. As sociologist Zaire Zeni Dinzey Flores, an expert on the phenomenon of the use of gates in private and public housing, puts it, "Historically, gates have assumed an enemy inside, an enemy outside. In elite neighborhoods, retirement communities, resorts, and even on military bases and bulwarks, gates have been intended to create a safe and protected sanctuary. In prisons, as in neighborhoods, and even in schools, gates are a mechanism of control and discipline of those inside."[104] Hence, when the gates fail, the police step in. When African Americans can't just be locked out of the suburbs or locked in place in the cities, they are locked up (that is, incarcerated), and, as has recently captured the public's attention (though many of us concerned about antiblackness have known this to be true for a long, long time), they are simply snuffed out. What I have in mind here, for example, is the murder of Trayvon Martin in 2012 in a gated suburban community in Florida by a member of the neighborhood watch.[105]

I haven't spoken to this issue enough thus far, but the fact is municipal policies aimed at excluding blacks have always required mechanisms of policing and enforcement. Law enforcement officers generally do this policing, but sometimes vigilantes do it. As sociologist James W. Loewen demonstrates in his sweeping study of "sundown" towns and suburbs defined as "any organized jurisdiction that for decades kept African Americans or other groups from living in it and was thus 'all-white' on purpose," both citizen and police violence have always been necessary to keeping communities white "on purpose."[106] I think of this as a kind of localized border patrol. Perhaps it's not surprising that it was in New Jersey that the very notion of "racial profiling" was first given national attention.[107]

Ironically, although white suburbanites often envision their communities as having been built by hardworking, self-reliant individuals, the fact is their communities are a result of active state engineering. They are "white on purpose." The suburbs were a response to the changing racial landscapes of urban centers that had experienced the Great Migration of African Americans from the South. They were not only a place to secure housing for the emergent middle class after World War II, but also the consolidation of whiteness among the descendants of European immigrants who constituted the other "great migration" of the early twentieth century. The Irish, Italians, and others who once figured outside the boundaries of what was properly white and "American" could literally claim a new place as Americans through a home in the suburbs. In other words, the suburbs became a place where these groups could become authentically and genuinely white.

Processes of suburbanization continue apace and they continue to exacerbate racial segregation.[108] Even when racial covenants were dropped, New Jersey suburban municipalities used legal and other mechanisms to exclude African Americans. These instruments of exclusion form the backdrop to contemporary anti-immigrant, local ordinances and other kinds of racist and xenophobic politics in New Jersey's suburbs. It is crucial to situate what has been happening more recently in New Jersey within this broader historical context. However, what is distinctive about race and suburban politics with respect to immigration today has to do with more recent trends, particularly the increasing hegemony of neoliberalism.

The Political Economy of Neoliberalism and Its Casualties

As I discussed earlier, anti-immigrant local ordinances have intensified in the wake of 9/11 immigration policy but are deeply connected to mid-1990s immigration reform as manifested in IIRIRA. There have been longstanding concerns about immigrants' use of public goods and services like welfare programs, schools, hospitals, and the like in local communities. While scholars rightfully connect today's anti-immigrant local ordinances to IIRIRA, they often miss the fact that IIRAIRA was passed alongside antiblack welfare reforms, yet some of the same arguments used to justify attacks on programs meant to ameliorate poverty in the African American community were used to justify attacks on programs beneficial to immigrants.

The rise of "Reaganomics," the economic policies implemented by President Ronald Reagan in the 1980s, marked the beginning of aggressive attacks on public goods and services including but not limited to welfare.[109]

Reaganomics are informed by neoliberal ideology.[110] "Neoliberalism" refers to the logic that individuals, not the government, are expected to assume primary if not sole responsibility for themselves and their families' livelihood and security. Following neoliberal logic, it is expected that good American citizens will not to turn to the government for support during difficult periods of their lives. As journalist Matt Taibbi puts it, in his 2014 book, "[I]n our new corporate dystopia the inner secret crime is need, particularly financial need. . . . The more you need, the more you owe, the fewer rights you have. Conversely, the less you need, the more you have, the more of a free citizen you get to be."[111] The "new corporate dystopia" he refers to is neoliberalism. Though Taibbi describes it as "new" it can trace its beginnings to the Reagan era. Under Reagan's leadership, the social safety net established in the New Deal and Great Society eras was systematically dismantled. In sum, "the ideal of the social welfare state, dominant in some guise for much of the twentieth century in the United States, has generally yielded to that of the neoliberal state."[112]

A key constituency that promoted Reagan into the presidency were suburban whites who not only sought to defend the "political integrity and fiscal autonomy of white suburban areas" but also devised "strategies for new upward redistributions of power and income through shifting tax burdens, privatizing collective consumption, and removing obstacles to the exploitation of cheap local labor."[113] In other words, Reagan's white suburban backers, veritable "suburban warriors," secured entitlements for capital and the wealthy even as they actively fought to roll back and eliminate the modest reforms (such as Lyndon B. Johnson's Great Society programs) that the government was forced to concede to the civil rights movement.[114] As geographer Ruth Gilmore puts it, "urban dwellers of color who had seized a portion of public resources began to weather the long attack on their right to share in the social wage."[115] Although many social programs established in response to the civil rights and social justice movements may not have represented the fundamental structural transformations that activists envisioned, they nevertheless attempted to level the playing field between the races (and classes). Let us not forget that Reagan made his political career as governor of California on a fundamentally antiblack political platform.[116]

According to legal scholar Michelle Alexander, Reagan and his allies, though adept at using nonracial, seemingly "colorblind" language, demonized African Americans for their use of government antipoverty programs, playing into whites' fears that the civil rights movement had gone too far.[117] Republicans accused African American women of being "welfare queens."[118] They were figured as "deviant anti-citizens," bad Americans who failed to take adequate responsibility for themselves.[119] Disenfranchised working-class and urban poor African American men were equally, if not more, vilified. They were represented as criminal elements partly to blame for African American women's reliance on public assistance. Indeed, they represented the worst sort of deviant anticitizen who deserved to be punished and locked up. During his presidency Ronald Reagan took a tough law-and-order stance that disproportionately put African American men behind bars.[120] In fact, it was a stance Reagan assumed early on in his political career while he was still governor of California, in response to rising African American militancy in the state's cities. The Black Panther Party established in Oakland in 1966, for instance, organized its membership around a radical agenda that not only created "serve the people" programs to address needs that the government failed to address but also encouraged blacks to defend themselves "by any means necessary" including taking up arms to protect themselves from both police and vigilante violence. According to historian Lisa McGirr, "Calls for 'law and order' and cries against 'rising criminality' often served as coded language that played to white suburban fears of the black masses of the inner cities."[121]

Notably, during the period when Reagan commenced his rampage on African Americans, he championed the restoration of the Statue of Liberty and Ellis Island. He forged a state-corporate alliance to accomplish this task. Led by the president and Lee Iacocca, the Chrysler Corporation's CEO during the 1980s and a child of Italian immigrants, the restoration of Ellis Island was an ideological project meant to support Reaganomics. It was "the ultimate statement that the private sector could accomplish work that the Government had traditionally done and that it could accomplish it better."[122] Just as importantly, however, both Iacocca and Reagan were invested in imbuing the Statue of Liberty and Ellis Island with a specific interpretation of immigration history. Restoring these national icons, Iaccoca stated, "gives us a chance to honor those who came before us and the values they cherished: individual enterprise, hard work, and voluntary sacrifice."[123] According to this logic, white ethnic immigrants "made it" because they had the proper values. African Americans struggle, this logic suggests, not as a consequence of white supremacist, capitalist exploitation and violence, which led to their enslavement and *forced* (not voluntary) migration, but as a consequence of their own failures. Meanwhile, Asian and Latino immigrants who face adversities in the process of settling into a new life in America, this logic suggests, must simply internalize the attitudes of the white ethnic immigrants who preceded them and bide their time because racial discrimination is but a temporary setback.

It has been quite some time since I visited the Ellis Island museum myself. To be clear, it is not as if the museum failed to depict the immigration of people from beyond Europe. There were even displays on the nativism and xenophobia that both white and nonwhite immigrants confronted when they arrived. The museum can therefore be considered "inclusive" in the sense that it reflects the diverse origins of America's immigrants as well as acknowledges their common struggles. It is important, however, to recognize, as literary critic Ali Behdad reminds us: "It is striking, if not ironic, that the liberal discourse of immigration, which so celebrates the nation's cultural identity, is often produced during times of xenophobia and national prejudice." He continues:

> Like every national myth, the myth of immigrant America blots out the historical conditions of its formation and masks the politics of exceptionalism that motivate its celebratory discourse. The nation's humanitarian acceptance of immigrants, I argue, should therefore not be treated as an oppositional force in the formation of American national consciousness. It too carries the binary logic of "us" and "them" in a *symbolically* violent discourse that either reproduces the stereotype of the immigrant as the "wretched refuse" in need of help from benevolent Americans or else tokenizes the "model minority" to bolster patriotism and national pride.[124]

Whatever the Ellis Island museum looks like now, it is vital to situate the restorations of Ellis Island and the Statue of Liberty within their historical context. What Iaccoca and Reagan propagated through the restorations was a model of the assimilated white ethnic immigrant (and his family) against the black, single-mother "welfare queen." Iacocca made sense as a major backer of the restorations projects. His biography is the classic Horatio Alger narrative of a white man descended from a white ethnic immigrant family (albeit Italians who were considered "not quite white" and suffered discrimination) who achieves greatness in spite of it.[125]

Even during the Democratic Bill Clinton administration of the 1990s, the attacks on so-called "entitlements" that began with Reaganomics did not wane but were, instead, accelerated. Clinton introduced major reforms to the system of welfare in the form of the Personal Responsibility Work Opportunity Reconciliation Act (PRWORA) in 1996, three years after he was elected to his first term as president. In fact, "ending welfare as we know it" was a feature of his presidential campaign.[126] In line with neoliberal logic, for example, PRWORA's title emphasizes "personal responsibility." Sociologist Lynn Fujiwara argues, "With *good citizenship* defined as wage earning, mothers who used welfare were deemed irresponsible and in need of strict punitive measures."[127] Also targeted were immigrant women of color. Indeed, if African American mothers were vilified for their use of welfare programs in the 1980s, immigrant women of color were demonized as noncitizens in similar ways in the 1990s. Latina immigrant mothers in particular were depicted as being dangerously fertile women who strategically crossed the border to give birth to "anchor babies" in the United States in order to access social services reserved for American citizens.[128] Undocumented immigrants, and to some extent even legal immigrants, were thus excluded (and continue to be excluded) from a range of federal, state, and local public programs and benefits through PRWORA.[129] It is not coincidental that PRWORA was enacted in 1996, the same year as IIRIRA. Antiblack policies and policies against immigrants of color often work in tandem. More precisely, antiblackness is foundational to anti-immigrant politics and policies.[130] At the same time, antiblack policies and policies against immigrants of color have been enacted by Republican and Democratic administrations alike.[131]

The punitive aspects of both PRWORA and IIRAIRA need to be underscored. If these laws were aimed at cutting back allocations for "entitlements," those allocations did not just go back to the national coffers. According to Alexander, "the reality is that government was *not* reducing the a amount of money devoted to the management of the urban poor. It was radically altering what the funds would be used for. The dramatic shift toward punitiveness resulted in a massive reallocation of public resources."[132]

If undocumented immigrants came to be characterized as "criminal" elements not only for their legal status but also for their purported "illegal" enjoyment of public goods and services in the mid-1990s, the undocumented immigrant is today often synonymous with "terrorist." Under the Homeland Security State, to secure the "homeland" is to police the nation's borders (at its edges and in its interior) against immigrants, who are increasingly thought of as simultaneously "illegals," "criminals," and "terrorists" by lawmakers, police, and citizens alike.[133] The "immigrant/criminal/terrorist" is often figured as male and always figured as brown.[134] Whether they are considered terrorists, criminals, or both, the undocumented immigrant is increasingly presumed to be the primary suspect for disturbing domestic peace.

Moreover, older stereotypes of the undocumented, particularly undocumented women, as being "criminal" for partaking of public services continue to prevail under the Homeland Security State. During the Republican primary race of 2016, candidates made "anchor babies" a major issue. [135] However conservatives have been concerned about the legitimacy of undocumented immigrants' U.S.-born children's claim to citizenship since the 1990s. As the federal government debated immigration and welfare reform during that time, it also debated proposals to amend the U.S. Constitution to end the conferral of citizenship automatically to anybody born on American soil. These proposals were motivated by allegations that undocumented Latina immigrant women strategically gave birth to U.S. citizen "anchor babies" who would not only take advantage of social services restricted to citizens but would eventually apply for their family's legal permanent residence in the United States. Proposals to eliminate birthright citizenship introduced in the 1990s were not successful, but that did not stop conservatives from introducing similar bills in the 2000s, after 9/11.[136]

While "illegal immigrants" have been the target of expanded enforcement efforts under the Homeland Security State, it is also true is that under this new immigration regime, the distinction between "illegal" and "legal" immigrant has become increasingly blurry. Legal residency is a precarious status. Seemingly mundane administrative violations like the failure to report a change of address to immigration authorities can render a legal immigrant "illegal" and therefore subject to detention and ultimately deportation.[137] In other words, similar to African Americans, immigrants are being locked up. However, because immigrants have links to other countries, they are then shipped out. Indeed, immigrant detention and deportation needs to be linked to the foundational logics that underlie the mass incarceration of blacks. These connections are not sufficiently explored in the immigration scholarship.[138]

If, after 9/11, Americans feel insecure about threats to national security as embodied by the immigrant, they are also feeling more and more insecure economically. Although this feeling of economic insecurity was perhaps especially acute at the height of the financial crisis, the fact is that the privileges associated with American citizenship (and hence, whiteness) have been and continue to be under attack. The dismantling of New Deal and Great Society social programs disproportionately affected African Americans and immigrants of color, but the elimination of a social safety net created new pressures for working-class and middle-class white Americans too. African Americans and immigrants of color have been scapegoated as drains on public resources, but neoliberal reforms aggressively propagated by this country's leaders regardless of party affiliation are to blame for the increasing precariousness of everyday life for everyone living in America.[139]

Neoliberal reform is not only manifested in domestic economic policies but in global economic policies as well. Notably, the passage of PROWORA and IIRIRA came on the heels of the passage of the NAFTA (the North American Free Trade Agreement) in 1993 and the establishment of the World Trade Organization (WTO) in 1995. The U.S. government, with much backing from major U.S. firms, has propagated free trade and other kinds of economic agreements with other governments, which in turn has led to the relocation of American companies to developing countries where they can take advantage of cheaper labor and more lenient environmental regulations. This has meant that jobs that once offered a good wage and benefits, like those in the auto industry, are no longer available to people in the United States. Neoliberal globalization is the term that scholars use to describe this phenomenon, which has exacerbated the economic insecurity experienced by working people in America (and in other countries of the world). In fact, neoliberal globalization is what has propelled greater international migration. The increased northern migration of Mexicans and Central Americans, for instance, is attributed to the passage of NAFTA.[140]

The intensification of the neoliberal agenda along with increasing immigration has precipitated a white backlash.[141] According to sociologist Andrew Barlow, "new focus on local autonomy and local control has become an increasingly important way for racially and nationally privileged people to fend off the downward pressures of globalization."[142] That is, as (white) Americans have felt increasingly threatened by the dramatic economic and demographic shifts unfolding in this country as a consequence of neoliberalism, they have tried to protect their ever-dwindling privileges though greater control over their state and local governments. And as we've seen through the history of suburbanization, this is how Americans always secured themselves. For example, citizens of the state of California introduced and passed Proposition 187 in 1994 through the state's ballot initiative process, which would have severely limited social services extended to undocumented immigrants (including denying their children access to public education) and was ultimately "a statewide attempt to control the border." [143] Though Proposition 187 was blocked from being implemented, its impact was far-reaching. The "new racialized conceptions of economic, cultural, and political citizenship created by Proposition 187" would crucially shape debates taking place in other states and at the national level.[144] Two years later, Californians would also vote Proposition 209 into law. The so-called California Civil Rights Initiative led to a state constitutional amendment that prohibited state institutions from taking race, sex, or ethnicity into consideration in public employment, contracting, and education.[145] That meant that state agencies could not take into account historical discrimination against different marginalized groups and try to remedy those inequities with programs like affirmative action. It is no coincidence that both IIRIRA and PRWORA were passed just a few years later. More recent anti-immigrant local ordinances are yet another manifestation of white backlash in response to neoliberalism.[146] Donald Trump's successful White House bid can be thought of as a scaling up of processes that have been underway at the state and local level for quite some time.

Suburban Imaginaries

Arguably, within the context of the Homeland Security State and neoliberalism, American citizenship is most fully achieved through a house in the suburb; it is the very pinnacle of American neoliberal citizenship.[147] To be a full-fledged American (neoliberal) citizen is to be one who is fully self-reliant and self-sustaining. Job, home, transport, health insurance, and the like are to be secured through individual, private means. One is guaranteed safety and education for one's children only by choosing "good" neighborhoods where one pays a premium in property taxes. If neoliberal citizenship guarantees any rights, it is the right to consume. Neoliberal citizenship is about having opportunities to consume (that is, business-friendly environments) and to live with others who have similar consumptive capacity (that is, "class"). Neoliberal citizenship can also be thought of as "consumer citizenship." Citizenship can only be fully enjoyed in local communities by those with the means to do so. Perhaps not surprisingly, New Jersey is where ideas of "consumer citizenship" were forged historically, as it was the site for the expansion of mass suburbanization.[148]

The ideal suburban home is often thought of as bordered by a white picket fence. The history of the suburb suggests that this fence is not merely some decorative item but a social divide built through local laws and other practices meant to protect suburban residents against those thought to threaten them. In today's post-9/11 context, the "borders" (and therefore "border enforcement") that are most meaningful to many Americans are the "borders" that demarcate the places where they live, the boundaries and fences that enclose their communities and homes. These borders are ultimately divides that do not just define and demarcate geographic space but also define and demarcate the difference between citizen and noncitizen; these borders are racialized divides defining whites as citizens and nonwhites as noncitizens.

From Jim Crow segregation to localized "Juan Crow" anti-immigrant policies, citizenship is organized through spatialized apparatuses. As Dianne Harris notes, spatial apparatuses "not only reflect, but reinforce and even create racially-based practices of exclusion, oppression, minoritization, and privilege in a variety of realms."[149] Immigration and citizenship policies may be determined nationally, but they are lived in places and are defined (and contested) locally. Suburban governments and residents have actively engaged in defining the borders of their communities and thus who can and cannot claim citizenship within their borders.[150] Anti-immigrant local ordinances and other kinds of racialized exclusions are aimed at defining who belongs to specific suburban communities and who has the right to enjoy access to jobs, housing, schooling, and safety. In many cases, however, local ordinances take the form of race-neutral language and do not necessarily identify immigrants as a specific target. Suburbanites fight for "historic preservation" or engage in "quality of life" campaigns that disproportionately affect immigrants of color.

Many suburbanites have come to feel that their lifestyles are under threat. This is certainly true in New Jersey. The state's suburbs are increasingly home to large numbers of first- and second-generation immigrants from Latin America and Asia who are bypassing cities to settle directly where their predecessors have begun to plant roots.[151] In addition to seeing immigrants as stealing jobs or sucking up local public resources that ought to be reserved for (white) residents in their towns, suburbanites believe immigrants' distinctive cultural practices undermine American norms and values. Suburbanites also fear the danger that lurks just outside of the boundaries of their towns. They fear cities like Newark and Camden and the black underclass that populates them.[152] They fear, too, Islamic terrorism. After all, men purportedly linked to one of the 9/11 attackers (specifically Mohamed Atta) lived for a time in Jersey City.[153] Moreover, though across the board, people in America are losing out as a consequence of neoliberalism on both a national and global scale, whites experience this loss as a form of victimization. Donald Trump's election to the office of U.S. president capitalized on this sense of victimization. For the whites who support him (indeed, the majority of his supporters are in fact, white), Trump speaks to their sense that social goods are being "taken away" and that immigrants are the primary culprits.[154] They feel a great degree of alienation and focus their energies on shutting out the "alien-nation" they believe is responsible.[155]

Of course not all white suburbanites are actively engaged in anti-immigrant campaigns. In fact, I worked closely with white suburbanites who actively engaged in immigrant rights activism. Nevertheless, all whites, regardless of their political orientation with respect to immigration, inherit a racialized suburban order that privileges them. All of us living in the United States are subject to a racial pecking order. Race is a fundamental organizing structure of American life.[156]

When local governments prohibit the settlement or facilitate the expulsion of immigrants, it is their citizens' "homes," both figuratively and literally, that they believe they are protecting. "Homeland security," as it is understood locally, is literally about safeguarding the lifestyles and houses associated with suburban home ownership. When homeowners assert their power as taxpayers and mobilize support for anti-immigrant policies, they are asserting themselves as neoliberal consumer citizens.

Within the context of neoliberalism, immigration enforcement under the Homeland Security State involves the policing of the geographic borders of the United States as a nation-state, but, just as importantly, it involves the policing of the geographic borders of localities. Ultimately, this new form of immigration enforcement is about the policing of the boundaries of social citizenship as they are most intimately experienced and understood on an everyday basis: at the level of the suburban community. What is perhaps distinctive about the Homeland Security State is that it is not merely tasked with protecting the "homeland" (that is, the nation-state), it is being tasked with protecting the "home" (that is, neighborhoods and local communities). What political science scholar Alfonso Gonzales called "anti-migrant" hegemony is secured at the level of suburban government through seemingly "common sense" policy proposals aimed at "reducing crime" or "increasing property values"—race-neutral policy proposals that disproportionately affect immigrants.[157]

The border politics of the suburbs are linked to what sociologist William Walters calls "domopolitics." He argues that "domopolitics implies a reconfiguring of the relations between citizenship, state and territory. At its heart is a fateful conjunction of home, land and security [. . .] it has powerful affinities with family, intimacy, place: the home as heart, a refuge or sanctuary in a heartless world; the home as our place, where we belong naturally, and where, by definition, others do not."[158] The "homeland" or nation elicits affective sentiments, but it is the notion of "home" (neighborhoods, communities) that can be especially emotionally charged for citizens. While the home (especially for women) might sometimes be an oppressive and violent space, it is nevertheless the site of intense affective attachment, intimacy, identity, or nostalgia and therefore a place/space to defend and secure. Domopolitics characterizes neoliberal citizenship as it is defined in America's suburbs.

This book is ultimately a close examination of the domopolitics of citizenship using New Jersey, the state that literally lies in Lady Liberty's shadow, as a case study. The passage of anti-immigrant policies at the local level in New Jersey took place long before the state of Arizona made national headlines for its anti-immigrant legislation in 2010, but what has occurred in New Jersey hasn't elicited the same sustained attention from the media or scholars.[159] Unlike Arizona or other states, such as North Carolina or Alabama and other southern states where anti-immigrant policies are being introduced, New Jersey is far from the U.S.-Mexico border and it is not part of the American South. Although distinctive in so many ways, New Jersey is a microcosm of contemporary American suburban life and is a good place to start to make sense of how race, immigration, and citizenship are being lived out in other places around the country. Immigration was hotly debated nationally and in small cities, towns, and boroughs during the 2016 presidential election. It is likely to continue to be debated.

Taking pause to examine how immigration politics have unfolded in New Jersey can shed light on these debates. It can even help us make sense of police and citizen violence against African Americans. Understanding the racial politics that left Trayvon Martin dead in a gated community in Florida and his shooter, Mark Zimmermann, acquitted of murder charges, as well as police violence from Ferguson to Baltimore, must be understood as symptomatic of processes linked to suburbanization.

Scholars who have been tracking anti-immigrant local ordinances in all of their forms all agree that it is not an easy task. We have all employed a variety of methods to determine exactly how many counties and municipalities have proposed or passed them. We have poured through local news media accounts, examined the transcripts of county and municipal meetings on certain issues, drawn from information shared by immigrant rights' advocates and most importantly, from immigrants themselves. However, anti-immigrant local ordinances (whether they are explicitly anti-immigrant or "back door" policies) only offer a partial perspective on what life is like for immigrants living in different communities. The broader context and culture of anti-immigrant sentiment at the county or municipal level (measured, for instance, by whether or not local police actively cooperate with ICE, the presence of anti-immigrant groups, or incidents of hate crimes and bias attacks) is also important. Taking all of these factors into account, I have tracked anti-immigrant politics and policies in twelve of New Jersey's twenty-one counties and there could be more. I do not focus on all of these counties in this book. I have selected a few case studies. My selection of cases is driven largely by my work with immigrant rights' activists. These were the cases where the hardest battles were fought. At the same time, I wanted to highlight anti-immigrant politics and policies as they played out in very different types of suburbs and against a diverse set of immigrant groups.

Chapter 2 examines how several white suburbs have engaged in local immigration and immigrant enforcement. I pay especially close attention to Freehold, New Jersey, which was ground zero for several local ordinances aimed at limiting immigrants' employment and housing. While I pay attention to traditional white suburbs, this book also casts light on racial politics in suburbs where "minorities" are now emergent "majorities."[160] In "ethnoburbs," a term scholars have coined to describe suburbs that are increasingly nonwhite (indeed, more precisely, increasingly Asian), new kinds of relations between "immigrant" and "native," as well as between and across racial lines, are being forged. Many immigrants immediately settle in suburbs to join their relatives. These relatives have not only purchased homes and raised their children in the suburbs but have also established businesses. In some cases, their grown American-born children are being successfully elected to public office. The election of second-generation immigrants in these new American suburbs, however, had been incredibly fraught. On one hand, U.S. born second-generation immigrants in the post-9/11 period are often seen by their white counterparts as "forever foreign," not quite able to authentically represent Main Street, a term some might use to describe suburban living. A prevailing idea is that these second-generation immigrants' parents have taken over their communities. On the other hand, the new diversities that characterize suburbs make for complex political landscapes. Ethnic minorities' shared immigrant roots, experiences of racialization, and party affiliation have proven to be insufficient bases for coalitional politics between and across ethnic and racial lines. I tackle issues of this kind in chapter 3, which focuses largely on Edison, New Jersey.

How does it feel to be an immigrant in New Jersey given this broader context of anti-immigrant hostility and xenophobia? The experiences of immigrants as narrated in their own words, including those who have been caught by the immigration enforcement dragnet, become the focus of chapter 4. In chapter 5 I look at how immigrants persevere and try to make New Jersey home despite the face that there are forces stacked up against them. I pay attention to novel approaches to historic preservation in Bridgeton, New Jersey, while also tracking different forms of activism across the state. I then offer up in chapter 6 a conclusion that helps to connect this New Jersey study to the debates that currently rage in this country under the Trump administration.

2

My Hometown

Immigration and Suburban Imaginaries

Bruce Springsteen's song "My Hometown" is a deeply nostalgic one. The song, from his *Born in the U.S.A.* album, is performed from the perspective of a man wistfully recalling his childhood hometown. He begins the song by describing the sense of pride that his father instilled in him about the town where he grew up. But the song takes a melancholic turn when the protagonist recalls rising racial tensions in his town resulting in the shooting of an African American student at his high school and the town's eventual economic decline. He ultimately decides, however reluctantly, to leave his beloved hometown. Springsteen himself said of Freehold, New Jersey, the borough where he grew up, "I used to think that once I got out of town, I was never going to come back. . . . I realized I would always carry a part of that town with me no matter where I went or what I did."[1] "My Hometown" reflects the ways the borough of Freehold has left its indelible mark on Springsteen's life.

For some observers, "My Hometown" also reflects tensions that continue to haunt the town of Freehold.[2] For more than a decade, Freehold has

PHOTO 3. Main Street, Freehold (Photo credit: Carolina Alonso)

been the site of conflict between some of its white community members and Latino immigrants. During a research trip to Freehold on a particularly blustery late winter day in 2009, scenes of racial conflict conjured up by the song were eerily replayed. I was on the corner of Throckmorton Street and West Main Street about a hundred yards from where many Latino men used to gather for employment. I stood alongside three Latino day laborers waiting to cross the busy intersection across which runs the Freehold and Jamesburg Branch freight railroad line. As we waited for the light to turn so we could cross the street, a large SUV, perhaps a Chevrolet Suburban (aptly named) pulled up at the crosswalk. As we continued to wait, all of us noticed the window of the back seat slowly roll down. I suppose we noticed because it was a cold day and it made no sense that anyone in a warm vehicle would open a window. In the back seat of the SUV sat what looked like a young teenager, perhaps fourteen or fifteen years old. He looked directly at the men I stood on the corner with. He formed his fingers in the shape of a gun as boys do when they play some version of shoot 'em up, whether it is the classic game of cops and robbers or cowboys and Indians, or a newer version of the game (as I observed at my son's taekwondo school) called border agents and illegals. He pointed his gun at the men and wordlessly "shot" them. Bang. Bang. Bang. The light then turned green and the SUV sped away. We stood there stunned and shocked. The men started twittering in Spanish to one another, outraged yet uncertain whether they had actually seen what had transpired. They turned to me and I nodded in affirmation. Yes, I had seen it and yes, I thought it was what we all thought it was. Yet cops and robbers is not a game in Freehold Borough. None of us could just brush off the episode we had witnessed as simply some childhood prank. Not when the local community had introduced and passed numerous anti-immigrant ordinances.

The new logics of immigration enforcement under the Homeland Security State are defined by interiorization (that is, the shifting of "border enforcement" into the nation's interior as opposed to the nation's "exterior," its national borders) and localization (that is, the passage of municipal policies to address immigration in addition to federal laws governing immigration enforcement). These logics have shaped the context for the passage and implementation of anti-immigrant policies in New Jersey's suburbs.

That anti-immigrant ordinances have been passed at the local level in New Jersey, however, are not simply a consequence of new approaches to immigration enforcement being enacted at the federal level. Whereas the migrants targeted for exclusion in earlier years were African Americans from the South, today suburban residents have turned their attention to excluding immigrants from Latin America. To exclude first African Americans and now Latino immigrants from suburban life is to limit the enjoyment of the rights and privileges of belonging and citizenship to white suburbanites. After all, the most prized aspects of American citizenship, from the right to secure the American Dream of home ownership to the right to an education, as well as the right to a decent and dignified livelihood, are increasingly best enjoyed in the suburb.

This chapter examines the passage of a spate of local ordinances restricting immigrant settlement in different suburban municipalities in the years since 9/11. In addition to overviewing the anti-immigrant policy landscape of New Jersey, I will delve more deeply into two case studies of towns where municipal campaigns to expel and prohibit immigrant settlement have been especially heated. One case study in this chapter focuses on Springsteen's hometown of Freehold, where day laborers have been at the center of controversy. Ironically, the very labor required to make the suburb (home construction, home improvement, and so on) is problematic to those who reside there. Much like the protagonist in Springsteen's "My Hometown," Freehold borough residents are nostalgically invested in a specific vision of the community and it becomes a basis for justifying municipal ordinances that negatively impact immigrants. In my discussion of Freehold, I examine the ways historic preservation campaigns, while not explicitly anti-immigrant, are one mechanism to restrict the settlement of Latinos.

The other major case study in this chapter is of Morristown, New Jersey. Morristown, like Freehold, is invested in bolstering its borders against Latino settlers but draws on different logics toward that end. In Morristown, homeland security discourses are deployed. This is perhaps not surprising given that Morristown residents, like those of many other New Jersey municipalities, were among the victims of the 9/11 attack. More than once, people have told me that smoke emanating from the World Trade Center marred the Morristown skyline that fateful day. Whether it is actually true or not, citizens of communities directly impacted by the attacks are not the only ones to invoke national security concerns in local immigration politics. This invocation of national security concerns in local immigration politics in places like Morristown is also symptomatic of deeper shifts in the ways that Americans debate immigration in wide range of communities across the country especially after 9/11. I focus on these two case studies because they are among the sites where the most vociferous debates around immigration were taking place in post-9/11 New Jersey. Though it has been over fifteen years since the Twin Towers were attacked, the Latino immigrant residents of Freehold still live in fear of being expelled from their community and Latino immigrant residents of Morristown are still being characterized as dangerous elements.[3] Although Freehold and Morristown may be distinctive for the especially aggressive behavior of their municipal governments and citizens, the kinds of debates that took place and continue to take place in both communities are emblematic of similar processes occurring in many other places around the state and the country. I reference these other examples as much as possible throughout the chapter.

Latino Immigration Historically

Before discussing the contemporary politics of immigration in New Jersey, it's important to provide a brief sketch of Latino immigration to the United States and New Jersey historically, with particular focus on the largest Latino immigrant groups in the state. When the U.S. Census counts people of "Hispanic or Latino" origin, those respondents can be of any racial background. In other words, there can be white Hispanic/Latinos (such as Argentinians), black Hispanic/Latinos (for example, Dominicans), or even Asian Hispanic/Latinos (for example, Japanese Peruvians).[4] According to the Pew Hispanic Center, 18 percent of New Jersey's population is Hispanic. A majority (57 percent) are in fact native-born. In addition, a majority of the state's Hispanic populations is non-Mexican. In order of size, the "Hispanic/Latino" population is as follows: Caribbean, South American, Mexican, and, finally, Central American.[5] More specifically, the top three "Hispanic" ethnicities are Puerto Rican (434,092), Mexican (217,715), and Dominican (197,922).

The United States has, from its very inception, relied on racialized labor, particularly for dirty, dangerous, and demeaning occupations. It has forcibly removed people (notably enslaved Africans) from their homelands to work in this country and produced conditions in less powerful countries that ultimately force people to leave, which is the experience of most immigrants from throughout the Third World.[6] In the case of Latin America and the Caribbean, histories of colonialism, neocolonialism, militarism, and foreign investment have produced conditions for emigration. At the same time, U.S. businesses have actively recruited workers from different countries, and U.S. immigration policy makers have typically tried to accommodate their interests.

Puerto Rican migration to the United States and ultimately to New Jersey traces its beginnings to the rise of U.S. imperialism in the late nineteenth century.[7] With the conclusion of the Spanish-American War and the signing of the Treaty of Paris in 1898, the United States acquired Puerto Rico, along with Cuba and the Philippines, as colonies. During the colonial period, U.S. agriculturalists actively recruited Puerto Ricans to work on sugar estates in Hawaii.[8] Today's Puerto Rican communities in the United States, including New Jersey, however, trace their origins to the mass migration from the island during World War I. As out-migration from Europe decreased, Puerto Ricans, along with other populations from throughout the Caribbean, were recruited to work in menial and agrarian jobs in the United States. Following the war, as immigration from other parts of the world (all of Asia and southern Europe) was increasingly restricted as a result of growing racism and xenophobia, Puerto Rico became a preferred source of labor. In early 1917, with the Jones-Shafroth Act, Puerto Ricans were officially recognized as U.S. citizens and therefore exempt from immigration restrictions.[9] Meanwhile, the Great Migration of African Americans from the South also became a source of labor for industrializing cities in the North. During World War II Puerto Ricans were recruited once again to work in the United States due to labor shortages. They worked in agriculture as well as in industry in the Northeast, and in the war's aftermath, they were recruited for low-wage jobs due to postwar expansion efforts in manufacturing and services.

One of the "pushes" off the island in the post–World War II period was a U.S. Cold War project, the "Point Four Program," which attempted to make Puerto Rico a showpiece of the U.S. vision of Third World capitalist development. As part of that program, both the Puerto Rican government and the U.S. government encouraged Puerto Ricans from the poorest areas to migrate in order to create conditions for the upward mobility of those left behind. With visible forms of poverty abated, Puerto Rico could emerge as a symbol of all that was right about U.S.-styled development. Between family reunification, familial and social networks, and the ease of travel (because Puerto Ricans possess U.S. passports), migration from Puerto Rico has continued.[10]

Dominican immigration was driven in large part by the turmoil that ensued following the assassination of the dictator President Rafael Trujillo in 1961. Both the United States and U.S.-friendly Dominican elites who replaced the dictator believed that encouraging out-migration could alleviate any further social unrest and promote political stability.[11] Indeed, different Third World governments have encouraged out-migration to essentially "export" potential political threats.[12] At the same time, the failure of economic development initiatives in the Dominican Republic (initiatives that were aggressively encouraged by the United States) left many in the country unemployed.[13] A number of these people would join their families in the United States. With the passage of the Immigration and Nationality Act of 1965, all racial exclusions that had characterized U.S. immigration law were dropped and new opportunities for immigrants to sponsor their relatives to join them were introduced.[14] Scholars have found that once both familial and other social networks have been established between immigrants in the United States and their relatives, friends, and town mates in the country they left behind, "migration flows can be self-sustaining and virtually unstoppable."[15]

Mexican immigration, which has elicited the most debate in the United States with regard to immigration from Latin America, has a long history in the United States.[16] In the late 1910s to early 1920s, California agribusiness, which had become increasingly powerfully politically, played a key role at the state and national level in sourcing labor from Mexico. The agricultural industry was a primary driver in shaping the migrations of Asians into both the U.S. territory of Hawaii and the state of California beginning in the late nineteenth century. However, Asian migration was met with fierce xenophobic and racist opposition. From 1919 to 1939, agribusiness transitioned from importing Asian labor (specifically Filipinos) and imported Mexican workers instead. Employers successfully argued that Mexico was a more favorable source of labor because Mexicans could more easily be deported if and when they posed either social or economic problems. They were able to ensure that immigration policy reflected this logic.[17] By 1942, agribusiness, along with railroad corporations, was able to secure government support for the Bracero Program, a guest-worker program that marks the beginnings of large-scale immigration from Mexico to the United States. As a guest-worker program, it included provisions to facilitate the recruitment of laborers from Mexico as well as provisions to facilitate their deportation. The program lasted until 1964.[18] Even though the Bracero Program has formally ended, its existence has had deep impacts on Mexican communities on both sides of the border, ensuring continued flows of workers northward, including migration without formal authorization.

Pressures for emigration from Mexico were heightened in the 1990s as a consequence of the North American Free Trade Agreement (NAFTA), which was signed in 1993. NAFTA has made it even more difficult for people to make a decent living whether it is off the land or in factories in Mexico. International migration has become the only option for many Mexicans to support themselves and their families. Meanwhile, continued demand for low-wage, racialized labor in the United States draws people north despite the heavy militarization of the U.S.-Mexican border. Because the United States does not currently have a program that allows Mexican immigrants to come into the country to work as unskilled workers, they come surreptitiously and are undocumented.[19]

Mexican immigrants have been settling primarily in California and other border states, but they are increasingly settling in new destinations, including many suburban communities in the Midwest, South, and Northeast. In the late 1990s into the early 2000s there was much demand in the construction, manufacturing, and service sectors in these regions.[20] Increased Mexican migration to New Jersey is attributed in part to these broader processes. Another factor that pushed Mexican migrants to settle in New Jersey was to escape anti-immigration sentiment in California, where Mexican migrants often first went to settle after crossing the U.S.-Mexican border.[21] Recall that in the mid-1990s, the California electorate passed Proposition 187, a voter-sponsored legislation that would have required all state employees effectively play the role of immigration enforcement agents. Although its implementation was stopped by the courts, Proposition 187 reflected Californians' growing hostility toward Mexican immigrants. What these immigrants may not have anticipated, however, is that once they settled in New Jersey, they would draw the ire of anti-immigrant forces in that state as well.

The Homeland Security State of New Jersey

The logics of localization and interiorization characterizing federal approaches to immigration enforcement after 9/11 manifest in several ways in New Jersey. The first is the formal and informal cooperation between local police units and federal immigration authorities; the second is anti-immigrant municipal politics and policies that attempt to prohibit immigrant settlement in (and ultimately lead to their expulsion from) a community by limiting immigrants' ability to find work or secure a home, or send their children to school.

Federal-Local Cooperation

The Homeland Security State in New Jersey is characterized by formal and informal cooperation between federal immigration enforcement agents (ICE) and local (county and municipal) police. In 2007, the New Jersey attorney general issued an official directive stating that "all county and municipal police officers are expected to either enforce or assist other agencies in the enforcement of immigration laws," in effect making federal-local cooperation New Jersey state policy.[22] Seven months after Attorney General Anne Milgram issued this order, the rate at which local authorities were referring undocumented immigrants apprehended under an array of circumstances, including routine traffic stops, doubled.[23]

As if this policy declaration were not enough, some county and municipal governments sought to deputize local police officers to serve as immigration enforcement agents under the federal government's 287(g) program. The program was introduced in 1996 as part of the Illegal Immigration Reform and Immigrant Responsibility Act. According to the Department of Homeland Security, "The 287(g) program, one of ICE's top partnership initiatives, allows a state and local law enforcement entity to enter into a partnership with ICE, under a joint Memorandum of Agreement, in order to receive delegated authority for immigration enforcement within their jurisdictions."[24] In other words, 287(g) authorizes local police to act as immigration enforcement agents. As of August 2014, ICE had 287(g) agreements with thirty-five law enforcement agencies in eighteen states. Several law enforcement agencies in New Jersey have penned 287(g) agreements.

In February 2007, when Donald Cresitello was mayor of Morristown, located in Morris County in North Jersey, he was the first New Jersey official to apply to the 287(g) program. He openly called for "vigilant enforcement" of immigration law within Morristown during his term. Before the 287(g) proposal was submitted, however, the municipality attempted to regulate undocumented immigration through the stricter enforcement of local policies against overcrowding in rental properties. In addition it attempted to prohibit day laborers from gathering near the town's train station to seek work. Although neither of these ordinances expressly targeted undocumented immigrants in Morristown, they did disproportionately impact them. Cresitello, however, became more explicit about his aims to crackdown on and get rid of undocumented immigrants living in the community by applying to the 287(g) program. Morristown does not currently have a 287(g) agreement with ICE despite Cresitello's efforts. If it had been formalized, the agreement would have allowed local police selected to undergo ICE training to serve as immigration enforcement agents.

In New Jersey, the county governments of Hudson and Monmouth authorized 287(g) agreements with ICE. The agreement authorizes specific Hudson County Department of Corrections personnel as well as Division of Corrections personnel in the Monmouth County Sheriff's office who have undergone training with ICE, to identify which foreign-born inmates are undocumented and should be processed for removal. As of February 2016, the agreements are still in effect.[25] Kim Guadagno, who oversaw Monmouth County's application to the 287(g) program after being elected county sheriff in 2007 (serving in that capacity until 2009), ran for office on an explicitly immigration-enforcement platform. Indeed, Guadagno, a Republican, made 287(g) a centerpiece of her campaign. She claimed, "It's time to get serious about protecting families and residents of Monmouth County. . . . The implementation of this program [287(g)] will greatly increase the protection of Monmouth County families from potential terrorists."[26]

Even in places where 287(g) agreements do not exist, local police have informally cooperated with ICE on immigration enforcement matters. Undocumented immigrants seeking assistance from local police on criminal matters have found themselves in detention when police officers turn them into ICE after responding to their pleas for help. This was the case, for example, in Plainsboro for an undocumented immigrant from Guatemala. ICE put him into custody after local police who were assisting him with a flat tire handed him over to immigration authorities. This was also true for a Brazilian undocumented immigrant living in West Long Branch who sought help from local police to apprehend smugglers responsible for bringing his sister to the United States and holding her for ransom. After the officers seized the smugglers and saved this immigrant's sister, they turned him over to ICE.[27] In some cases, local police have apprehended and remanded undocumented immigrants to ICE agents after routine traffic stops. According to the Morris County sheriff, "We have found that we had been doing that [checking the legal status of suspected undocumented immigrants] prior to the [NJ Attorney General's] directive." It is no surprise that Morris Country is the county in which Morristown is situated. Within six months after the directive, Morristown had the most referrals to ICE in all of Morris County. This was even without the 287(g) being signed.[28]

In her research of a neighborhood in Trenton, sociology and anthropology professor Rachel Adler found that in some cases ICE agents dress to look like police in order to gain entry into immigrants' homes. Once they gain entry, ICE officers often subject all residents to interrogation even though they may have deportation orders for only a specific individual.[29]

Housing

Agencies beyond the police are being drawn into the work of immigration enforcement. Several municipalities attempted and in some cases were successful in introducing housing ordinances to expel immigrants from local communities. Morristown took measures to limit immigrants' ability to rent homes through the strict enforcement of policies related to overcrowding before it applied to 287(g). In 2006, Riverside, located in Burlington County in southern New Jersey, may have been the first town to introduce an anti-immigrant housing (and employment) ordinance, when the local council passed the Illegal Immigration Relief Act, which made hiring or renting property to an undocumented immigrant punishable by a $2,000 fine and jail time.[30]

The municipal government of Freehold did not necessarily introduce a new housing ordinance, but it did initiate efforts to actively enforce existing codes regulating overcrowding. Local officials and even local media attributed overcrowding to immigration. As reported in a New Jersey real estate blog: "Instances of residential overcrowding [in Freehold] have increased over the last ten years as the borough has seen an influx of immigrants, but not a corresponding increase in the housing stock."[31] Freehold residents can participate in the enforcement of housing codes through the borough's "Quality of Life" hotline. According to the borough's website, "Residents are urged to report quality of life complaints (loitering, public urination, overcrowding, loud noise, illegal parking, etc.) to a special hotline number. [. . .] Callers may remain anonymous if they wish."[32] "Quality of life" ordinances like those related to residential overcrowding do not always contain specific references to immigrants, but they are "coded codes," municipal codes that have discriminatory effects even though their discriminatory intent may be difficult to prove in court.[33] Freehold's Rental Property Advisory Committee recommended, furthermore, that anyone seeking rental housing or even seeking to buy property had to produce proof of citizenship or permanent residency to do so. The mayor of Freehold rejected the committee's proposal, which was also vigorously opposed by Latino residents and organizations, but it is an example of how local citizens attempt to use existing local municipal policy to prohibit immigrant settlement.[34]

Interestingly, the Rental Advisory Committee of Freehold during this period was made up of members of PEOPLE (Pressing Elected Officials to Preserve Our Living Environment). Although the group represents itself as committed to maintaining Freehold's quality of life, it is ultimately an anti-immigration group. Former councilmember Marc LeVine served as chair of PEOPLE and went on to be a member of the Rental Property Advisory Committee. He would later come under scrutiny for racist remarks on Latinas' promiscuity. LeVine has long believed that the issue of undocumented immigration in the town of Freehold ought to be addressed by local government and, as is clear with his work on the Rental Advisory Committee, has attempted to use local government apparatuses to do so.[35] Despite the rejection of the proposal that renters produce proof of citizenship or permanent residency to seek housing, community members that I interacted with indicate that there have been "clandestine" code enforcers who enforce policies related to residential overcrowding by reporting "violators" to local authorities. Immigrant advocates tried to contest these cases, but the borough lawyer insisted that the code enforcement was legal.

Other municipalities have also attempted to employ housing measures to limit immigrant settlement. By the year 2000, Latinos accounted for nearly 35 percent of the population in Bound Brook, Somerset County, a sizable number of whom were undocumented Costa Ricans.[36] In 2008, Bound Brook councilman Jim Lefkowitz introduced a resolution requiring landlords to determine the legal status of renters.[37] In making a case for the enforcement of housing codes, Lefkowitz argued, "There's a groundswell of people willing to turn the other cheek on illegal immigration. I will not do it. . . . I'm asking that overcrowding be enforced. I'm asking that landlords be accountable as far as illegal immigrant harboring, as that they be prosecuted to the fullest extent of the law."[38] Notably, the town had already been scrutinized for its discriminatory housing practices. The U.S. Department of Justice filed an action against the town. Court documents state: "The United States' Complaint alleges that defendant, the Borough of Bound Brook, New Jersey ("Borough"), discriminated against Latino residents on the basis of national origin, race, and color which constituted a pattern or practice of resistance to the full enjoyment of rights secured by the Fair Housing Act, 42 U.S.C. §§ 3601 *et seq.*; and a denial to a group of persons of rights granted by the Fair Housing Act, 42 U.S.C. §§ 3601 *et seq.*, which raises an issue of general public importance."[39] The municipality settled the case with the Department of Justice. Bound Brook did not admit guilt, but it agreed to pay a $30,000 fine and create a $425,000 compensation fund for victims of discrimination between 1996 and 2002. Lefkowitz's housing proposal was in part a response to the council's settlement with the DOJ; he claimed, "We're in danger of being considered a sanctuary [for illegal immigrants]."[40]

Schools and Jobs

In addition to limiting the settlement of new immigrants into their communities, municipalities have made it difficult for immigrant residents to enjoy public education and to seek employment. For example, in the town of Fairview located in Bergen County, the school superintendent, David Verducci, dismissed students from their classes during the first week of school after learning that their parents were undocumented.[41] Forty-eight percent of Fairview's residents are foreign-born. In an anti-immigration website, an article titled "America Educating the World—At Taxpayer Expense" and supporting Verducci states,

> David Verducci is a victim of U.S. immigration law. No, he's not an Italian who snuck into the U.S. illegally, or one of the millions turned back in the 1920s, the last time Americans decided that their country needed a breather between waves of mass migration. In fact, David Verducci is an American citizen, and a public official—a conscientious schools superintendent in Fairview, New Jersey, whose good name and career prospects were trashed because of immigration law. You see, he foolishly tried to obey it. Even worse, David Verducci tried to enforce it. To execute the laws duly passed by our representative government, judged constitutional by our courts, and binding on all U.S. residents. He tried to do his job—and found himself made out as a monster before a national audience.[42]

Children are constitutionally guaranteed the right to a public education regardless of their legal status, yet Verducci's supporters try to invoke the Constitution to claim that denying public education to immigrant children on the basis of their immigration status is legal. Notably, the piece quoted here draws the distinction between the "taxpayer" and the immigrant who, it is assumed, does not pay taxes and burdens local public resources. Immigrants, both legal and undocumented, do pay taxes, but in this case, the "taxpayers" are presumed to be citizens and therefore the only ones deserving of the right to an education.[43]

In 2014, the New Jersey chapter of the American Civil Liberties Union (ACLU) found that more than 130 school districts in the state engaged in discriminatory practices that created barriers to the enrollment of children with undocumented parents.[44] These districts did not necessarily engage in practices as extreme as Verducci's, but they had the same outcome: they denied immigrant children the right to public education. In Freehold, I learned from local activists that immigrants were even being cited by local police as "illegal taxi drivers" for carpooling their children to school. This not only penalized the students but their parents as well.[45]

However, the most contentious issue in Freehold was less related to educational access than to access to work opportunities. Indeed, the phenomenon at the heart of the immigration debate in Freehold has been the increased presence of day laborers. In 2003, the municipality closed a "muster zone" where immigrant day laborers typically gathered to seek work. Local police leafleted the zone with flyers in both Spanish and English warning jobseekers that if they persisted in trying to secure employment in the area not only would they be ticketed, but their names would be forwarded to ICE.[46] The borough was forced to reverse its decision to close the muster zone when immigrant rights' advocates sued them. Three years later, in 2006, the borough decided to settle with the plaintiffs in the lawsuit, agreeing to pay their legal fees as well as establishing a fund to reimburse day laborers who had been fined after the closure of the muster zone. Marc LeVine, who was a council member at the time, responded to the borough's decision to settle with outrage and disgust, saying, "This case and the feelings from advocates from outside this community be damned." LeVine stated, "We are going to steamroll over this issue, and we are going to make this a town that is desirable to young families that are going to come into this community and not be transient."[47] LeVine kept his vow to "steamroll over this issue" through his work in PEOPLE. Significantly,

LeVine characterizes the lawsuit as having been brought by people "outside this community." From one perspective, his comment can be construed as suggesting that non-Freehold residents are responsible for advocating on behalf of day laborers' rights. Yet from another perspective, his comment can be construed as suggesting that day laborers are themselves the outsiders. Moreover, LeVine states that he is invested in the migration and settlement of "young families" in Freehold. He does not say so explicitly in this case, but it becomes clearer upon examining LeVine's statements and positions in other cases as I discuss later in this chapter, that it is "young *white* families" he is most invested in.

Day laborer muster zones have been the target of protests by local residents and anti-immigrant activists in other municipalities. In Palisades Park, local anti-immigration forces joined a national day of action in 2006 calling for the enforcement of immigration laws by local government and police. Picketing took place near a muster zone for day laborers as part of a national "Stop the Invasion" protest called by the Connecticut Citizens for Immigration Control. Protest attendee Ron Bass, a resident of Linden, New Jersey, and the founder of the United Patriots of America, an anti-immigrant group affiliated with the Minutemen Project (an organization of civilians engaged in patrolling the U.S.-Mexico border), stated: "It's time for mayors, county executives, and police chiefs to enforce the laws of our country."[48] Even though there were non–Palisades Park residents, like Ron Bass, among the protestors, many others were residents of the town. As one day laborer notes, "We recognized a couple of them. They live in this town."[49]

In a move related to restrictions to education and jobs, one municipality passed what is essentially an English-only ordinance. In Bogota, Mayor Steve Lonegan called for a boycott of the local McDonald's when it posted a Spanish-language billboard. He stated, "McDonald's should realize that in promulgating bilingualism, they are empowering the left wing that sees bilingualism as one more arrow to the heart of our democracy."[50] Bogota's town council supported a resolution demanding that McDonald's replace the sign with an English-language one.[51]

Freehold: A Case Study of Suburban "Preservation"

As I've discussed earlier, the municipal government of Freehold has practically introduced the entire gamut of anti-immigrant ordinances. Just

PHOTO 4. Main Street, Freehold (Photo credit: Carolina Alonso)

as importantly, it has engaged in practices that may not initially seem anti-immigrant but prove to have the effect of excluding immigrants. Specifically, "historic preservation" projects are a means by which local white residents exclude immigrants from Freehold's civic landscape.

New Jerseyans, like many Americans, are invested in the upkeep and improvement of their homes. Homes, as most Americans know, can be an important financial investment. The market value of one's home can serve as a guarantee for other kinds of goods as homeowners borrow against the equity of their houses to pay, for example, for their children's college tuition. When the housing market is in trouble, homeowners invest in the maintenance and improvement of their homes in order to maintain (or possibly increase) their market values.[52] Not surprisingly, home improvement as an industry expanded along with the expansion of new suburban developments.[53] What suburb doesn't have a local Home Depot or Lowe's? Moreover, television has seen a proliferation of home improvement shows, as well as shows related to real estate investment, sales and purchase where the question of home values is front and center.

In Freehold, residents aren't just invested in their individual homes but in the town's revitalization through historic preservation. According to the National Park Service, the federal agency that governs historic preservation,

> Preservation is defined as the act or process of applying measures necessary to sustain the existing form, integrity, and materials of an historic property. Work, including preliminary measures to protect and stabilize the property, generally focuses upon the ongoing maintenance and repair of historic materials and features rather than extensive replacement and new construction. New exterior additions are not within the scope of this treatment; however, the limited and sensitive upgrading of mechanical, electrical, and plumbing systems and other code-required work to make properties functional is appropriate within a preservation project.[54]

Private institutions like the National Trust for Historic Preservation also define and promote preservation standards.[55]

Idealized suburban life is often represented through specific temporal logics. In today's popular culture, the period that is especially idealized (what we think of as "the good old days") is the postwar era of the 1950s, the decade immortalized in television shows like *Adventures of Ozzie and Harriet* and *Leave It to Beaver*. Maybe that's to be expected. After all, the 1950s was the decade of postwar prosperity, a time when the promise of upward mobility in American society for the (white) working class—especially at the height of the Cold War—was actually possible. It was a time before the restive 1960s when race, gender, and sexual mores were being revolutionized, and anti-imperialism was reaching a peak. If the suburb was once a place that represented the future (and therefore development, evolution, and progress), some of today's suburbs represent themselves as harkening back to a more ideal past whether its the "happy days" of the 1950s or even earlier.

The suburb is also represented through geographic logics. Stacy Denton, for example, argues that a "dichotomy in which the rural was at times implicitly cast as a white space, an undeveloped realm that existed outside of a modern world associated with both the sub/urban and the middle class" was deployed in representations of the "urban" versus the "rural." Indeed the suburb can appear, "to align itself with such a rural place in its attempts to separate from the 'problems' of urban centers."[56]

Representations of the suburb abound in popular culture, and those representations rest not only in defining what the suburb is but also in defining what it is not. By extension, through representations of the suburb, suburbanites define who they are and who they are not: "The suburban middle-class subject knows its inner-city other through an imposed system of infinitely repeatable substitutions and proxies: census tracts, crime statistics, tabloid newspapers and television programmes, and lastly, through the very ground of the displaced aggressions projected from suburban moral panic itself."[57]

The borough of Freehold imagines itself in specific temporal and spatialized ways. The very name of the borough goes back to a moment in history when it was much more rural. In contemporary representations of itself and its work in historic preservation the borough prides itself in preserving and sustaining its collective memory as a once-rural small-town that was presumably safer, more peaceful, and decidedly white. In 2005, the borough conducted a "Reexamination of the Master Plan"; among the issues raised were concerns for "preserving the historic fabric" and preserving the "character of individual structures and streetscapes."[58] By 2007, the borough council had declared a portion of the town an "Area in Need of Rehabilitation." Plans for the town's "rehabilitation" included ensuring that specified historic buildings in the borough's designated "historic district area" would be preserved. The historic district area encompasses most of Main Street and several blocks of both Throckmorton Street and South Street.[59] The borough's Historic Preservation Advisory Commission is charged with helping to oversee this aspect of "rehabilitation" work. The borough identifies the first purpose of designating an historic district area as "[safeguarding] the heritage of the borough of Freehold by preserving resources within the borough which reflect elements of its cultural, social, economic, and architectural history."[60]

Encompassing only about two square miles, Freehold Borough is home to 10,976 residents and 3,695 households. Its downtown looks and feels like a quintessential American Main Street with its locally owned businesses and few major national chains. Within walking distance of downtown are brightly painted, well-maintained Victorian houses. Freehold Borough is a far cry from its closest neighbor, Freehold Township, from which it separated in the early twentieth century.[61] Indeed, driving to Freehold Borough on Route 79 as you go through the township, you pass dozens of McMansion housing developments. Meanwhile, if one approaches

Freehold Borough from Route 9, one passes a series of strip malls. If the Springsteen song is about Freehold Borough, there is truth to the line in "My Hometown" that indicates that the town was once in decline: "Now main streets whitewashed windows and vacant stores / Seems like there ain't nobody wants to come down here no more." This decline began in the 1960s with the closure of a local rug mill.[62] Today, however, Freehold has a thriving Main Street, and it actually is its name.

It is very clear that Freehold Borough residents take great pride in maintaining it as the very picture of hometown America. Not only that, walking around Freehold, it is very obvious that it is especially invested in its authenticity as an historic American city. Seemingly all the businesses proudly bear patriotic red, white, and blue bunting and American flags. You feel as if it's the Fourth of July even when it is not. In addition to the town's official Historic Preservation Advisory Commission, other town residents are devoted to preserving the town's history. The website www.welcometofreehold.com contains photos, oral histories, and more (including quite a bit about Springsteen, "The Boss"). It's not really clear who maintains it, but it certainly isn't the Freehold Borough Historic Preservation Advisory Commission's site. Local residents memorialize the town in books; local writer Kevin Coyne proclaims Freehold is "one of the oldest towns in the country."[63] The Monmouth County Historical Association's library is located in the borough and it maintains a historic house museum, the Westcoven House, in the town.[64]

Coyne's observation that Freehold Borough is "one of the oldest towns in the country," reflects the particular sense residents have of their town. The name "Freehold" itself is significant according to locals: "In early America, the right to vote was restricted to property owners. These were seen as responsible men who held their possessions free and clear. In a very literal sense they were 'Freeholders.' This expression has lasted through the years and is used extensively in this part of New Jersey."[65] That Freehold's name derives from the idea of freeholders, that is, citizen-property owners, seems quite apt. It captures the ethos of suburban membership: that only property owners can properly belong in the town. Freehold Borough residents are concerned with preserving specific sets of histories. In particular, Freehold holds on to the town's Revolutionary War past. Freehold's history therefore is a patriotic one and its residents, true American citizens.[66]

Interestingly, the "Reexamination of the Master Plan" occurred within a few years of major debates around the Latino day laborers. Indeed, the muster zone in question as well as Latino immigrant-owned and -oriented businesses fell squarely within the designated "Area in Need of Rehabilitation," which closely corresponds with the "historic district area." I don't think it's totally coincidental, especially given the wide array of strategies employed by some Freehold residents to prohibit immigrant settlement in the borough. There is much evidence that historic preservation has been used, particularly in urban settings, to justify the displacement of the poor and blacks. Leland Saito argues, for example, that "labels placed on buildings and communities can lead to their destruction or preservation."[67] The designation of different areas in Freehold as needing "rehabilitation" or requiring "preservation" has potential impact on the degree to which Latino immigrants can live or even do business in those areas. When a building is labeled in need of rehabilitation it often means that its inhabitants may be forced to relocate. Though it can be argued that it is better to have people vacate buildings that are truly dangerous and uninhabitable, the fact is they are often removed without being able to actually return to their homes. They are highly unlikely to return to the building after renovations are complete because rents are typically raised. Meanwhile, immigrant entrepreneurs who own or lease commercial properties within a designated historic district are required to conform to strict regulations about building and renovation, which may be especially costly. Rehabilitation and preservation programs in suburbs like Freehold are no different from urban renewal programs in New Jersey's cities, which have a long record of displacing African Americans and the poor.

This is why, from my view, New Jersey's history as a state of suburbs becomes relevant when trying to make sense of anti-immigrant local ordinances. Some of New Jersey's suburbanites, like those in Freehold, fear the specter of increasing numbers of brown folks in their streets. Suburban living has always meant being safeguarded from the dangers typically associated with the city: working-class people and their presumed vices as well as racialized minorities and their presumed propensity for criminality. Suburbanites believe working-class Latino immigrants are an insidious threat they must combat by any means necessary, and indeed Freeholders have used every means at their disposal to get rid of them. When all other policies failed, historic preservation became their tool of choice.

With McMansions in Freehold Township and historic preservation efforts ongoing in Freehold Borough, there is much demand for construction, home repair, and landscaping labor. Low-wage, undocumented immigrant workers from Mexico as well as Central America have fit the bill. Consequently, the 2010 census estimated that 42.9 percent population of Freehold Borough was Latino. This is up from 28.1 percent as counted in the 2000 census.[68]

Not surprisingly, the Latino population is highly visible. It is not unusual to see Latinos strolling down the streets of Freehold Borough's designated historic district with their children, or sitting on park benches in front of the borough's hall of records. Within blocks of downtown, along the railroad tracks and not far from construction supply wholesalers and equipment rental outlets, is a day laborer muster zone. Yet, the presence of Latinos on the streets of downtown Freehold probably feels incongruous to (white) Freeholders against the backdrop of a streetscape that attempts to preserve a history that long predates the large-scale migration of Latinos to the area.

The presence of Latinos in Freehold's historic district, however, is ultimately necessary. Historic preservation requires labor for building, remodeling, and upkeep. Suburbia more generally requires much labor for construction, improvement, and maintenance. Home construction, improvement, and maintenance are *work* and require tremendous effort. Although many Americans take pleasure in DIY (do-it-yourself) projects, many others seek out workers to finish the job. Nationally, according to the National Day Labor Survey spearheaded by the Center for the Study of Urban Poverty at UCLA, most day laborers are "picked up by homeowners or small contractors to do home repairs and landscaping work. About 43 percent of day laborers are employed in temporary construction jobs."[69] Indeed, scholars attribute the rise of Latino immigration to New Jersey in the mid-2000s (the same period when Freehold Borough residents began to aggressively introduce anti-immigrant local ordinances), particularly increasing numbers of day laborers, to the construction boom.[70] It has to be underscored that home improvement doesn't only involve home construction or repair but also requires the maintenance and upkeep of the entire property. Lawns and gardens need to be kept up to sustain the suburban aesthetic of cleanliness and order. Home improvement and maintenance is about sustaining a community's "quality of life" (against the disorder and chaos of the city, for instance) and because property values depend on it. It is not surprising that among the goals of Freehold's historic preservation plans is "to stabilize and improve property values within the historic district and foster civic pride in the built environment."[71] Home improvement and maintenance are projects that are never fully achieved, ceaselessly demanding investment not only to preserve but also to increase property values.

The work of home improvement and maintenance reveals the tenuousness of suburban lifestyles. Danger lurks not merely at the suburb's edges (that is, the city) but, perhaps more menacingly, within. There is the danger of being unable to sustain the never-ending work of home improvement and maintenance, which is generally performed if not managed by (white) women. There is also the threat of (racialized and gendered) outsiders, in this case, Latino day laborers, who are nevertheless indispensable (if disposable) for the maintenance and improvement of suburban life. No matter how necessary day laborers are to supporting suburban lifestyles in New Jersey, they are not welcome as neighbors, as evidenced by the different ordinances that Freehold Borough has introduced.

Locals engaged in restricting immigrant settlement deploy different kinds of discourses that draw on racialized and sexualized logics, even as they may pass seemingly race-neutral policy measures. They draw on what anthropologist Leo Chavez describes as the "Latino Threat Narrative" through which Latino immigrants' "social identity has been plagued by the mark of illegality, which in much public discourse means that they are criminals and thus illegitimate members of society."[72] Although immigrant laborers are essential to the maintenance and improvement of suburban life, they are considered threatening to it as well. Immigrant day laborers in Freehold are figured particularly as a criminal menace.

Even at the state level, officials play up cases where immigrants have been found guilty of crimes to lobby for anti-immigrant legislation. In 2006 State Senator Christopher J. Connor, a Republican representing District 9 (Atlantic, Burlington and Ocean counties), reintroduced "a bill to prohibit the state from granting any license, contract, loan or tax abatement to New Jerseyans who cannot prove they are legal residents." It was prompted by the beating deaths of two (white) New Jersey boys by an undocumented immigrant from Mexico.[73]

Latino immigrant men are also figured or "racially profiled" as sexual threats, represented as predators ready to pounce on neighborhood women. It is perhaps because the work suburbanites require is generally the labor of men, particularly unattached single men (since the expectation is that they won't settle in the communities where they work), whereas the suburban homestead is the domain of the (white) woman and family, that these men's proximity to domestic spaces makes them sexually threatening.

Local media play a role in producing and reproducing notions of Latino men and other immigrant men of color as sexual predators. For instance, the *Tri Town News* featured a 2004 article on arrests made in Monmouth County with the headline, "Federal agents nab nine sex offenders: All immigrants, six in country illegally, face deportation for crimes."[74] The article then noted the country of origin for each of the men (mainly Latin American and African countries). According to ICE's public affairs spokesman who was quoted for the piece, "These groups have a history of being sexual predators."

Even if men are in fact attached to female partners, their partners are likewise characterized as exhibiting problematic sexualities. For example, Freehold Borough Council member Marc LeVine publicly remarked, "There is definitely a very promiscuous flavor in—at least—parts of Hispanic culture."[75] Here, the Latino Threat Narrative is not so much the single, male predator but the attached male who forms part of a couple that has the potential to reproduce prolifically. In other words, it is the Latino family that becomes threatening.[76] These families are seen as products of sexually unruly and deviant people. LeVine's concerns about Latinos' "promiscuity" echo larger concerns about so-called anchor babies, that is, U.S.-born, second-generation Latino children who might serve as "anchors" for their undocumented parents. With their legal claim as U.S. citizens, these American-born children can potentially legalize their parents' status, something that those opposed to Latino undocumented immigration find problematic. Even if legalization for their parents is not forthcoming, the American-born children of undocumented immigrants are entitled to other kinds of public goods (education, health care, and the like), which anti-immigrant forces believe ought to be reserved for more "authentic" Americans. Juxtaposed against Latino families' settlement in Freehold, LeVine encourages the settlement of "young [white] families," which, can be interpreted as a neo-natalist argument for the sexual reproduction of whites as a kind of antidote to the perceived overpopulation of brown families.

That Latinos are considered a threat is in suburban spaces like Freehold must be linked to longer histories of racial segregation in the United States. Suburbs have always been considered "white space." According to sociologist Elijah Anderson,

> Whites and others often stigmatize anonymous black persons by associating them with the putative danger, crime, and poverty of the iconic ghetto,

> typically leaving blacks with much to prove before being able to establish trusting relations with them. Accordingly, the most easily tolerated black person in the white space is often one who is "in his place"—that is, one who is working as a janitor or a service person or one who has been vouched for by white people in good standing. Such a person may be believed to be less likely to disturb the implicit racial order—whites as dominant and blacks as subordinate.[77]

Latino laborers who settled in Freehold are, like their black predecessors, considered violators of "white space" because they are not "in their place" as mere laborers. The racialized and sexualized profiling and representation of African American men has, arguably, shaped the constructions of all men of color. It is important to note that the same sorts of characterizations were even applied to turn-of-the-twentieth-century Asian immigrants such as the Chinese and Filipinos as well as Southern European immigrants, like the Italians. The Latino Threat Narrative, it must be emphasized, is not a recent one. During the Great Depression, campaigns in California supporting the deportation of Mexican immigrants, deployed themes similar to the ones I have tracked in New Jersey. According to communication scholar Lisa Flores, "Public perception was that the European immigration/race problems had been largely solved; however, fears that unassimilable and undesirable aliens might pollute the stock and dilute the character of Americanism had not disappeared. Thus, these fears could be easily drawn upon and transferred to Mexicans. Unfortunately, the commentaries and tropes that had highlighted the supposed problems of degeneracy, illiteracy, and other forms of pollution could now be transferred from the Asian and European menace to the characters in the narratives of the Mexican problem."[78]

Morristown: A Case Study of Local Antiterror Campaigns

The Latino Threat Narrative is not always the operating discourse for proponents of anti-immigrant policies in New Jersey. Post-9/11, immigrants, including Latinos, are figured as national security threats as well. This has been the case in Morristown. Located about an hour west of New York City, it has a population of nearly 20,000. Whites make up 62.5 percent of the population. The next largest group is Hispanics/Latinos, at about 34 percent. Notably, the foreign-born population is also 34 percent. Like

Freehold, Morristown boasts of its significance to the nation's beginnings. The town's website boasts, "Washington did sleep here," noting that Morristown served as George Washington's headquarters on different occasions during the Revolutionary War.[79] Moreover, the National Trust for Historic Preservation, a private nonprofit organization (distinct, for example, from the National Park Service, a federal agency that manages the National Register of Historic Places) named the town one of its Dozen Distinctive Destinations in 2002.[80] Communities earn this distinction "by combining dynamic downtowns, cultural diversity, attractive architecture, cultural landscapes, and a strong commitment to historic preservation, sustainability, and revitalization."[81] At the same time, Morristown is home to Morristown National Historical Park, run by the National Park Service, which is notable for being the country's first national historical park.[82] Morris County, of which Morristown serves as the county seat, also celebrates the county's historic roots in tourism material touting the area's history during the Gilded Age and the Industrial Revolution, though the county's role in the Revolutionary War takes pride of place. The Morris County Tourism Bureau's logo is an American flag. That logo, along with Morristown's logo of what appears to be a profile of a Revolutionary soldier, suggests that the place's identity is especially tied to America's beginnings. As historian Howard Zinn reminds us, however, "There is no surer way to obscure the deep divisions of race and class in American history than by uniting us in support of the American Revolution and all its symbols."[83]

Alongside its strong investment in its Revolutionary War roots, Morristown sees itself as offering a more urbanized lifestyle than most suburbs for both young childless professionals and professionals with families. Morristown offers easy access to Manhattan as it is one of the stops on New Jersey Transit's Midtown Direct train service. It has invested in publicizing its proximity to New York City and appealing to prospective residents who work there. One of the few news items that the current Morristown leadership posts online, for example is a 2012 *Wall Street Journal* piece that highlights its cultural life, presumably to assuage urbanites' fears that moving to Morristown would mean giving up the pleasures of city living.[84] Walking around Morristown's downtown area while doing research, I recall how busy it seemed for a relatively small community. I took note of major new construction of slick-looking residential units, which I imagined were meant to appeal to a younger demographic. Indeed, an ad I picked up for the 40 Park apartments located downtown confirmed my suspicions. The ad features mainly young, white people in tastefully appointed residences. It reads, "40 Park's regal lifestyle begins just steps from legendary parks, restaurants, shops and theaters . . . all just minutes from Morristown's train station with direct service to Manhattan."[85]

As mentioned, Morristown is the county seat for Morris County, a county that has consistently been counted among the wealthiest in the entire country.[86] Morris County's self-representation is similar to that of Morristown. The county's official guide depicts five different images. Three of the images are of the county's Revolutionary War and rural roots. One is an image of a performing arts center. The final two are of people who are ostensibly the county's current residents, all of whom are white.[87]

Morristown's leaders appear to have succeeded in fashioning their town in a particular manner as a recent *New York Times* real estate article picks up on precisely the sorts of characteristics Morristown has attempted to project. Titled "Morristown, N.J., Historic with a Lively Downtown," it opens with an interview of a new homeowner, a man in his mid-twenties, who commutes into New York and was looking to live in community that was, "lively."[88]

Morristown, like Freehold, is a place where residents have debated the influx of Latino immigrants, particularly day laborers. White residents' concerns about day laborers stem from the belief that Latino workers mar their civic landscape in a range of ways. Michael Rockland, a Morristown resident and American Studies professor, describes, for instance, how Morris Street, a main artery in Morristown, is populated by "a multitude of short, swarthy men dressed in work clothes and baseball caps," who are "jostling each other" for work. He goes on to describe how Morris Street leads up to the town's "lovely Colonial-era Green, the epicenter of the downtown business district," and ultimately hits Speedwell Avenue, where many Latino businesses and residences and located. In contrast to the "lovely Green," Rockland's describes the area of Speedwell Avenue (using his own words and the words of other residents), as a place where people live in "overcrowded conditions," "shout on their cell phones all the time," and "urinate in the backyard." Meanwhile, although its eateries (and other businesses) have given new life to the area, according to Rockland, they serve "barely tolerable" food.[89] He says he's ambivalent about the presence of Latino immigrants in his town; however, the contrasts Rockland draws between the different communities in the town are quite stark. Wittingly or unwittingly, he reproduces elements of the Latino Threat Narrative, specifically the notion that Latino immigrants' presence in the United States signals the "devolution of society" when he describes (or quotes others who describe) Latinos as people who "shout on their cell phones all the time" or who "urinate in the backyard" and who eat unpalatable food. Moreover, the title of his piece, "Those People" serves to reinforce the notion that Latinos do not belong.

When Mayor Don Cresitello, a Democrat at the time, announced in 2007 that he was applying to the federal 287(g) program, which would deputize local police as immigration enforcement officers, he was one of the first mayors in the country and the first in New Jersey to introduce an initiative of this kind. Although coming under heavy criticism by immigration rights activists and others, Cresitello believed his action was justified by the New Jersey attorney general's directive clarifying the expectation that local police cooperate with ICE in immigration enforcement. In an interview, Mayor Cresitello remarked that the directive "is an acknowledgement of what I have been saying all along. Morristown has a right to do this."[90]

In a major national media interview Cresitello stated, "People are just fed up with the illegal immigration. They feel violated. They just don't like the fact that somebody can walk across the border. It's as if they've opened a door and walked into your home and sat down at your table and said, 'feed me.'"[91] In this statement, Cresitello reproduces the Latino Threat Narrative about undocumented migrants' criminality, narratives circulated as well in Freehold. Undocumented immigrants' supposed criminality is among the leading reasons Cresitello put forward to justify his proposal to deputize local police as immigration enforcement agents. In the same interview, he described a crime committed in his own neighborhood as a motivating factor for him. He stated, "This [where Cresitello lives] is a very residential neighborhood and yet—somebody will buy a single family home and put fifteen people in it." He continued, "This—this particular house had—activities that—allegedly, because the trial hasn't taken place yet, involved prostitution and drug dealing—money laundering and false documents."[92] Although Cresitello tried to make it seem in this particular statement as if he was not jumping to a conclusion about the criminal activities of the immigrant household's members, he made it clear that he associates undocumented border crossing with criminality in his public remarks at a town hall debate on the topic of 287(g). In response to opposition to the program he stated, "Don't tell me we don't need to enforce immigration laws. There are thousands of people crossing the line, who are criminals."[93] For Cresitello, undocumented immigrants can never be presumed innocent. They are always, already criminals. It is important to index here how this thinking has always been applied to African Americans, particularly African American men.[94] As I have suggested earlier in this book, the racialized logics applied to Latinos and other immigrants of color are imbricated in the racialized logics applied to blacks.

Cresitello presumes that undocumented immigrants are all criminals and likens their threat to the nation-state as a threat to a person's home. This is a prime example of the post-9/11 "domopolitics" that Walters describes. Cresitello draws heavily on national security discourses in justifying the need for 287(g) in Morristown. He states plainly, "First of all, it's . . . a homeland security issue. Morristown manages an airport; for police protection. It's a major hospital, major office buildings and certainly, we want to be working closer with Homeland Security." He goes on to mention an alleged terrorist plot against Fort Dix, also in New Jersey, to further justify his actions.[95]

In 2007, six Muslim men from New Jersey and Pennsylvania were arrested for allegedly plotting to attack and Fort Dix, a U.S. military installation in southern New Jersey. Major media reports on the plot, not surprisingly, detailed each man's ethnicity and immigration status.[96] More recently, alternative claims have been made suggesting that the men were in fact entrapped by the FBI and not "predisposed to commit a terrorist crime."[97] Nevertheless, what transpired became an issue that Cresitello used to justify 287(g). He stated: "As was indicated with Fort Dix a week ago, these problems can be uncovered at a local level. It'd be easier if there's cooperation." Moreover, in the same interview he stated, "Also, with the increased problems with day laborers, with stacking, federal, criminal violations of federal immigration law we felt and I personally felt that it was better if we would be directly in contact with and participate with ICE in any investigations going to take place in Morristown."[98]

Cresitello suggests that the threat of Islamist terrorism is of a piece with undocumented Latino immigration. In both cases, immigrants of color are cast as dangerous Others who need to be rooted out of the community. Different groups represent different sorts of threat (Muslims are represented as a national security threat whereas Latinos are represented as a threat to public safety), but they are nonetheless a threat that requires local government's response. As ethnic studies scholar Irum Shiekh argues, the racialization of immigrants "creates a climate of fear in which the general public assumes that the state is protecting them from dangerous individuals. The general public therefore consents to provide the state with unprecedented and unchecked powers in the name of national security."[99] Shiekh writes here specifically about Muslim or "Muslim-looking" immigrants, but I would argue that this extends to Latino immigrants as well. Moreover, when she refers to "the state," she means the federal government. Yet, her argument is perhaps especially relevant to local governments. When residents of suburban communities feel threatened and unsafe, it is to their local law enforcement that they turn for help. Cresitello was keenly aware of this fact when he applied to the 287(g) program in the mid-2000s. To what extent his 287(g) proposal was a shrewd political ploy to bolster his constituent base in Morristown, is not entirely clear. After all, Cristello is known for switching political parties. This particular policy priority may have been aimed at garnering more support given his political ambitions. It did not work as his U.S. Senatorial bid in 2008 as well as his bid to get reelected as Morristown's mayor both failed. What is clear is that weighing in on immigration is something local politicians are doing across the state. Cresitello portrays himself as at once safeguarding the citizens of his town from dangerous criminal elements and performing his patriotic duty to fight terrorism through the defense of "home/land security." As American Studies scholar Amy Kaplan puts it, "Although homeland security may strive to protect the domestic nation from foreign threats, it is actually about breaking down the boundaries between inside and outside, about seeing the home in a state of constant emergency, besieged by internal and external threats that are indistinguishable."[100] For Mayor Cresitello, Morristown is "besieged by internal and external threats." Those threats are immigrants of color, who are "indistinguishable." That they are not citizens makes them both not American and ultimately un-American.

Arguably, terrorism fears can be more easily stoked in a place like Morristown given its very real connections to the World Trade Center attacks. Several Morristown residents were killed on 9/11. Regardless of connection or proximity to the site of the terror attacks, however, scholars have found that people who identify very strongly with an American national identity tend to support policies to intern Arab Americans or Arabs suspected of having terrorism links. Notably, these same individuals may actually define "being an American" as including, among other traits, respecting other people's cultural differences, or seeing people of all backgrounds as American. In other words, having a kind of multicultural definition of what it means to be an American has not exempted people in this country from supporting policies that would lead to Arabs' mass incarcerations.[101] That Cresitello is a Democrat yet supports policies that are not typically associated with the Democratic Party may have to do with his investment in this idea of what it means to be "American." His bravado in putting forth a 287(g) application, moreover, may well reflect his Morristown constituents, who, though perhaps more urban and cosmopolitan than people in other municipalities, possess a sense of "Americanness" that is nevertheless exclusive. It may well be that Cresitello's party affiliation has less to do with political ideology and more with political expedience. Cresitello previously won an election bid to the town council as a Republican then was later elected to the office of mayor as a Democrat. In an earlier bid for the mayor's seat, he ran as an independent. What is certain is that Cresitello drew on homeland security discourses to justify his application to the 287(g) program. Moreover, symbolic politics, as sociologists have documented, can activate anti-immigrant sentiment in a community. In her review of the sociological scholarship on symbolic politics and immigration, Elizabeth Fussell finds that "an in-group's sense of threat from immigrants can be elicited not only by their presence but also by politics. Symbolic politics theory proposes that political elites employ symbols, words, and laws to evoke predictable emotional reactions in target audiences and assign blame or responsibility for social problems."[102]

Immigrant rights advocates both locally and nationally contested Cresitello's proposal. Local advocates were especially concerned that it could influence neighboring towns in Morris County to make similar moves.[103] Even Morristown's chief of police seemed reluctant to publicly support the 287(g) application, stating that the local police's relationship with the ICE was already strong and that "What we're doing now seems to be very affective."[104] Moreover, the Morris County sheriff, a Republican, refused to support the mayor's application to the 287(g) program on the grounds that it would be too costly and that it would become the "target of protests and lawsuits by civil rights groups."[105] However, anti-immigrant groups both locally and nationally were actively supportive of Cresitello's initiative to apply to the 287(g). Not long after Mayor Cresitello officially announced his plan, the ProAmerica Society of New Jersey organized a rally to support him.[106] The slate of speakers for the event included representatives of a number of anti-immigrant groups. Cresitello made the following statement at the rally: "I am here today because this is the military capital of the American Revolution." He actually makes direct reference to the Boston Tea Party, stating, "A few people in Boston threw some tea in a harbor and started a revolution. We are here today to continue the efforts of these individuals."[107]

Most notably, the rally included Peter Gadiel, the founder of the group 9/11 Families for a Secure America; Gadiel lost his son in the attack on the World Trade Center.[108] According to the 9/11 Families for a Secure America website, the group was formed "because every illegal alien is a person whose true identity has never been verified by competent federal officials, any illegal alien may be a terrorist or violent felon. It is not possible to keep terrorists out of the United States without denying entry to all illegal aliens." The site further states, "Because the massive number of illegal aliens present in the United States has caused the ending of interior enforcement of immigration law the millions of illegals in our country acted as an 'ocean' which allowed the 9/11 terrorists to hide in plain sight."[109] At the ProAmerica rally, Gadiel practically repeated the narrative of the 9/11 Families for a Secure America website, stating that to be an undocumented immigrant "means that your true identity is unknown, it has never been verified by any competent authority which means that every illegal alien, every undocumented immigrant, any illegal alien may be a criminal or a terrorist and many of them are and some of those terrorists murdered my son on 9/11." Like Cresitello in the interviews cited earlier in this chapter, the organization links migrants' legal status with a propensity for criminality, terrorism, or both. If Cresitello and other anti-immigrant forces in New Jersey and beyond deploy state-defined and sanctioned notions of "security," a consequence of these discourses is that immigrant community members are rendered insecure.[110] I explore questions of security and insecurity as immigrants struggle and negotiate with it in their everyday lives in chapter 4.

Conclusion

This chapter has examined the municipal landscape of immigration policy in various communities in New Jersey. Enabled in part by the emergence of the post-9/11 Homeland Security State, local governments have introduced a host of policies aimed at expelling or excluding immigrants from their communities. At the same time, these municipal policies aimed at delimiting the rights of belonging and citizenship to the select suburban few are linked to a longer history of racial segregation in the United States.

Local government officials have often taken the lead in initiating anti-immigrant local ordinances. They draw on a variety of discourses to garner support for these initiatives including the "Latino Threat" and national security/antiterrorism narratives. Other actors are equally involved in shaping the policy landscape of post-9/11 suburban New Jersey. On one hand, there are local explicitly anti-immigration groups involved in municipal struggles to prohibit immigrant settlement. These groups are either homegrown or are local branches of national organizations. On the other hand, there are groups that do not necessarily make immigration their central issue yet are proponents of measures that would prevent immigrant settlement. These groups deploy what might be considered "postracial" languages to make their claims. What they promote are historical preservation or "quality of life" concerns. These groups engage municipal governments directly, but they also organize and participate in public events like forums or direct pickets of immigrant spaces.

Immigration continues to be highly contested in both Freehold and Morristown. In Freehold, local residents rejected measures aimed at expanding the borough's public schools to better accommodate its growing immigrant population in two referendums. The state's education commissioner, David Hespe, was forced to step in to nullify the referendums. In his decision, Hespe wrote, "[T]he failure to act will deprive children in this community of the educational opportunity that they will need to succeed in life," and would be a violation of their constitutional rights.[111] Meanwhile, in Morristown, the anti-immigrant banner is being taken up by at least one local resident. In the fall of 2015, Morristown resident Gregg Bruen covered his porch with signs that many in the Latino community found offensive. Accusing the municipality of not doing enough to address undocumented immigration in the community, Bruen called for those who share his view to support Donald Trump for president because, "He is the only candidate who is really aware of what undocumented people are doing in this country."[112]

Immigration politics is likely to continue to be a major issue of concern for communities around the state. Though 2014 census figures do not specify exactly who is exiting, between 2013 and 2014 at least 55,000 left New Jersey to live elsewhere. What the census does indicate is that new immigrant settlement in the state accounts for stable population growth.[113] An article reporting on this census data does not explicitly address the issue of race, but it is certainly a concern among readers. Though the comments section for the article are moderated and therefore do not comprehensively capture reactions to the piece, it is clear that what is at stake is the racial composition of the state. Readers who have weighed in assume that the white population is declining and that the changing composition of the state, most notably the increasing number of Latinos (who the readers assume to be undocumented), is leading to the state's economic and social decline. It has been ten years since my research for this chapter first started and the dominance of the Latino Threat Narrative has hardly waned.

3

The New "Main Street"?

Ethnoburbs and the Complex Politics of Race

Named after the great American inventor Thomas Edison, Edison, New Jersey, has its strip malls with retail giants like Walmart, Target, and others. Much of Edison looks no different from what many might consider a typical American landscape. Yet look a little more closely and Edison reveals itself to be rather atypical. On the weekend, it is not unusual to pass public parks crowded with cricket players in their starched whites. Usually they are South Asians. Turn onto Oak Tree Road and you find strip malls not just with Dunkin' Donuts or McDonald's restaurants, but also with eateries like Bengali Sweets and Moghul Express.[1]

Edison has attracted mainstream media attention for its dramatically changing landscape. A 2008 *New York Times* article describes how Indians "have spearheaded the transformation of Edison—an overwhelmingly blue-collar and middle-class white community a generation ago—into a town with a decidedly Asian flavor."[2]

Several years later, an Edison native satirically commented in a *Time* magazine article, "My town is totally unfamiliar to me. The Pizza Hut where my busboy friends stole pies for our drunken parties is now an Indian sweets shop with a completely inappropriate roof. The A&P I shoplifted from is now an Indian grocery. The multiplex where we snuck into R-rated movies now shows only Bollywood films and serves samosas. The Italian restaurant that my friends stole cash from as waiters is now Moghul, one of the most famous Indian restaurants in the country."[3]

The article outraged many in the Indian community.[4] This prompted both *Time* magazine and the author, Joel Stein, to respond:

> TIME: We sincerely regret that any of our readers were upset by this humor column of Joel Stein's. It was in no way intended to cause offense.
>
> JOEL STEIN: I truly feel stomach-sick that I hurt so many people. I was trying to explain how, as someone who believes that immigration has enriched American life and my hometown in particular, I was shocked that I could feel a tiny bit uncomfortable with my changing town when I went to visit it. If we could understand that reaction, we'd be better equipped to debate people on the other side of the immigration issue.[5]

It interesting to note that Stein's nostalgic ruminations on the petty crimes he committed in his youth in his now "unfamiliar" hometown were published on July 5, a day after the Fourth of July, a major American holiday. I wonder about its publication during the week that Americans probably feel especially patriotic; whether the unrecognizability of Stein's hometown and the anxieties it elicits are anxieties that become especially acute during a major national holiday? Though it was meant as a satirical piece, the tensions the article reflects and reproduces are only the tip of the iceberg. If Edison was feeling practically "unfamiliar" to Stein, an Edison "native," it is a feeling shared by other Edison residents, including local leaders. A white former local official responded to a question about what defines Edison as a "community" in the following way: "Mostly race, somewhat ethnicity, but most definitely the changes that occur [in the] neighborhood."[6]

Indians in particular have borne the brunt of the fears and resentments Edison's whites feel because of this "unfamiliarity" and race-based sense of "community." Edison's Indian community has had to contend with hate crimes perpetrated by local white residents, municipal restrictions on Indian cultural practices, and tensions with the local police. Despite their position as a more economically privileged group of legal, and generally English-speaking immigrants, Indians in Edison experience marginalization and exclusion like that experienced by their undocumented Spanish-speaking working-class Latino counterparts in other parts of New Jersey. Moreover, they experience this marginalization and exclusion in the context of a suburb where minorities have overtaken the "majority." The Indian community's "unfamiliarity," as written by Stein, expressed by the former local official and encoded in local laws, is also linked the racialization of Asian Americans as "forever foreigners"; that is, no matter how many generations Asian Americans may have been living in the United States (and as I will discuss later, we have been in this country for over a century), they/we are automatically assumed to be foreigners.[7]

Even for Indians beyond New Jersey, Edison figures prominently as a place they can call "home." It is a key node in the Indian diasporic geographic imaginary. In other words, many Indians in the diaspora recognize Edison as a significant Indian American community. For example, a major Indian television series about the Indian diasporic experience was set in Edison. It is not the experience of a fully assimilated American suburban existence, but of a distinctively ethnic and racialized American suburban experience. As Sam, a middle aged Indian immigrant interviewed for this book, put it, when asked where "Indian places" are in New Jersey, "Edison was the main place, but now you go to Old Bridge, it's full of Indians. You go to Jersey City, it's full of Indians." Edison, notably, was the first place he identified.

I grew up in Edison's Filipino equivalent in California: Union City. The corner of Dyer Street and Alvarado Boulevard looks and feels like a "little Manila." Two major Filipino grocery stores sit diagonal to each other (that's how many Filipino people live there). Moving to Highland Park in New Jersey when I got my job at Rutgers was a fun novelty to me. From my perspective as a Californian, I thought it was quaint. Highland Park looks and feels like the version of "America" that I grew up watching on TV and in movies, but not a version of America that I actually experienced. Edison borders Highland Park, and in many ways it felt much more like home to me. If parts of Edison are populated with large concentrations of Indian residents and businesses, other parts are populated with other kinds of Asians, including Koreans and Chinese.

I enjoyed the drive on Route 27 into Edison from Highland Park as English-language signs would give way to signs in Chinese. Some of the best Chinese food I've had in my life, I've eaten in Edison. I did my grocery shopping there because it's where I could find the flavors of home (home being Union City, not the Philippines; I was born in California). It was a big event for me when H-Mart, a Korean grocery store, opened at the edge of Edison close to Highland Park. It meant being able to have even better access to Asian groceries. I experienced Oak Tree Road not as some unfamiliar place; rather, it was vaguely familiar. Places like Edison and Union City, America's "ethnoburbs," share many characteristics. According to geographer and ethnic studies scholar Wei Li, an ethnoburb is defined as "suburban ethnic clusters of residential areas and business districts in large metropolitan areas."[8] Edison, like Union City, fits this definition, and though I'm not Indian, it still felt like home.

Although Edison counts among the nation's increasing numbers of "ethnoburbs," it is hardly a postracial context even with its "majority minority" population. It is not a place where racism doesn't matter anymore. It's perhaps for this reason that I found Edison interesting as a site of study. Maybe I was just young and naïve, but I do not recall when I was growing up witnessing or experiencing the kinds of tensions that I would uncover while studying Edison, though it's important to recall that California is hardly immune from these tensions.

In places like Edison, immigrants' entrepreneurship and long-term settlement change the civic landscape in highly visible ways that provoke negative, visceral reactions from "natives."[9] Long-term (generally white) residents desperately hold on to the last vestiges of their community, which they believe immigrants undermine and threaten. In other words, I look at how Edison's "unfamiliarity" as Joel Stein describes it manifests in everyday life as well as in local politics. I analyze anti-immigrant local ordinances introduced and passed by the Edison government that target Indian residents. However, concerns about Asian immigrants more generally spilled into the political arena in the mid-2000s during the Edison mayoral campaigns of Jun Choi, a second-generation Korean American. The high-achieving child of immigrant entrepreneurs, this "model minority" Asian American political candidate was not exempt from racist marginalization and exclusion in his own hometown, something I examine in this chapter as well.

Even though Indians and other Asian immigrant groups face similar forms of marginalization and exclusion, interethnic coalitions between these groups are quite fragile. In Edison, despite the fact that Mayor Choi was racialized at different points of his tenure as representing "Asian" interests, which presumably includes the interests of the Indian community, he would in fact draw ire from that community over various issues. Indians' distancing from Choi belies the pan-ethnic identity that non-Asians who opposed his candidacy assumed he represented. Indeed, "Asian American" as a collective, pan-ethnic political identity is situational and contingent in Edison. Both ethno-racial as well as class tensions make pan-ethnic coalitions difficult to forge and sustain.

Race in Ethnoburbs

Residential or spatial assimilation, what many scholars consider the opposite of residential segregation, is the degree to which people of color live in close proximity to whites. While research has typically measured the degree to which immigrants and other racialized minorities have achieved economic and political parity with whites (in other words, are economically and politically assimilated), residential assimilation has often been considered an important indicator that group boundaries and the hierarchies that organize them are destabilizing.[10]

If racial groups live in close proximity to each other they have more contact. The "contact hypothesis" posits that with more contact, tensions between groups are likely to lessen.[11] Moreover, if racial groups live in close proximity and have more contact, the chances that they may cross racial boundaries and intermarry are greater. It is through intermarriage that group boundaries are breached and ultimately destroyed. Alongside the "contact hypothesis" advanced by scholars, civil rights activists have championed desegregation as a primary means by which equality can truly be achieved between/across racial groups. As I discussed in chapter 1, suburbs have typically been highly segregated and many suburban residents have engaged in efforts to keep them that way. Yet, despite these efforts, suburbs are changing quite rapidly.

African Americans have been able to make inroads into the suburbs. In fact, what was once Levittown, New Jersey, is now Willingboro. Whereas various Levittowns were known for being almost exclusively white in large part due to racial covenants encouraged by Levittown developer William Levitt, today's Willingboro is predominantly African American.[12] When African Americans weren't able to breach the boundaries of white suburbs, they have created their own.[13]

Cities were the initial stop for many generations of immigrants who then moved to the suburbs after achieving some degree of upward mobility economically. Many of the more privileged and highly educated immigrants, like immigrants from Asia, are bypassing cities altogether and settling directly in suburbs because they have the human and social capital to do so. At the same time, many immigrants settle in emerging ethnic communities in the suburbs because it gives them access to people who share their background, as well as goods and services they desire.[14]

Asians are more likely than most other immigrant groups to live in suburbs than in cities.[15] New majority minority, "melting pot" suburbs have begun to emerge.[16] In the Middlesex-Somerset-Hunterdon County region of New Jersey, where Edison is located, the Asian suburban population is over 10 percent.[17] The diversification of many New Jersey suburbs, particularly those defined as part of the "Greater New York metropolitan region," which includes Edison, is a process that has progressed since the 1970s. It is not a new phenomenon.[18]

Although contact theorists might have predicted that ethnoburbs are sites where racialized boundaries are weakening and hence group conflict (specifically between whites and racialized minorities) may be lessening, residential assimilation has not necessarily led to the weakening of boundaries, but, seemingly, to the bolstering of them. Residents, particularly white, native-born residents in ethnoburbs, engage in bitter battles to define the identities of their communities. This is certainly true in Edison.

What contact theorists may not be accounting for is that residential assimilation is not just about having more nonwhite neighbors. When more minorities move into a neighborhood, they can engage in a host of practices that dramatically reshape the look and feel of a place. For example, along with residential assimilation can be the establishment of businesses by racial and ethnic minorities, which cater to both their own and the broader community.

Minority businesspeople, like the Indian entrepreneurs that enliven Edison's Oak Tree Road, are generally thought to embody the "American" ethic of entrepreneurship and are typically held up as "model minorities."[19] Even the White House celebrated Asian American entrepreneurs, calling them "leading actors in the U.S. economy."[20] Unlike their undocumented Latino counterparts, these immigrant entrepreneurs are often depicted in broader public discourses as truly contributing to the United States. According to the White House, they provide jobs, and "[a]s the U.S. faces difficult economic times, these contributions are a vital catalyst to economic recovery."[21] These aren't the immigrants that "take jobs away." The immigrant entrepreneur, particularly the Asian American entrepreneur, is often held up as a model racialized citizen, not only in contrast to low-wage undocumented Latinos immigrants but also native-born Latinos and blacks. Indeed, Asian immigrant businesspeople themselves often try to use their entrepreneurship to stake a claim as authentic Americans.

Yet, immigrants' businesses also raise concerns among "natives" because they reshape suburban landscapes in very visible ways. Ethnic businesses have ethnic signage, ethnic patrons from beyond the neighborhood, and the like. The issues raised by Joel Stein, for instance, are issues related to Edison's landscape as it has been reconfigured by Indian businesses. As ethnic studies scholar Wendy Cheng argues, based on research of a Chinese ethnoburb in Southern California, struggles over landscapes "are also struggles over power in which questions of race, history, and identity are implicated, and the stakes include specific and unequal material outcomes."[22] The suburban-scape is constituted by commercial landscapes (those to which businesses contribute through buildings, signage, types of retail activity, and the consumer base they attract), residential landscapes (the types of houses people live in), and civic landscapes (government buildings and other public spaces including how they are occupied and used). In Edison, changing landscapes have been a source of a range of conflicts and have been at the heart of local electoral battles.

Asian Immigration Historically

Before I discuss tensions in Edison over Asian immigration, I will provide a brief overview of Asian immigration to the United States more broadly and into the state of New Jersey more specifically. It is the European narrative of immigration through Ellis Island that perhaps forms the basis for popular understandings of immigration for people who live in Lady Liberty's shadow, so a historic discussion of Asian immigration, which traces its beginnings to the western United States, seems appropriate here.

Asians have been immigrating to the United States for several centuries. Some of the earliest immigrants were those who jumped ship at the height of colonial global trade. For example, Filipinos escaped Spanish galleons and settled in Louisiana in the 1700s.[23] Large-scale Asian immigration to the United States, however, began in the latter half of the nineteenth century, after the Civil War. The rapidly industrializing and once-again unified country, fulfilling its "Manifest Destiny," required labor to do the arduous and often dangerous work of building the transcontinental railroad as well as picking fruit and vegetables in the fields to connect and feed a growing and expanding nation.[24]

The United States has always had a contradictory stance toward immigrants from Asia, however. While Asian immigrants were actively sought to fill labor needs, they were simultaneously reviled. When they came in large enough numbers, they were seen not as only economic but also cultural threats embodying norms and mores that could undermine the American nation. They were thought of as sources of disease who would infect the broader population and as potential sexual predators who could victimize innocent white women. As a consequence, Asian immigration has been marked by fits and starts. Different Asian groups arrived in the United States in succession as different Asian ethnic groups were recruited and then subsequently excluded in the wake of the Civil War.[25] Although the Chinese arriving in the United States through Angel Island off San Francisco generally sought employment in the American West, many ultimately made their way to the East Coast, seeking new opportunities for employment as well as, in some cases, respite from growing anti-Chinese violence in the western United States.[26] After several decades of immigration to the United States, the Chinese were met with highly organized racist nativism that eventually led to the Chinese Exclusion Act of 1882. Although prior to exclusion most Asians immigrated to the United States through Angel Island, Ellis Island became a more direct entry point for Chinese immigrants into New Jersey (mainly from Latin America and the Caribbean). Ellis Island, which opened in 1892, ten years after the passage of the Chinese Exclusion Act, had "Chinese inspectors" whose job it was to ensure that the Chinese Exclusion Act was being implemented properly on the East Coast.[27]

After the passage of the Chinese Exclusion Act, U.S. employers sought other sources of labor in Asia and looked to Japan. By 1898, however, the United States extended well beyond the North American continent into the Pacific and the Caribbean. Hawaii was annexed in 1898, and the Philippines, Puerto Rico, and Cuba were colonized the same year. The annexation of Hawaii led to the closer integration of its economy with that of the mainland. Japanese workers were brought in to work in the sugarcane fields of Hawaii; later many came to California to work in the fruit and vegetable fields. Like the Chinese before them, the Japanese would face the wrath of the white nativist lobby, which would successfully secure the passage of the Gentleman's Agreement of 1907, prohibiting the immigration of the Japanese.

The fact that it was called a "Gentleman's Agreement" (as opposed to an outright "Japanese Exclusion Act" like the first anti-Asian immigration law, which prohibited Chinese immigration) reflects Japan's relative higher status and a degree of diplomatic civility between the two countries that did not exist between China and the United States. Nevertheless, the outcome was the same: the prohibition of specific forms of Asian immigration. Some highly resourceful Japanese among those who had entered prior to the passage of the law transitioned from farm laborers to farm owners. This provoked hostility among local whites and led to the Alien Land Law of 1913 in the state of California.[28] This law, and other land laws passed by different states, prohibited "aliens ineligible for citizenship" from both owning and leasing land. Indeed, both the Chinese and the Japanese were considered people who could never qualify for U.S. citizenship no matter how long they lived and worked in the United States.[29] Although the Fourteenth Amendment of the Constitution, adopted in 1868, guaranteed the citizenship and equal protection of African Americans, the right to citizenship and equal protection would not be extended to Chinese and Japanese immigrants until 1952 with the passage of the McCarren-Walter Act. Attempts were even made to try to deny rights to the American-born children of Asian immigrants. Court challenges of the Alien Land Law tried to prevent Asian American children from holding title to the land their parents worked.[30]

With two sources of Asian labor closed off, employers sought yet another source of workers and turned to the Philippines. Filipinos, considered U.S. "nationals" as a consequence of American colonization in 1898, could not be prohibited from immigrating on the basis of being "foreign," although they were not considered full citizens. In other words, Filipinos would have the "right" to work as low-wage laborers in Hawaii and the continental United States—but they wouldn't have the right to vote, to marry whites, and more. And so they were brought into the United States by the thousands. Many arrived on the West Coast to work in agriculture, but many others came to the United States as students. These *pensionados* were sponsored by the U.S. government to be educated for the purpose of later returning to the Philippines to partner with the Americans in the colonial administration of the Philippines. Filipino immigration in the Northeast was typically that of *pensionados*.[31] Like their Chinese and Japanese predecessors, however, Filipino workers in California were met with both vigilante violence and organized nativist forces that would champion the passage of an immigration exclusion law against them.[32] Excluding immigrants from the Philippines, however, would require that the United States first let go of the Philippines as formal colony. Only when the Philippines was considered an "independent" nation whose citizens could then be rendered "foreigners" and not U.S. nationals could they be eligible for exclusion. Filipino exclusion was secured in this way through the Tydings-McDuffie Act of 1934.

Korean and Indian immigration, though much smaller in number than that of the Chinese, Japanese, and Filipinos, began in the early twentieth century. The Koreans had been recruited to work in Hawaii's agricultural industry around the time that the Japanese were recruited to work there. Indian men would also make their way directly to the United States to work in the fields of California, even intermarrying with Mexican women.[33] Other Indians went to Washington, Oregon, and later California via Canada to escape from anti-Indian riots in Vancouver in the early 1900s.[34] A smaller number of Indians came as traders or jumped from British ships in New York City.[35] However, with the introduction of the Immigration Act in 1917, Indians would be barred from entering the United States. The Immigration Act of 1917 created the so-called Asiatic barred zone that defined the geographical scope of Indian as well as Asian immigrant exclusion more broadly. The zone went from South Asia and Arabia to Southeast Asia and extended to islands in the Indian and Pacific Oceans.[36]

As if the 1917 Immigration Act wasn't enough, the 1924 Immigration Act was passed to further bolster U.S. borders against the incursion of Asian immigrants. This act included a provision that prohibited the immigration of those "aliens ineligible for citizenship." Unlike their European counterparts, Asians already living and working in the United States were not eligible to naturalize and become U.S. citizens. Hence, after the passage of the 1924 Immigration Act, people from the continent of Asia could not enter the United States.[37]

It would take several decades before all of this would change. World War II had an impact on changing, in part, Americans' attitudes toward some Asian groups. As is well known by now, the Japanese (even their U.S.-born and thus American-citizen children), were considered enemy aliens. They were corralled and put into internment camps. The Chinese and the Filipinos, allies of the United States, were seen in a more positive light during the war as well. Indians also enjoyed a more favorable assessment from Americans with the increasing popularity of India-based spiritual beliefs and practices.[38] Notably, it was during World War II that new kinds of Asian "migration" would take place to New Jersey. Japanese Americans as well as Japanese Latin Americans who had been interned in other parts of the country were brought to Seabrook, New Jersey, to work, and they ended up settling there after the war for generations.[39]

After World War II, at the height of the Cold War, U.S. immigration policy took a dramatic turn. Racist exclusions were dropped. The policy shifted, opening up to fuel the U.S. Cold War economy through the recruitment of highly skilled immigrant workers and at the same time to address critiques of domestic racism. While America's urban centers as well as the Jim Crow South were seething with tensions, the U.S. Congress passed the Immigration Act of 1965. This act dramatically reshaped the United States as a whole, making a decisive impact on the Northeast, including New Jersey. Not only did the act lead to Asian and Latino immigration in greater numbers than initially anticipated, it also shaped the class character of that immigration. Asian immigrants after 1965 were a far cry from the Asian immigrants of a century before. If Asians had been recruited to fill the needs for cheap, physically demanding, low-status, and often dangerous work in a fast-industrializing economy in the late nineteenth century, in the latter half of the twentieth century Asians were being recruited to fill the needs for highly skilled health and science professionals in a deindustrializing economy. Although often figured in popular culture as "model minorities" who have some sort of genetic or cultural characteristics that make them successful, Asian American achievement is actually a result of what one scholar calls "state engineering."[40]

By 2010, the Asian population stood at 5 percent of the U.S. population (excluding multiracial individuals), becoming the largest wave of immigrants to the United States.[41] A small group compared to others, Asians were the fastest-growing population group in the state of New Jersey. From 1990 to 2000, the Asian American population in New Jersey went from 3.5 percent to 5.7 percent of the population. By 2011, 8.5 percent of the population of New Jersey was Asian.[42] Every county in the state of New Jersey had seen double digit increases in its Asian American populations during that period of time.

Asians would come to settle in different pockets of the state. In a 2008 article about the increasing population of Asians in different parts of New Jersey, Howard Shih, the Census Information Center manager of the Asian American Federation, is quoted as stating, "instead of immigration into traditional ethnic enclaves in cities, they're moving directly to the suburbs and setting up enclaves there."[43] By the 2000 census, Palisades Park located in Bergen County was over 40 percent Asian.[44] Fort Lee, also in Bergen County, which by the 2010 census was nearly 40 percent Asian, became a major place of settlement for Japanese and Korean immigrants. Indeed, of the total population of Fort Lee, 23.5 percent are Korean.

Indian Americans are the largest among Asian groups in New Jersey and have been since the 1980s.[45] They have had an especially significant presence in Middlesex County, where Edison is located. In 2000, there were 57,053 Indian Americans living in Middlesex County. That nearly doubled by 2010, to 104,705. Not surprisingly, four of the five New Jersey municipalities with the largest Asian Indian populations were in Middlesex County: Edison (28,286), Woodbridge (15,827), South Brunswick (11,040), and Piscataway (10,662).[46] The Indian Americans settling in Edison draw from the professional classes and many are indeed entrepreneurs, or as S. Mitra Kalita describes them, "suburban sahibs."[47]

By the time I began paying close attention to race and immigration politics in New Jersey in the mid-2000s, Indians had become a major part of the fabric of Edison. People had spent time in Edison raising their families, establishing businesses and simply being a part of everyday life. Though they were becoming the norm, they made the town feel "unfamiliar" to past and present residents.

Violence Against Indians

(White) Edison residents have met the growth of the Indian population with concern, disdain, and in some cases outright violence. Federal statistics indicate that the state of New Jersey has the nation's third highest rate of bias or "hate" crimes, which Congress has defined as criminal offenses against a person or property motivated in whole or in part by an offender's bias against a race, religion, disability, ethnic origin, or sexual orientation.[48] While state authorities contend that the rate has less to do with actual incidences of hate crimes than with the state's reporting practices, it is nevertheless troubling. Immigrants of color, not surprisingly, are among those who have been most victimized by racist attacks.

Anti-Indian violence in particular has increased since 9/11 as a consequence of racial/ethnic "misrecognitions" of Indians (particularly turbaned Sikhs) as Arab Muslims. It is perhaps more precise to say that it is not "misrecognition" (and therefore the misapplication of proper racial categorizations) as much as it is about the normal operation of the U.S. racial categorization system, which is socially constructed and changes over time.[49] According to anthropologist Junaid Rana, in the contemporary moment Indians are racialized in such a way that they are conflated with "those from a broad geography of the Islamic world most readily combined with the abstract Middle East."[50] For example, the Sikh Coalition, a national advocacy group that formed in the wake the September 11 terrorist attacks, documented more than three hundred cases of violence and discrimination against the Sikh community in just one month following the bombings of the World Trade Center.[51] Of course, this number excludes attacks that simply do not get reported.

Unfortunately, violence is familiar to New Jersey Indians and was occurring well before 9/11. Numerous cases of anti-Indian violence have been documented around the state. One highly publicized series of hate crimes was committed in the mid-1980s by the so-called Dotbusters in Jersey City. The group of men, made up of both whites and nonwhites, was responsible for the brutal killing of Navroze Mody. Following Mody's murder, Indians in Jersey City suffered from a rash of attacks over the course of the year. One non-Indian, white resident of Jersey City explained anti-Indian violence in this way: "We're just jealous because they [Indians] have more money than we do."[52] That Indians are perceived to be outpacing whites economically and that that perception triggered violence is a crucial point here.

It is important to note that this economic explanation of anti-Indian sentiment is not new (that is, not, corresponding with more recent immigration from India), nor is it one that has been used only against Indian immigrants. It is a familiar narrative and whites have historically used it to explain (and justify) anti-Asian immigrant violence more broadly. The immigration of Asians since the late nineteenth century has been met with vigilante violence similar to that inflicted on Navroze Mody because Asians were considered both an economic and a cultural threat. Historical sociologist Rick Baldoz's research on the experiences of Filipino immigrants in California in the 1930s reveals, for example, how white vigilante groups used to terrorize Filipinos' labor camps and literally try to run Filipinos out of town. In one case, a young Filipino man was murdered.[53] Early Chinese, Japanese, Korean, and Indian immigrants all contended with similar forms of violence. Even as Navroze Mody's death can be historically linked to this history of anti-Asian violence shared by all Asian groups, legal scholar Deborah N. Misir argues, "The racialization of Indians into a discrete, identifiable group highlights . . . that the paradigm of a pan-Asian American unity does not reflect political and social realities."[54] This issue of the limits and challenges of pan-ethnicity, that is, the notion of inter-Asian ethnic minority collective experience and identity, is something I will take up in greater depth in a following section of this chapter, but it is important to index the point here.

More recently, anti-Indian violence has spilled into suburban sites in New Jersey. For example, in Wayne, New Jersey, a Hindu family was targeted with hate mail for several weeks that culminated with their house being spray-painted "We Kill U," "We will fire your house," "Watch your kids," and "I hate Indians."[55] In North Brunswick, an elderly Indian man was knocked down, beaten on the head, and left bleeding. His attack was one of several in the area.[56]

In the Edison area, tensions with the Indian community have been taking place since the early 1990s. In 1992, the so-called Lost Boys attacked an Indian man behind a convenience store and drove through an apartment complex where hundreds of Indian families live to yell out racist epithets. An investigator from the New Jersey Office of Bias Crimes attributed the Lost Boys' violence to the visible presence of Indians as business owners. He stated, "Now these people come in, they are perceived to be different and they are doing well in hard economic times." White business owners, meanwhile, believed their businesses had suffered substantially from the entry of Indian business owners. They thought that Indians got tax-free small business loans and other special entitlements to establish their businesses and therefore had an unfair advantage over whites.[57]

Significantly, the Lost Boys were made up of ethnic whites, Anglos, an African American, and two individuals with Filipino backgrounds.[58] This suggests that what was at stake was even more complicated than the bias crimes investigator suggested. What might have been at issue was not simply anti-Indian sentiment on the part of whites, but the racialization of Indians as Others by members of other minority groups. Indeed, the Dotbusters also included nonwhite individuals.[59] On one hand, Indians, as Asian Americans, are "triangulated" vis-à-vis both whites and blacks in American society. According to Claire Kim's notion of "racial triangulation," Asian Americans experience discrimination along two axes, the first on the basis of race and the second on the basis of citizenship. They can be racialized as "closer" to whites and hence can be seen more positively than blacks. Yet relative to both whites and blacks, Asian Americans, including Indians, can be seen as "forever foreign" and never "authentic" Americans.[60] The white members of the Lost Boys may very well have considered Indians as less than American and therefore threatening. At the same time, Indians have a phenotype distinctive from other Asian ethnic groups. Members of these groups may think of Indians as falling outside what is typically defined as "Asian American."[61] This disidentification with Indians may explain why Asian Americans joined the ranks of the Lost Boys. It is crucial to point out that ultimately it is the ideology of white supremacy that practically "recruits" people of color to be pitted against each other, reinforcing racialized understandings and leaving white supremacist thinking intact.[62]

Even Hightstown, a community that passed a "sanctuary city" ordinance for immigrants in 2007, is not immune to these everyday forms of violence. In 2008, a Sikh high school student's turban was set on fire.[63] Hate violence and other forms of harassment and intimidation, however, are rare. Perhaps more common are the daily indignities, the everyday racisms or what some call "racial microagressions" that Indians face.[64] For example, Rajinder Singh, a fifty-seven-year-old Indian immigrant who works as a chemist and holds two Ph.D.s, commented in an interview about discrimination toward turbaned Sikhs, "You could see people—their lips inside their car—that this person is swearing at me."[65]

Prohibiting Cultural Practices

Individuals' everyday experiences of racism are important, but of more concern in this book are structural and institutional forms of racism and the ways they manifest in specific localities to exclude immigrants. However, it is important to bear in mind that there is a continuum between hate crimes and the immigration enforcement regime that has emerged at the local level since 9/11. There are formal mechanisms by which immigrants are policed, yet the formalization of these mechanisms also normalizes nativist, xenophobic, anti-immigrant sentiment and produces a context that is favorable to hate crimes as well as militia and paramilitary activities against immigrants. The discussion in this section focuses on the ways the "natives" of Edison have used both formal and informal mechanisms to limit or prohibit Indians' cultural practices.

In 1991, members of a Hindu denomination organized a lavish thirty-day Cultural Festival of India. The festival featured booths that displayed both traditional forms of handicraft and more "modern" examples of Indian technological production; there were also food booths featuring Indian cuisine and booths featuring Indian intellectual and religio-cultural traditions (with an emphasis on the specific brand of Hinduism associated with the festival organizers).[66]

According to cultural critic Sandhya Shukla, even as the festival highlighted Indians' ethnic difference the overarching message communicated through the festival was one that ultimately aligned with neoconservative politics, emphasizing private property and entrepreneurial achievement. It also aligned with a postracial multiculturalist understanding of race relations in the United States, that is, the notion that since the "success" of the civil rights movement, American society is no longer characterized by racial inequality and is in fact a "melting pot" or "salad bowl" of cultural diversity. Shukla argues, "Indian and North American conservative critiques of the current state of affairs in the United States converged in exhortations about contemporary culture" that took place in the festival.[67] Moreover, as ethnic studies scholar Monisha Das Gupta points out, even within the Indian community, class-based tensions exist and more economically privileged Indians, including entrepreneurs, employ a "politics of [cultural authenticity] . . . to exclude and vilify working-class South Asians."[68]

Despite the event organizers' ideological alignment within conservative, postracial multiculturalist discourses in late 1980s and early 1990s America, they could not escape processes of racialization and exclusion. In 1992, the city of Edison introduced an ordinance to limit future Indian religio-cultural activities, notably the observance of the Navratri festival. The Navratri festival is centered on the female deity Durga and celebrates the triumph of good versus evil; it draws thousands of adherents and has become an annual activity in Edison. It was the observance of Navratri that became an issue of controversy when Edison passed a Public Entertainment Ordinance.[69] Although festival organizers were able to secure permits for three years (1992–1994), they faced serious challenges in 1995 when additional restrictions were placed on how they could conduct the festival. Township council members claimed that the restrictions were necessary to respond to residents' noise complaints. When festival organizers requested reports of the complaints, the files were never sent. On June 19, 1995, white Edison residents attended a meeting organized by three of Edison's council members to voice their complaints. Among the issues raised by a council member was that the festival had negative consequences for area residents and posed a threat to "homes that people have worked so hard for."[70] Here, the council member portrayed Indian immigrants as outsiders, as if they haven't also "worked so hard" for the home they've made in Edison.

The Indo-American Cultural Society filed a suit against the township on the basis that it was violating Indian residents' right to free speech. U.S. District Judge John C. Lifland ruled in the Indian community's favor and supported its claim that the township had indeed violated its First Amendment rights.[71] The township attempted an appeal in 1997, on the first day of the Navratri festival that year, but it was denied. Eventually, on June 19, 1998, a settlement was signed.[72] Among the negative responses to the settlement in a local paper was a letter written by a local clergyman about Indians' "obeisance to their heathen gods."[73] The issue has hardly disappeared and has resurfaced time and time again. In 2007, the township denied festival organizers a permit to hold the event in response to noise complaints from more than a hundred local residents.[74] The event has been held since that year, but complaints about noise levels continue to be raised by non-Indian Edison residents.[75]

As sociologist Prema Kurien lays out in her study of the practice of Hinduism by Indian Americans, there are multiple mechanisms through which Hinduism gets defined as outside "American" religious practice and hence those who practice it are defined as "un-American." Kurien suggests, "For religious groups to be meaningfully incorporated into the national fabric . . . they need to be publicly recognized by the state."[76] In the United States, the Internal Revenue Service (IRS) has specific rules that outline what organizations qualify as nonprofits, including which entities can qualify as churches or religious organizations and therefore can be eligible for tax-exempt status.[77] Kurien finds that Hindu Americans engage in a number of strategies to try to get Hinduism officially recognized by the state as a religious organization for tax and other purposes but that the policies regulating this process are ultimately biased against the sorts of practices Hindus engage in. Meanwhile, some Americans, like those in Edison opposed to the celebration of the Navratri festival consider Hindu to be a "heathen" religion.

The notion that Indians are heathens because they are non-Christian harkens back to older forms of anti-Asian discrimination that characterized Asians as a cultural threat and became one of the bases for anti-Asian immigration legislation. Yet in the contemporary moment, Indian spirituality (embodied, for example, by New Age thinkers like Deepak Chopra) has been depicted in popular culture as an antidote to the alienation people experience in an advanced capitalist society.[78] In other words, Americans have had a contradictory stance with respect to Indian religious and spiritual practices. However in Edison, when Indians' religious practices spill into the public arena they become a cause of concern and can even be considered threatening. The struggles over the holding of the Navratri festival in Edison demonstrate the limits of American cultural citizenship. While hate crimes might be attributed to irrational individuals, policies that dissuade particular forms of religious practice exposes the limits of "religious freedom," a core value around which American citizenship is purportedly oriented.[79]

Even seemingly more innocuous cultural practices, like playing cricket, have raised concerns among Edison residents. Cricket is actually a European sport, but in Edison it is played mainly by immigrants (specifically Indian immigrants), which has made the sport a highly contested political issue. When the township of Edison approached a youth softball league to sign an agreement ensuring that other groups (including cricketers) would also have access to the field they played on, a former (white) softball coach who helped start the league stated, "We built it up. Now they're going to come and take it?"[80] The field is township property, but the league has had practically exclusive access to the field, which it helped build and maintain. The idea that "they're going to come and take it," was not merely in reference to the local government attempting to open up access to the field: it was racially charged. Supporters of the softball league accused the township's Korean American mayor, Jun Choi of initiating the agreement as a political ploy to "win Asian votes" by opening the field to Indian cricket players.[81]

The controversy surrounding Edison cricket players' access to public fields parallels the struggles Latino immigrants have when it comes to playing soccer, which I will discuss in the next chapter. At the same time, some scholars contend that Americans' characterization of cricket as an un-American sport has a history that predates its association with immigrants. They attribute American's favoring of baseball over cricket as an anticolonial means by which to "sever all sporting connections with the [British] empire to emphasize an independent American identity."[82] In either case, cricket is characterized as a fundamentally foreign and un-American sport.

Changing Political Landscapes

If the cultural landscapes of Edison have been transforming and increasing the indignation of white residents, impending political changes angered them and they responded to these changes in often vociferous ways, especially during the mayoral campaign of Jun Choi in 2005.

Choi, the son of Korean immigrants, arrived in the United States with his parents when he was three years old. He graduated from high school in Edison, then went on to earn a degree in aeronautical engineering from the Massachusetts Institute of Technology (MIT) and a master's in public administration from Columbia University. His parents owned a dry cleaning business in Edison. In many ways, as an entrepreneurial family, they are an example of the "ideal immigrant" model-minority family, not unlike many Indian American families in Edison. Paradoxically, immigrant entrepreneurs and even their second-generation children, especially when their businesses provide goods and services primarily for other immigrants, are seen as undermining local communities. When members of the Asian "model minority" attempt to engage in American life not merely as economic actors but as political actors, they are perhaps seen as even more threatening.

Choi, considered by many to be a political outsider in multiple senses, ran in the Democratic primary and edged out the incumbent Democratic mayor by a 56 to 44 percent margin, despite the fact that the incumbent mayor was endorsed by most county and state Democratic organizations. The only Democratic endorsement that Choi secured was that of Senator Bill Bradley and a few labor unions. Choi's primary victory over the Democratic Party–favored, longtime incumbent was a first in Edison history.[83] Indeed, Choi's opponent in the final race was not a Republican but William Stephens, a former Democrat who became an independent to try to defeat Choi.[84] Stephens described his candidacy as being about "saving Edison." In an article about his candidacy, he waxes nostalgic about the Edison he grew up in that no longer exists, much like Joel Stein.[85]

Choi was not simply an outsider to the Democratic Party establishment, but viewed by some as an outsider because he was Asian American. His candidacy was met with vocal opposition by local radio 101.5 FM talk show hosts Craig Carton and Ray Rossi who refer to themselves as the "Jersey Guys," ostensibly because they represent the "typical" New Jersey resident. In an on-air rant, Carton and Rossi characterized Choi, Asian Americans, Arab Americans, and other minority groups as "fringe groups." Carton stated, "No specific minority group or foreign group should ever, ever dictate the outcome of an American election." He continued, "I don't care if the Chinese population in Edison has quadrupled in the last year, Chinese should never dictate the outcome of an election. Americans should."[86]

To radio's "Jersey Guys," Asians (for which the term "Chinese" is a stand-in) are "forever foreigners." Despite Choi's local roots, he is characterized as part of a "foreign group" who can never adequately represent the interests of authentic Americans. A major protest campaign was organized in response to the Jersey Guys' comments. Pan-ethnic Asian American groups like the New Jersey/National Taskforce Against Hate Media and the Coalition for Asian-American Civil Rights led the charge to demand an apology from the radio station and to call for advertisers to pull their ads from the station.[87] The radio station was forced to make a public apology and pledge "to cultural-diversity and competency training for many employees, a stronger policy against racially derogatory speech, and on-air promotion of New Jersey events involving Asian-Americans." In a public statement, Andrew Santoro, group vice president for Millennium Radio New Jersey, stated, "The station is steadfastly committed to promoting racial and ethnic tolerance within New Jersey and will continue to work toward long-term improvement in cultural awareness and diversity that benefits the station's listening audience and the various ethnic communities in New Jersey."

Despite being considered an outsider as an Asian American and an outsider to the local political party machine, Choi ending up winning the Edison mayoral race in 2005, albeit by a very narrow margin (a mere 273 votes). Analyses of Choi's successful mayoral bid attribute it to the mobilization of Asian American voters. Perhaps not surprisingly, Choi's co-ethnics, that is, other Korean Americans, supported him, but the Indian community did too. According to exit polls, 100 percent of South Asian American respondents polled voted for Choi compared with 87 percent of Chinese American voters. Overall, 97 percent of all Asian American respondents supported Choi.[88] The Jersey Guys' racist comments seemed to have galvanized the Asian American community in Edison to support Choi's mayoral bid.[89]

Labor unions were another major source of support for Choi, according to analyses of the election.[90] Choi's campaign included major opposition to the entry of Walmart into town.[91] Choi made good on his stance and actually became subject to a lawsuit when Walmart developers claimed that along with the township he was personally responsible for blocking the issuance of a building permit; Choi's predecessor, Mayor George Spadoro, had signed the permit right before leaving office. Edison's Planning Board was responsible for approving Walmart's site plan before then.[92] Walmart has become an iconic example of the growing dominance of big-box retail giants over "mom and pop" business owners. As one major anti-Walmart activist puts it, "Walmart is destroying hometown America. . . . It's destroying the unique sense of place in this country. It's making every town indistinguishable and it's also doing a number on our economy."[93] Yet in Edison, there was a group of residents that favored the corporate powerhouse over the small businesses owned by Indians and other minorities.

In a small research project that one of my undergraduates, Justine Abrams, conducted, Edison residents were asked if they felt Walmart threatened their sense of community. An interview of a former white public official revealed that he was less concerned with Walmart's opening and more concerned about the changing racial character of local businesses. Reminiscing about his favorite pizzeria, he recalled his disappointment when the place stopped serving meat and when workers no longer spoke Italian-accented English but spoke Indian-accented English instead. At that point, he stopped patronizing the pizzeria. Interestingly, another finding in Abrams's study was that among the issues raised by those opposed to Walmart was not Walmart's displacement of local businesses or even its unfair labor practices, but the sort of clientele that Walmart would draw to Edison: "People who wouldn't otherwise be in Edison are now coming to Edison just to go to Walmart. . . . Ya know, like the Asian people. If you go into Walmart, you already know you're going to see a lot of Indians." Despite Walmart's potential for destroying "hometown America" (that is, local businesses), "hometown America" for these Edison residents has already been undermined by other, seemingly more threatening "outsiders": immigrant entrepreneurs and the clientele they attract.

As American studies scholar Wendy Cheng argues, "struggles over race, geography, and history are intertwined in the contemporary identities of places and integral to the shaping of civic landscapes."[94] In Edison, the civic landscape has been a site of contestation. The presence of Indians, not merely as residents, but as entrepreneurs whose businesses shape the suburban landscape in distinctive ways, disturbs natives' sense of what Edison *ought* to look and feel like. "Asians and Asian space [are] seen as a foreign threat."[95] Yet, even a putatively all-American business like Walmart poses a similar threat because of the kind of workers it employs and the clientele it attracts. If Walmart has been posed as a threat to "hometown America," it is considered threatening to some Edison residents for its associations with working-class immigrants of color, and not for its threat as a global corporate giant.

Tenuous Pan-Ethnicity

To what extent Choi's election reflects a solid Asian American pan-ethnic identity in this "majority minority" community, and therefore a postracial landscape is not especially clear. Although Choi's election was buoyed up by pan-ethnic support, which was bolstered both locally and nationally by the Jersey Guys' racist tirade, that support waned and tensions emerged between Choi and the Indian community after he was elected.

In 2006, the Indian American community accused an Edison police officer, Michael Dotro, of police brutality during the apprehension of an Indian immigrant man, Rajnikant Parikh, who had participated in an illegal fireworks display at an apartment complex. The police officer in question had arrested Parikh on charges that Parikh attacked the officer and attempted to incite others to attack him as well. Parikh countercharged that he was in fact a victim of violence at the hands of the police. An internal investigation ultimately cleared the police of any wrongdoing.[96]

The Indo-American Cultural Society, the same organization that engaged in the federal suit against the township on charges of violating its First Amendment rights, organized protests against the Edison police. The group accused Dotro of a pattern of anti-Indian violence. Sixty Indian protesters were met with a counterprotest of about forty police supporters. At least one of the counterprotesters called out, "How many of you are illegals? You must've slid under the border to come here!" Others held signs that echoed this message.[97] Here, we see how the specter of the illegal/criminal immigrant is conjured in municipal struggles. What was supposed to be a local police matter becomes an immigration issue. Police supporters justify their defense of Dotro's action on the basis of their belief that Indian immigrants are "illegals" who are therefore undeserving of decent treatment. Indeed, the local police summoned immigration agents who then arrested Parikh during the rally. In response, Peter Kothari, one of the organizers of the protest, exclaimed, "This is another mockery of law and justice. This is ridiculous, a type of intimidation—you ask for justice, we'll get you another way. Wake up Asian-Americans!"[98] By 2008, the Asian American Legal Defense and Education Fund (AALDEF) filed suit on behalf of Parikh against the Town of Edison, several officers of the Edison Police Department, and officers of ICE for civil rights violations as well as for what AALDEF characterized as Parikh's wrongful, retaliatory immigration arrest.[99]

The tenuousness and fragility of Asian American pan-ethnicity becomes evident in this case. On one hand, Kothari invoked Asian American pan-ethnicity during the course of the protest when he calls not on Indian Americans but on Asian Americans to "wake up." Moreover, it was the AALDEF that filed the suit on behalf of Parikh, not an Indian-specific community organization. On the other hand, Indian Americans in Edison expressed dismay about the way that Mayor Choi handled the matter. Moreover it was Choi's administration that had to respond to the AALDEF's lawsuit. Although whites accused Mayor Choi of pandering to the Indian American community on some presumed basis of pan-ethnicity, the mayor and some sectors of the Indian American community were not entirely in agreement about how to handle the case. Mayor Choi was arguably in a rather difficult situation, as he had to manage competing interests during the matter, but in some ways the tensions that emerged between the mayor and the Indian American community also reflect tensions that characterize relations between Indians Americans and their East Asian American counterparts due to their differential racialization. Sociologist Sofya Aptekar argues, in a study of the organizational life of Asian Americans in Edison, that although Indians and other Asian ethnic groups are racialized in similar ways, Indians are often singled out as a distinctive more dangerous "Other" as compared to groups like the Chinese. According to Aptekar, "Indeed, colour is colour and Asian Indians, with their dark skin, are racialized in a very different way than the light-skinned Chinese and other East Asians."[100] The racialization of Indians in Edison has resulted in "reactive mobilization" which has translated into new forms of entre into the local political arena, but these political engagements are not always consistently of the pan-ethnic variety.

Of course, New Jersey's Asian Americans have engaged in pan-ethnic politics on many different issues. For instance, though some of the most highly publicized hate crimes in Edison involved Asian Indian victims, Asian American pan-ethnic groups like the AALDEF and the Asian American Political Coalition publicly decried the crimes and took a lead in pressing for tougher hate crime laws. By 1990, the state's hate crime law was expanded with more stringent sentences for those found guilty of assault or harassment.[101]

Interestingly, one former Edison public official claimed,

> There has been a huge change in perception among Edison due to the influx of the Asian community. They haven't become involved in politics, and are more focused on educating their children and working. In the Asian community overall, there is a huge caste system and they look down on politicians. We have been trying to change that, and now we have an Indian on the council and Asian on the Board of Education, but they really never work together. Because of their different beliefs, they will never be able to take over government. They'll never have enough voters.[102]

Despite the Jersey Guys' fear-mongering or the fear felt by other white Edison residents (from Joel Stein to the supporters of Officer Dutro) of an Indian/Asian/immigrant takeover, at least this local political insider seemed less worried. His comments indicate that he does not necessarily see Asians as posing any actual threat because he believes they lack any kind of pan-ethnic unity. Just as important, however, this local political insider also refers to Asians as being encumbered by a backward, premodern "caste" system. One could interpret the statement that "they never really work together" less as a comment on the difficulties of pan-ethnic politics than as a characterization of Asians being saddled by tribalism, hence his use of the term "caste" to describe the divisions between them. Caste is often figured as the polar opposite of class. If class is figured as flexible and characterized by mobility (though it can just as easily mean downward mobility as much as upward mobility), caste is an intractable, unchanging system. Class-based systems are represented as modern and democratic (in other words, Western and ultimately American), whereas caste systems are backward, archaic, and are hence, foreign.

Jun Choi's mayoral tenure was ultimately short-lived. He was unable to secure the support of the township's Democratic Committee when he tried to run for reelection, and he lost the primary in what was characterized as one of the most heated elections in the county that year.[103] Moreover, his mayoral stint has not necessarily transformed racial politics in Edison. A recent bid for mayor by Sudhanshu Prasad, the only Indian American town council member, was met with anti-Indian sentiment as campaign signs were defaced with "Never in Edison!" and "DOTHEAD!"[104]

Different Town, Same Story

Asian Americans in ethnoburbs outside Edison have experienced similar yet in some ways different dynamics. Palisades Park, like Edison, is an Asian American ethnoburb in Bergen County, New Jersey. It is located less than twenty miles northwest of New York City. Based on the 2010 census, the Asian population is at nearly 60 percent, with a vast majority from Korea. As in Edison, Korean immigrant business owners are transforming Palisades Park's civic landscape. Also as in Edison, their presence has raised the ire of local residents, and the municipal government has intervened to regulate their activities. In the mid-1990s, during the same period when Edison's Indian community was dealing with the municipal government essentially trying to shut down their religio cultural festival, the Palisades Park municipal government introduced an ordinance that prohibited retail business like Korean-owned karaoke bars from being open past 9:00 P.M. Meanwhile, it restricted restaurants from being open past 3:00 A.M. Many of the businesses owned by Koreans were twenty-four-hour operations. Notably, there was a clause in the ordinance that excluded diners from this restriction, hence allowing the one Greek-owned establishment to stay open at all hours. The Korean American opponents of this municipal ordinance believed it to be racist; the mayor countered that it was merely a "quality of life" matter.[105] As I have discussed previously, "quality of life" issues are often a form of color-blind racism, a means by which local governments and residents introduce policies that are in fact aimed at excluding communities of color. The racialized politics of the twenty-four-hour ordinance are clearer in the statement of the borough attorney, who commented with respect to the exception granted to diners: "'a diner is a diner is a diner: everyone knows what it is. The fact that nobody really knew what those other places did, or that people had suspicions about what they did—that was probably part of the consideration for the ordinance.'"[106] The borough attorney's comment reflected numerous logics that have been used in the racialization of Asians as Others. He deployed the idea of the "inscrutable Asian" whose cultural practices are not immediately legible and therefore are potentially threatening.[107]

Significantly, the ordinance regulating the operating hours of specific businesses in the municipality came on the heels of another municipal ordinance that directly targeted Korean business owners. In the late 1980s, the municipality passed an ordinance that required all businesses with Korean signage to put up English signage alongside their original signs. In 1994, the borough passed an amendment to the original ordinance requiring that the English signage needed to be in a font size equivalent to the Korean. Notably, Palisades Park was not the only municipality to make English-signage an issues. Several neighboring towns, also dealing with an in-flux of Asian business owners, did the same thing.[108] Despite the linguistic diversity of the state, officials in suburbs attempt to ensure that civic and commercial landscapes conform to a narrow understanding of authentic, local culture.[109]

Conclusion

Anti-immigrant sentiment extends beyond the white suburbs and is alive and well even in places where immigrants constitute the majority. In fact, although Asian Americans are often thought of as a "model minority" compared with their Latino counterparts because they are typically better educated, are legal permanent residents or naturalized citizens, and at least in the case of Indians can generally speak English, they are nevertheless "forever foreign." Asian entrepreneurship, like the Indian-owned businesses on Edison's Oak Tree Road or the Korean karaoke joints in Palisades Park, is not interpreted as a mark of assimilation but rather a menacing threat as the businesses they operate cater mainly to other immigrants and disturb the civic and commercial landscape with "foreign" aesthetics. In some cases, nativists have used physical violence against Indian immigrants to express their resentment at their perceived success. Asian cultural practices, especially those that take place in the public sphere, equally disturb white residents' sensibilities and whites have used local municipal codes to prohibit those practices. Meanwhile, attempts by Asian American candidates to break through the political leadership, as Choi did in Edison, have been met with racist opposition because they are considered outsiders in their hometowns.

Even when an ethnoburb is constituted by a single "majority minority" racial group (Asians in the case of Edison), political alliances across ethnicity cannot be assumed.[110] Although Asians assert an Asian American panethnic identity in many cases, often in response to animus from whites, there are times when that identity is abandoned in favor of ethno-national identities. Among Asian immigrants and even their second-generation, U.S.-born children, there are divisions that are tied to the distinctive ways "brown Asians" (that is, South Asians) are racialized. These divisions have been especially heightened in the post-9/11 context. Although the election of Korean American Mayor Jun Choi can be considered a major advance for Asian American representation in a community where Asians as a racial group are nearly a majority, he only lasted a term and lost his bid for a second term.[111] Both Asian and Latino leaders in New Jersey are attempting to increase the numbers of Asian and Latino legislators by redrawing legislative districts, but Mayor Choi's experience illustrates some of the challenges that candidates are likely to face even in places where victory might seem to be assured.[112]

4

Being the Problem

Perspectives from Immigrant New Jerseyans

In *The Souls of Black Folk*, W. E. B. Du Bois's classic early twentieth-century book on African Americans' experiences of racialization, Du Bois poses the question "How does it feel to be a problem?"[1] At the turn of twenty-first century, Moustafa Bayoumi, writer and professor of English at Brooklyn College, poses the same question for post-9/11 Arab Muslim immigrant youth in his 2008 book, *How Does It Feel to Be a Problem?: Being Young and Arab in America*. In describing why he draws inspiration from Du Bois's work, he writes, "[B]eing a problem is a strange experience—frustrating, even. This book was conceived out of my frustrations, but it is not about me . . . I know what it is like to be Arab and Muslim today, but what is it like, I wonder, to be young, Arab, and Muslim in the age of terror?"[2] Similarly, as a child of immigrants whose last name is Rodriguez and as a woman of color, I know what it feels like to be figured as an outsider.[3] I know how frustrating it can be, infuriating really, to have to contend with so many different kinds of negative stereotypes associated with the various groups to which I am linked. This chapter is specifically aimed at bringing to the foreground immigrant New Jerseyans' everyday experiences with these stereotypes and the policies they are used to justify.

In much of the national debate on immigration today, particularly among those positioned on the right of the political spectrum, it is generally assumed that immigrants are racialized (classed and gendered) minorities. The prevailing images that the term "immigrant" conjures up are that of the "illegal" Mexican (or Latino) man working as a day laborer or perhaps of a Mexican (or Latina) woman working as a domestic and who is mother to a large brood of children. When the question of national security and terrorism gets thrown into the mix, the dominant image that the term "immigrant" conjures up is that of a turbaned and robed Arab Muslim man.[4] Immigrants are generally thought to be outsiders, "Others." They are people who do not belong. They are threatening. They are dangerous. They are people who ought to be expelled from the United States or, in extreme cases, eliminated altogether. These representations are circulated with particular vitriol during political contests (generally by Republicans in recent decades, but Democrats are by no means immune), as in the case of the Republican primary campaign of 2016.

Donald Trump, the 2016 Republican presidential nominee, now president of the United States, singled himself out and was singled out by the in the media for his seemingly extreme positions on immigration policy. According to Trump, "For many years, Mexico's leaders have been taking advantage of the United States by using illegal immigration to export the crime and poverty in their own country (as well as in other Latin American countries)."[5] Consequently, Trump believes in aggressively deporting Mexican and other Latin Americans, and even prohibiting the U.S.-born children of undocumented Latino immigrants from being citizens.[6] In the wake of the San Bernardino mass shootings, he called for a ban on the immigration of Muslims.[7] While many observers have been especially critical of Trump's views on immigration, views that are typically attributed to the Tea Party and therefore not generally considered mainstream Republican views, it is important to underscore first that other Republican contenders for the nomination may have been less colorful in their policy pronouncements and called for more measured approaches as compared to Trump, but they nevertheless shared a fairly consistent stance on immigration: that enforcement efforts ought to be stepped up. Second, few Republicans have opposed President Trump's January 2017 directive to close the borders on refugees and suspend immigration from specific Muslim-majority countries.

An often-cited quote by Du Bois is: "The problem of the twentieth century is the problem of the color-line,—the relation of the darker to the lighter races of men in Asia and Africa, in America and the islands of the sea."[8] The color-line, or racial categorization, is not simply a problem of the twentieth century but a fundamental organizing structure of American life. Although the United States is supposed to be a nation of immigrants, the fact is that only a small fraction of modern-day immigrants and their U.S.-born children can actually claim membership in the nation as authentic "Americans." Of course, African Americans who were born and raised in the United States and have been in this country for generations—they are citizens—have never been able to claim full membership and belonging to the nation as "Americans" either.

Sunaina Maira, an Asian American Studies scholar who conducted an ethnographic study of South Asian Muslim youth as they were affected by post-9/11 cultural politics, offers a description of her work that resonates with my approach here. She describes her study as an "ethnography of imperial feelings" that attempts to reveal "the *intimacy of empire* by exploring the everyday encounters with the state that have increasingly dissolved the boundaries between 'private' and 'public' spheres for communities surveilled by the state, and the feelings of fear, dissent, complicity, and solidarity that emerge from the imperial."[9] Maira's notion of the "intimacy of empire" is a useful framework for thinking about the kinds of politics and policies that have emerged in suburban New Jersey after 9/11. Whether they attempt to kick people out of the houses or apartments they are renting simply because they are undocumented or they prevent people from playing soccer in the park with their children, anti-immigrant local policies are incredibly intimate in the sense that they disrupt immigrants' home lives. Inasmuch as this book focuses on the intimate realms of the neighborhood and the home, it is crucial to underscore that I have been documenting the everyday manifestations of *empire.* U.S. imperialism is not some abstract idea, or something that takes place "out there," somewhere else. It is a violent, organizing structure of post-9/11 life right here at home, in the United States, and literally in our homes; imperial violence is visceral, it is palpable, it is something immigrants confront in different forms on a daily basis.

It is important to highlight the ways race and immigration have shaped municipal governance in recent decades and have led to the increasing exclusion of nonwhite immigrants as I have done in the previous chapters. It is equally important to track how immigrants contend with the suspicions and mistrust their white neighbors have of them. It is important, in other words, to hear how immigrants experience what it feels like to be thought of as "the problem." Anti-immigrant sentiment is both a cause and a consequence of anti-immigrant policies. Clearly, it is what motivates people to advocate for municipal ordinances that negatively impact immigrants. At the same time, however, anti-immigrant sentiment becomes normalized among residents in towns that support these ordinances. It becomes normal for native-born and nativist Americans in those communities to think about immigrants in stereotyped ways or to discriminate against them. That's why the prepubescent white boy I observed in Freehold, for example, pretended to "shoot" immigrants from the back of his parents' SUV, or why the kids at my son's taekwondo school play "border agents versus illegals" without thinking twice and certainly without being reprimanded.

Every day, immigrants are forced to deal with stereotypes and discrimination in seemingly mundane ways. However mundane those experiences are, they are nonetheless violent because they have very real consequences for immigrants' lives. Sociologists Cecila Menjivar and Leisy Abrego introduce the notion of "legal violence" that informs my thinking here. They argue,

> To bring to the fore the complex manner in which the law exerts its influence and control, we examine the harmful effects of the law that can potentially obstruct and derail immigrants' paths of incorporation. We use the term *legal violence* to refer to these effects, as they are often manifested in harmful ways for the livelihood of immigrants. Importantly, although we note cases of interpersonal aggression, or physical violence, we concentrate on those instances that are not directly physically harmful and that are not usually counted and tabulated; indeed our analysis draws attention to the accumulation of those damaging instances that are immediately painful but also potentially harmful for the long-term prospects of immigrants in U.S. society. We trace immigrants' experiences to the laws, their implementation, and the discourses and practices the law makes possible.[10]

In this chapter I examine the experiences of a range of immigrants as well as other foreign-born individuals living in New Jersey. On one hand, I examine how immigrants have coped in the broader context of the highly racialized (classed and gendered) landscape of suburban New Jersey. As I have noted in previous chapters, even as 9/11 ushered in a Homeland Security State and new logics of immigration enforcement, a different yet related sort of border policing organized suburban New Jersey. At stake are not simply national borders but the borders that separate racialized groups within and between communities—boundaries defining the suburbs—that are meant to keep out undesirables to secure the lives and livelihoods of the whites contained within them. Many of the immigrants interviewed here share experiences of what it is like to be figured outside those boundaries. On the other hand, I examine how immigrants contend with what Menjivar and Abrego call "legal violence," that is, the violence wrought by post-9/11 immigration legislation at different levels of governance. I lift up the voices of documented and undocumented immigrants as well as those who are living in the United States on a temporary basis such as migrant workers and foreign students. Although anti-immigrant public discourse and municipal ordinances often attempt to make distinctions between legal immigrants and "illegals," what I found is that when it comes to everyday encounters between immigrants and their American (white) citizen counterparts, those distinctions are meaningless. Immigrants of all legal statuses (especially immigrants of color) experience hostility and discrimination from whites. In fact, even immigrants' American-raised children experience alienation and exclusion. Though they have spent most of their lives in the United States, the children of immigrants don't feel protected from the anti-immigrant animus that their parents face. In addition to giving voice to immigrants of varying legal status, I give voice to immigrants from a wide-range of ethnic and racial backgrounds. If anti-immigrant public discourse and municipal ordinances have focused on "illegals," it has often been specifically Mexican "illegals" or Arab Muslim immigrants (irrespective of legal status). Yet I find that all nonwhite immigrants experience different forms of stereotyping and discrimination in the suburban communities where they live, whether or not those communities have introduced, debated, or implemented anti-immigrant ordinances. Finally, I give voice to those immigrants who have been expelled from their communities and put into detention. Immigrant detainees are perhaps the most voiceless population among immigrants. As with all other incarcerated populations, immigrant detainees are always already untrustworthy people. Regardless of whether they are innocent or guilty of immigration violations, misdemeanors, or felonies, that they are behind bars makes them unworthy to be listened to. Yet from their vantage point behind bars they perhaps offer us some of the most poignant and compelling perspectives on the nature of (in)justice in the post-9/11 period. Most of the people I discuss in this chapter would not call themselves activists or community organizers. I look at the work of activists and organizers in the next chapter. The immigrants here do not always have the vocabulary of their activist/organizer counterparts, yet they display an acute understanding of their everyday world and often can link their experiences to broader structural processes occurring both nationally and globally.

Anti-Immigrant Sentiment in Everyday Life

Anti-immigrant ordinances passed in some New Jersey towns create a climate of hostility toward immigrants even in places where they have not been introduced or passed. Anti- immigrant politics have come to be normalized in daily life throughout the state. Public parks, for example, are sites from which some (white) community residents attempt to exclude their Latino neighbors. Soccer players, from youth to adults, are scrutinized much more closely by park personnel than those playing what some might consider genuine "American" sports such as football or baseball. Soccer players, many of whom are immigrants or children of immigrants, feel as if they are more likely to be asked whether they have permits to use public facilities. Some have their residency (and therefore their right to use parks in specific towns) questioned.

A former student of mine who assisted with some of the research for this book once observed that well before the debates around the 287(g) programs, as more and more immigrants began to use the public parks in her hometown of Morristown, she noticed new signs being posted indicating that use of the park's fields was subject to permit. Although we were not able to confirm whether the town's officials discussed the need for such signs as related to concerns about immigrants' use of public space, that my student (a white woman) attributed the signs to increasing numbers of immigrants is important.

I observed firsthand how the politics of race and immigration shaped suburban youth soccer leagues. My son played soccer for the Highland Park Hawks between the ages of eight and eleven. His team was made up almost entirely of second-generation (U.S.-born children of immigrants) or 1.5-generation (children who immigrated to the U.S. at a young-age) children from Latin American, Asia, Africa, and Europe.[11] Because it was a competitive team, the Hawks played games all around the state.

PHOTO 5. Highland Park Hawks (Photo credit: Robyn Rodriguez)

Far too often, when the boys played in white suburbs, they would be subject to taunting by their opponents (and even their opponents' parents) who made fun of their Spanish names. In some cases, their opponents actually made monkey noises, suggesting that the boys of our team were less than human.

As I discussed in the preceding chapter, contestations over public parks were an issue in the town of Edison with respect to playing cricket, which is considered un-American. Arguably, at issue with respect to soccer is that it is not so much considered an "un-American" sport as it is a sport generally associated with affluent suburban life in this country. After all, the notion of "soccer mom" does not conjure up images of a low-wage Latina immigrant employed as a domestic worker and living not far from her place of employment in the suburbs. "Soccer mom" typically refers to a middle-class (or even upper-middle-class) stay-at-home mom whose life's work is devoted to shuttling her children around from one after-school activity to another. Indeed, studies indicate that soccer in the United States has been concentrated in specific places and among specific socioeconomic groups—the suburbs and middle-class suburbanites—who think of soccer as more closely aligned with their values and sensibilities, unlike "urban" (that is, black and working-class) sports like basketball or football.[12] Practices aimed at excluding immigrants from playing soccer may have less to do with soccer being a foreign sport and more with the notion that it is considered a quintessentially suburban American sport that ought to be played only by white suburban youth.

Anti-immigrant sentiment insinuates itself in many interactions as I will demonstrate throughout this chapter. My own observations at my son's soccer matches and even recounted by the people interviewed here reveal anti-immigrant sentiment being expressed by people I would least expect to feel it: school-age children. An article on bullying programs in elementary schools describes how an eleven-year old girl suffers from bullying at her school. She says, "It's hard to ignore them. They call me 'immigrant,' and girls tell me, 'You're so ugly, your clothes don't match.'"[13] In addition, it appears that in places where local anti-immigrant ordinances have been passed, violence against immigrants by nativist youth is normalized. In Pennsylvania, one of New Jersey's neighbor states, at least one study documents the introduction of twenty-four anti-immigrant local ordinances.[14] Hazelton, Pennsylvania, like Morristown, gained national attention for its 2006 ordinance.[15] Less than twenty miles away, Shenandoah, Pennsylvania, passed an ordinance in the same year making English the official language. In 2008, three teenagers were arrested and charged in the beating death of a Mexican undocumented worker in that town.[16] They were later acquitted of charges of murder and ethnic intimidation. Instead, they were found guilty of misdemeanor assault.[17] Rene Flores's research of the effects of anti-immigrant local ordinances in Pennsylvania finds that politicians' depictions of immigrants as criminal, dangerous elements leads to increases in gun purchases in the counties where anti-immigrant ordinances are formally considered.[18] He even finds similar patterns in South Carolina. Though quite different from Pennsylvania demographically, socioculturally and politically, South Carolina's municipalities have been introducing anti-immigrant local ordinances like Pennsylvania's. Though South Carolina does not publish data on handgun sales, it does release information on concealed gun permit applications. Flores finds that proposals for anti-immigrant local ordinances, and the fear-mongering rhetoric that typically accompany them, leads to the significant increase of concealed gun permit applications in the counties where they have been introduced.[19]

Anti-immigrant sentiment also shapes the media in New Jersey. While municipalities debated and deliberated on anti-immigration ordinances, disc jockeys on local radio station 101.5 FM called for people to report on those in their neighborhoods they suspect to be undocumented. Calling their campaign "Operation Rat a Rat/La Cucha Gotcha," Craig Carton, one of the disc jockeys forming the so-called Jersey Guys duo discussed in the preceding chapter, made the following comment in response to public outcry: "If you're here illegally, you are breaking the law—no better, no worse than the guy who robs the liquor store or the guy who waits to case your house out and robs you of your belongings." He said, "You are a criminal."[20] The Jersey Guys' antics reflect broader trends in the public fomenting of anti-immigrant sentiment. Political scientist Roxanne Lynn Doty argues, "Talk radio has become a venue for the anti-immigrant message that at times promotes extremism and outright violence against undocumented migrants."[21] Sociologist Christopher Bail found that in the years since 9/11, anti-Muslim organizations have come to dominate mainstream media portrayals of Islam and its practitioners on a national scale. A key tactic these groups deployed to capture media attention has been emotional displays of fear and anger in their print and video releases to the press.[22]

One of the first things I learned about race, particularly about racist extremism, when I moved to New Jersey was something a student taught me. I was teaching a Race Relations course and he shared something he had learned in another class: that New Jersey is home to a large number of white supremacist groups. In fact, it has the highest number of documented hate groups among states in the Northeast.[23] While a handful of these hate groups are classified by the Southern Poverty Law Center as "black nationalist," the rest are some variety of white supremacist including "racist skinhead," "white nationalist," "neo-nazi," and "KKK." During the period I was doing field research, New Jersey was the meeting point for neo-Nazis as part of a nationwide call for "patriot weekend" celebrations. In a *Village Voice* interview with one member of a neo-Nazi group, he expressed concern about an "immigrant invasion." Indeed, the *Village Voice* reporter who observed the "patriot weekend" celebrations in New Jersey noted that organizers believed that growing anti-immigrant sentiment in the state was helping their cause.[24] White supremacists would convene again in a rally at the state's capitol in Trenton in 2011. Immigration was a major topic for speakers representing the National Socialist Movement, which organized the demonstration. Jeff Schoep, the National Socialist Movement's national director is quoted as stating: "We have illegal aliens . . . streaming over our borders taking American jobs."[25] According to a 2016 report by the

New Jersey Office of Homeland Security and Preparedness, white supremacists are present in nine of the state's twenty-one counties. In 2015, they were actively recruiting members by leafleting in neighborhoods in Bergen, Burlington, Middlesex, and Monmouth.[26]

Although perhaps not classified as hate groups, anti-immigrant organizations have been formed throughout New Jersey; these include chapters of the New Jersey Citizens for Immigration Control or the United Patriots of America. Anti-immigrant rights organizations outside the state have supported local efforts. As I mention in chapter 2, the Connecticut Citizens for Immigration Control led a national call for anti-immigrant demonstrations, which was heeded by the Essex County–based United Patriots of America. The group organized a "Stop the Invasion" picket at a popular day laborer muster zone in Palisades Park. Even though a nonlocal group called for the picket, participants were local residents, people whom the day laborers (also local residents) recognized as their neighbors.[27]

Hate violence and involvement in anti-immigrant organizations are arguably extreme responses to immigrants. Though anti-immigrant ordinances are spreading, they are not quite the norm. Yet they do shape norms about the treatment of immigrants. Everyday life for immigrants in New Jersey includes the multiple forms of harassment, both subtle and overt, that they suffer. This harassment is my focus in the next section.

Invisibility and Hypervisibility: Contending with Everyday Racism and Discrimination

If Latino immigrants in towns like Freehold have become targets for expulsion from their communities as a consequence of their hypervisibility in suburban spaces, Latinos in other communities sometimes describe theirs as an experience of invisibility similar to the statement in Ralph Ellison's classic novel of the African American experience, *Invisible Man*: "I am invisible, understand, simply because people refuse to see me. Like the bodiless heads you see sometimes in circus sideshows, it is as though I have been surrounded by mirrors of hard, distorting glass. When they approach me they see only my surroundings, themselves or figments of their imagination, indeed, everything and anything except me."[28]

In describing his community of Somerville, New Jersey, a borough that is 66 percent white, 23 percent Latino, and the rest divided between

African Americans, Asian Americans, and others, Rolando, an undocumented immigrant from Costa Rica, says, "Most people just live their lives and ignore that I am even there, which hurts me." Yet, he adds, "I'd rather be ignored than treated badly because of my ethnicity." Similarly another Latina immigrant, this time from the Dominican Republic and a naturalized U.S. citizen living in central New Jersey, describes how "I have experienced bus drivers that arrive too late or they leave me standing in the cold and they avoid me although they see me standing there. I believe that it has happened because I may be Hispanic or maybe because they just don't care."

Immigrants have an acute sense of place, that is, they think of certain places as being racialized (and classed) in specific ways; thus certain communities in New Jersey can be either friendly or hostile to them. When asked whether she feels that she is treated differently in different public spaces like stores, restaurants, and the like because she is an immigrant, Luz, a naturalized citizen who comes from Colombia, states, "Well, it all depends on the place. I know that I do not speak perfect English and there have been times where I get ignored by people and it makes me desperate. Those are the places that do not speak Spanish and the people are just rude. I have never had to complain against a place that I go and people speak Spanish." When asked what surprised him most when he first moved to New Jersey from El Salvador, Cesar responds that he finds it troubling "how ethnicity and wealth changes between one town and the next." Notably, when Polina, a white immigrant woman from Russia married to an Italian American, was asked why her family decided to settle in Toms River, New Jersey, she admits, "I just heard that it was a good community to raise the children. They have a very strong feeling about schools. There the schools are good. Actually, we did research of racial percentage. It's like 90 percent Italian." Unlike her Latino counterparts, Polina considers a "good place" a white place, though not necessarily a place where people share her cultural background.

Of course, being hypervisible as a "problem" shapes the experiences of most immigrants in New Jersey. This is true for both Latino and Asian immigrants. A woman who emigrated from China describes how she believes Americans see her people as "poor and [that] they're not educated as people here." Meanwhile Sam, a middle-aged immigrant from India, believes that "sometimes they [Americans] feel like . . . [Indians] are not intelligent or are not capable of doing things. . . . They look upon Indians like, 'Oh they are . . . stupid. They don't know anything.' Or, 'They are from [a] very poor country.'" Anita makes a similar observation and attributes it to people in power. She provides a specific example of a joke made by Hillary Clinton in 2004. In a speech in which she quoted Mahatma Gandhi, Clinton quipped, "He ran a gas station down in St. Louis."[29] Anita suggests that "[w]hen people in power make statements like that the general public thinks that we are low-class and only know how to fill gas."

Latino immigrants share assessments like that of the Asian immigrants quoted above. Colombian immigrant Luz comments, "A lot of people in this country, [especially] the white people, look down on us. I am not saying everyone does but the majority of them do. So if the question is, have I ever felt like I have been discriminated against for being Hispanic? The answer is yes." Connie, a Honduran undocumented immigrant, similarly describes how "if you're going to the mall they have rich people, sometimes they look at you ah [lifts nose in the air] . . . because I [am] Spanish." Furthermore, immigrants believe that their status as immigrants impacts their wage earnings. Connie continues, "Say you are a citizen. You apply for a job and they tell you they gonna pay fifteen dollars but you tell them you want more than fifteen dollars. But if I go and apply for the same job and they tell me they are gonna pay eight dollars an hour because I don't have no papers or anything."

Both Latino and Asian immigrants interviewed feel that Americans see them as lower-status people. Notably, although Sue and Sam are Asian, their perspectives on how native-born whites see them do not conform with the model minority myth that is generally ascribed to Asian Americans. The myth is not meaningful for them. Rather than feeling celebrated, they feel reviled.

Immigrants are painfully aware that they are the center of negative media attention. Rolando, an undocumented migrant from Costa Rica, offers this perspective:

> The media should not put so much attention on ethnic minorities. It is not fair for normal people like me who are just here to make a better life for my family to be portrayed as illegal aliens and made to feel like a threat to Americans and their society. The media mostly reports negative things about minorities, which is not fair. There are positive parts of my culture which could be reported which might help people like me feel more comfortable in this country.

Immigrants experience a range of indignities and microaggressions in all arenas of social life. Shopping for food or clothing is no simple task, for instance, because immigrants have to deal with insults from people they encounter in and around different stores. Sue, a Chinese immigrant women in her early twenties who immigrated to the United States when she was a child, recalls how when out shopping for shoes she was reprimanded by a fellow shopper, a white woman, who stated, "I don't know what your habit is in your country, but in the U.S. you don't reach in front of people." Sue was stunned, as she had said, "I'm sorry," before reaching in front of the woman to take the pair of shoes. According to Sue, "I said sorry, like, my sorry was . . . equal to 'excuse me' in the U.S." Sam, an Indian immigrant in his late fifties who has lived in the United States for thirteen years, recalls, "When I was totally new, I went to a grocery store, a Shoprite store. People look at you like you are from another planet or something. Then after I came out of the store, I was walking and somebody was coming down the road, some young guys. They yelled out of their car, 'Go back to your country!'"

Sam believes his children, twenty-six and thirty-one at the time of his interview, have better adjusted to life in America over the course of their thirteen years in this country, but he describes how one of his sons struggled at the hands of bullies when he was in high school. Sam attributes this bullying to his son's immigrant status:

> The other kids were not treating him right and always giving him [a] hard time and trying to bully him because he was different. One even, one kid was like having some kind of argument with him in the class. They [tried] to instigate him or bother him and then after school one time they beat him up . . . he was alone and they just gathered at one point where he was and challenged him and everyone was watching like [it was a] fun thing. Then he was hit hard on the head. He had bleeding and all that. And he had to go to the hospital and he was fine luckily . . . and that had a very . . . adverse, very negative psychological effect on his personality.

Indeed, psychologists find that discrimination does affect individuals' mental health and that this is true for both immigrants and native-born Asian Americans. Moreover, depending on when a person experiences discrimination over the course of his or her life cycle (such as during adolescence), it can have a "more negative impact on psychological well-being."[30]

Surprisingly, a white college student who emigrated from England with her parents as a young child recalls a similar experience of bullying from her peers. "At school, I got made fun of a lot and it got annoying. That's why I left my first elementary school. The kids there were really mean. They would say things like 'immigrant' or 'why don't you go back to your country?' This one time a girl came up to me and was yelling at me in my face because I didn't used to say the Pledge of Allegiance."

Being a Problem after 9/11

Immigrants recognize that 9/11 prompted a major shift in immigration policy. As Menjivar and Abrego find in their research, immigrants often express a great deal of fear and trepidation about immigration enforcement. Different studies show that post-9/11 immigration enforcement policies are incredibly traumatic and detrimentally affect immigrants' mental health.[31] These findings are supported by the statements of immigrant New Jerseyans interviewed here.

Rolando arrived in the United States on a temporary employment visa in 1999 from Costa Rica but decided to overstay his visa, remaining in the United States beyond the specific time frame for which his visa was initially approved. Having violated his visa, Rolando, at the time of his interview in the late 2000s, was considered illegal from the perspective of the Department of Homeland Security. When asked to what extent he had to deal with the immigration bureaucracy he responded, "I avoid it. It is difficult now in this country more than when I first came here. Now that everything is more strict I am worried about deportation so I try to keep to myself and live day to day until I can go back to my own country when I am ready." Rolando had ambitions of working in the United States to save enough money to eventually set up a business in Costa Rica.

Whether or not they were directly impacted by post-9/11 immigration policy shifts, immigrants are acutely aware that since September 11, 2001, immigration policies have become more stringent. Jin, a long-term resident of the United States and naturalized U.S. citizen from South Korea, observes, "After 9/11 everyone knows that getting things done [with respect to immigration] is so much harder. I think I came at a good time, when the economy was good and it wasn't too bad to immigrate here." Similarly, Winnie, a Jamaican immigrant, states, "I came over the border to New York on a Canadian visa without declaring at the border and stayed here undocumented. You can't do that now." She further describes how immigration enforcement has affected people in her community. According to Winnie, "My good friend's son . . . got caught selling drugs and he was illegal. He got deported and can't come back to America now." When asked about the advantages of citizenship in the post-9/11 context she states, "Security . . . not being able to be deported." Recall that although 9/11 precipitated more aggressive immigration enforcement practices, the IIRIRA was passed prior to that, in 1996, and expanded the definition of immigrant criminality so that drug offenses that were once considered minor are now deportable offenses.

In response to a question about whether she knew people who had immigration difficulties after 9/11, Luz, a naturalized U.S. citizen from Colombia, reports, "I had a friend of the family who got in trouble in the United States on drug charges. He was a permanent resident but when he went to visit his country, since he had gotten in trouble with drugs in the United States, he was not given permission to reenter the United States." Similarly, Aziz, an Indian Muslim college student, recounts the experience of a "family friend, a lady who was ambushed outside her home and deported for ten years."

A woman who arrived in the United States from Kenya after having won a green card by lottery nearly a decade after 9/11, states, "I am shocked with what people go through to get a green card. Shocked! I would rather stay home. I would never go through that hell. I was least interested in coming. It was luck. My friend signed me up and I was the only one that got the green card."

Some groups of immigrants feel they experience discrimination more severely as a consequence of the 9/11 attacks. Rucha, a college student who arrived in the United States in 2003 from India, states, "Since 9/11 it has been harder for Indians because of the color of their skin. Even in middle school, there were kids who would say, 'Go back to the hellhole you came from.'" She explains, "Generally people think brown people are Middle Eastern, then they will discriminate against you in that way." As a Pakistani journalist reporting on the waves of apprehensions and detentions plaguing the South Asian community in New Jersey and New York taking place in the immediate wake of 9/11 put it, "There was 9/11. Then a post-9/11 era. And then there were the aftereffects of that post-9/11 era. . . . Crackdowns, deportations, people leaving the country." He continued, "then everybody was seen like suspects."[32]

As I discussed in chapter 3, one experience that Indian immigrants, specifically turbaned Sikhs, have is that they are racialized and culturally "misrecognized" or "misidentified" as being Arab and/or Muslim.[33] Anita, an Indian citizen who entered the United States to accompany her husband, a medical student, and who was later able to study in the United States herself, describes how in the immediate wake of 9/11, "People were thinking we are Muslims and you never know. Especially when a Sikh was killed in a gas station . . . he was killed because they thought he was from Afghanistan so we got a little conscious . . . they used to tell us whenever they see us, 'go back to Pakistan.'" As Jasbir Puar and Amit Rai put it, "The turban is now deployed as an integral component of racial profiling within surveillance technologies of counterterrorism." Moreover, "Sikhs are a sanctioned hate-crime target."[34] In other words, the state and citizens alike have profiled Sikhs as a terrorist threat to be at best expelled and at worst eliminated.[35]

Isaac, an Israeli graduate student who entered after 9/11, describes his experience of "misrecognition"; in his case, he is mistakenly thought of as Muslim though he describes himself as an Arab Jew." He states, "Sometimes it is as if I am being tested by my bosses at the library where I work. I have been asked about my opinion of President Bush, of the U.S. government in general, about Osama bin Laden." Sometimes this "testing" comes in the form of jokes. Isaac describes how, "One of my co-workers who is a Filipina American sometimes teases me and calls me a 'desert rat' or a 'terrorist.' She is also an immigrant. She came to the United States at the age of four and is multiply identified, as a Filipina and as an American, but she tends to be a defender of all things U.S."

If racial "misrecognitions" have characterized the experiences of Indians and others who are mistakenly thought to be Muslims or Arabs (or both) and treated with suspicion or even violence in the post-9/11 context, other immigrants similarly experience forms of racial misrecognition and suffer negative consequences for being mistaken for Latino. An immigrant woman who was born in Azerbaijan who arrived in the United States in 2001 describes bouts with racism when being mistaken as a Latina while she was shopping at the mall. "The woman was just rude in general . . . she never mentioned anything about my ethnicity, but I believe she assumed I looked maybe Mexican, because I have long black hair and I'm short and she just assumed I just stole something from the store." Indeed, people who hail from other parts of Latin America, as Cesar, a naturalized U.S. citizen from El Salvador, explains, people "automatically assume I am Mexican and illegal. They don't even know where El Salvador is. People have a lack of knowledge."

Limits and Possibilities of Immigrant Solidarity

There are times where immigrants draw lines of difference between themselves on the basis of religion, ethnicity, and legal status. Given the broader context of living under the Homeland Security State this makes sense even as it hampers the possibilities for immigrant solidarity. Yet there are times when immigrants see themselves as sharing common cause. When they organize collectively around a shared identity as immigrants they are able to effectively transform their local communities, as I will detail in the next chapter.

Although South Asians of different ethnicities are generally racialized by others in similar ways, Indian immigrant Anita often makes it a point to tell people that she is not a Muslim. She explains,

> Wherever we used to go, we used to mention ourselves as Hindus. You know, because, you know, like, maybe they're not asking us but we consciously used to mention, "We are Hindus. We are Hindus." I think it really, really affected our minds, that maybe they discriminated us. And we're not wearing any Indian dresses when we are going out for a while. Many people are from Bangladesh in New York and they are Muslim so we don't want to get identified with them. So it's very sad, but to save ourselves, we need to choose.

Though Anita expresses some shame in distinguishing herself from other South Asians, she feels that she has little choice. Here we see some of the limits of a South Asian pan-ethnicity. In the immediate wake of 9/11, Anita distances herself from Muslims from Bangladesh. She decides to identify herself as Hindu in social interactions without being prompted and tries to become ethnically invisible by refraining from wearing Indian clothes. Even though she has misgivings about actively dissociating herself from Bangladeshis, she considers it as a necessity for self-protection. Interestingly, when Anita herself asked a Pakistani doctor whether he would shave off his beard after experiencing repeated interrogations by airport security, he said no, but also said he feels pressured to do so by his wife: "She was also saying, 'Why don't you shave it off?'" And he said, "No, I want to keep it because . . . it's a part of my religious beliefs."

If Hindu Indians distinguish themselves from Muslim South Asians, legal immigrants including naturalized citizens often attempt to distinguish themselves from the undocumented. Winnie immigrated illegally to the United States via Canada from Jamaica before 9/11. With the help of lawyers she was able to adjust her status and become a naturalized U.S. citizen. When asked her opinion about the immigration debate, she expresses a contradictory response to undocumented migration:

> I think and believe that working illegally in this country and making money and getting the benefits, I'm against it. I paid all my taxes when I got my documents. I never took public assistance or any benefits. I felt I wasn't entitled. Everyone's riled up about immigration. I was illegal for a time but I did the right thing and got my citizenship. I came here for a better life and a better life for my kids and worked two and three jobs to make it. I volunteered to give back. I didn't go on welfare, Medicaid, or public housing. If you're a parasite doing the wrong thing then you should go. Arizona is wrong, going about it the wrong way.

Winnie's statement raises several issues. Though she distinguishes herself from other undocumented immigrants—she believes herself to be a "good" immigrant because she did not avail of public services, while others are "bad"—she is also opposed to harsh anti-immigrant policies like those introduced by the state of Arizona. Indeed, she emphasizes how she adjusted her status, but that is hardly an easy prospect for most immigrants, especially now.

She then makes a distinction between herself and other African Americans, stating, "That's why I don't have patience for black Americans who take things for granted. Those who take things for granted and don't have respect for all the opportunities that they have. I came to this country later in life and worked damn hard to get where I am. . . . I say that if I was born here or had come here earlier there is no telling how far I would have come. People should not waste or throw away opportunities; it just makes me mad to see that happening." Ironically, Winnie uses notions of deservingness that have been used to attack the modest gains African Americans achieved through the civil rights movement in terms of social protections.

Ruiz, a naturalized U.S. citizen from Peru, similarly makes distinctions between undocumented and legal immigrants. Like Winnie, he assumes that those who arrived in the United States without documentation are people who are unfairly partaking of public benefits reserved for legal permanent residents. In response to a question about whether he thinks immigration policies after 9/11 are fair, he answers, "Yeah, I think so. 'Cause I mean I busted my ass in this country. I think it's unfair for anyone who just comes now to get everything handed to them on a silver platter. You know, they have to work their ass off just like I did."

Patrick, an immigrant from the Philippines, shares both Ruiz and Winnie's opinions on undocumented immigration:

> Being Filipino or being from Asia, I guess, I'd like to have a stricter implementation of immigration rules because I feel that it is unfair for people who are trying to legally enter or legally acquire their immigrant status in the United States, versus people who are just crossing the border. Some people might think otherwise, but people from Asia who are being petitioned by their families are waiting ten, fifteen, twenty years to legally come here. Whereas some are being granted amnesty or being afforded the right to stay and be a resident of the United States when they just cross the border. One is through legal means and the other is illegal. I find it unfair that the person seeking legal means has to wait so long, while the other who entered illegally gets a faster process.

Patrick's observation that "people from Asia who are being petitioned by their families are waiting ten, fifteen, twenty years to legally come here" is an accurate one. Although the 1965 Immigration Act opened up opportunities for citizens as well as legal permanent residents to "petition" their family members in the countries they left behind, the wait time can be devastatingly long. In my own experience, my father petitioned his brother in the 1980s but my uncle's visa was not approved until the mid-2000s. By the time the green card came in the mail, he had passed away. In fact, many Filipinos and other Asian immigrants try to join their relatives in the United States by entering on tourist visas and overstaying rather than waiting decades to reunite with their family members. In short, because immigration bureaucratic processes are so slow, people are forced to come to this country as undocumented immigrants. What Patrick sees as a point of distinction between legal immigrants who "wait so long" and undocumented immigrants who "enter illegally," however, has more to do with the failures of the immigration system and people's desires to live with their loved ones than undocumented immigrants' criminality. Moreover, Patrick's notion that somehow specific immigrant groups are being awarded amnesty (though he doesn't make it explicit, he is clearly talking about Mexican immigrants when he refers to people who "just cross the border") is patently false. Yet immigrants like him buy into the incorrect narrative that privileges are granted to some groups over others.[36] White nativists articulate this narrative. They believe that immigrants are extended economic and other sets of entitlements that citizens cannot enjoy, yet it is not true.

Anita, an Indian immigrant who arrived in 1997 and eventually became a naturalized citizen, draws distinctions, paradoxically enough, between citizens and specific kinds of legal immigrants. She is opposed to increasing numbers of immigrants coming to the United States on H-1B visas. H-1B visa holders are essentially guest workers who are allowed to work temporarily in the United States in specified professional occupations. They can become legal permanent residents only if their employer sponsors them. Anita states, "At first I was against . . . people coming over on H1 visas. Actually I still feel that way. Because of them, people like us don't get jobs because the jobs fill up and we are citizens. It's not fair."

Cultural studies and ethnic studies scholar Lisa Marie Cacho offers an important explanation for the divisiveness exhibited by some immigrants of color. She argues that it should not be simply read as people "selling each other out" but rather that it reflects a deep understanding on the part of these groups that "recuperating social value *requires* rejecting the other Other." Racialized groups "are simply reasserting the truth of their existence, which has been erased or distorted not only by likening them to already not-valued others but also by not representing them when writing about differently devalued others."[37] In other words, there are dominant narratives, stories, or what we might think of as scripts about race and race relations in America, scripts that are white supremacist, antiblack, xenophobic (classist and gendered too) that peoples of color are forced to draw from when making sense of their experiences and their relations to other racialized groups. Institutions like the mass media and even public education, stage, rehearse, and perpetuate these scripts. Part of my task as a critical activist-scholar is to lay bare the operations by which these scripts are reproduced as well as to offer up alternatives. And there are alternatives. Even as immigrants draw divisions between themselves, they also make connections with one another.

For example, Anita asserts her Hindu-ness to distinguish herself from Muslim South Asians, yet Manjusha recognizes and is sympathetic to the injustices suffered by her Muslim counterparts. She states, for example, "I know for the Bangladeshi students, getting, because they are Muslims, job discrimination. Even my husband's uncle who's a doctor here, he was a director, he was in charge of the residency program, he told my husband like, though it's not a written law, we're getting an instruction about not hiring any Muslims." Even as some immigrants draw lines of difference and ultimately hierarchy between themselves across religious, racial, and ethnic lines, others do not.

Shared experiences of racialization shape Ghassan's connections with Latinos. An immigrant from Lebanon who had been in the United States for just over two decades at the time of his interview, he describes feeling close to Latino immigrants. On one hand Ghassan is often racialized as Latino, but on the other hand he works with many Latinos and thus, "I had to learn Spanish because a lot of Spanish people were here. [They knew] no English whatsoever and being that I'm in charge I have to understand what they are saying, if they need something. You can't always rely on sign language. It's good but you also have to speak something so I started learning. And if something I don't understand, I ask what does that mean and I translate it in my mind and know what the meaning is."

Immigrants notice the kinds of indignities suffered by fellow immigrants. Tri, a twenty-one year-old Vietnamese man from a refugee family observed "other people," specifically "Hispanic people," getting treated "differently" on public transportation. He continued, "The bus driver kind of like looks at those people as like they don't know what they're doing or like they don't know what's going on because of their lack of English." In describing his own experiences, he shared how "in the town where I live, people see that we're not that much . . . like most of us is not that educated 'cause we didn't grow up here or some of us don't go to college here."

When asked what her sense of the public's perceptions of immigrants are, Rachel, a white woman who emigrated from the United Kingdom as a young child, responded, "I think there's a lot of people who are really rude and anti-immigration. They really look down on them [immigrants]. Like at my job, at Bennigan's, there's a lot of Mexicans, the cooks and stuff. And I think a lot of them are illegal. I think people really look down on them because they don't speak English. That's more of an issue for them than it is for me. I'm more American because at least I've got the language." Of course, a point Rachel does not make but is significant: she is also white. Whiteness allows her to claim "Americanness" in a way none of the immigrants discussed thus far in this chapter have.

Settlement in Immigrant Spaces and Alternative Notions of Safety

"I think that Americans see us as inferior and not worth anything. They look at us like we are strangers or garbage. That is why there are certain places where only rich Americans live and other places where Hispanic people live," observes Lucia, a naturalized U.S. citizen originally from Colombia. If the suburbs are figured as "white" spaces in the popular imagination, it is a notion immigrants like Lucia fully understand. They know what spaces are white spaces and they know that those are places where they do not belong. They know that white spaces are places where they are not safe and face the possibility of apprehension, detention, and, worse, deportation. Immigrants construct alternative geographies and identify spaces where they can evade immigration authorities but where they can also enjoy some respite from discrimination and build ties with other community members who share their background.

Rolando, discussed above, was hyperconscious of where to settle, and his undocumented status made him especially vigilant about communities where he could feel safe. He states, "I knew that is was safer to live near a big city then to live in a small town if I planned on staying here longer than my visa allowed me to." He settled in Somerville because "this town also has Spanish restaurants and stores so I feel more welcome in this area than I would possibly somewhere else." Moreover, given his undocumented status and therefore his limited mobility, Rolando settled in Somerville because "I thought I would be more comfortable in an area like this . . . because I did not have a license to drive myself anywhere and I could get where I needed by walking. I thought I would have an easier time finding a job in this kind of place." Though there have been some legislative attempts to extend driver's license privileges to the undocumented, New Jersey currently does not issue driver's licenses to those who cannot prove they are in the United States lawfully.[38] Tri, the young Vietnamese man, explains that his parents settled specifically in their South Jersey town in close proximity to Atlantic City because of the casinos, which "provide good paying job[s] for people that are . . . mostly immigrant or people that [didn't] go to school or have education."[39]

Aziz, a twenty-two-year-old college student, speculates that his parents, originally from India, moved to the town of Montville because "there was a population of Muslims in the town." Similarly Ji-Hye, a Korean woman also in her early twenties, notes that her parents moved close to Palisades Park and Fort Lee because of the presence of "a strong Korean church" and Korean businesses. Both Aziz and Ji-Hye came to the United States as young children. Although they did not make the decisions to settle in the places where they grew up, they make sense of the fact that they live where they live because their parents wanted to be in communities where their co-ethnics had settled.

Living with co-ethnics is not necessarily desirable for immigrants. A middle-aged Korean immigrant said, "I like the non-Korean communities in America because there is less social drama and more privacy. If I were to live with Koreans, I would rather live in an actual Korean city in South Korea." Patrick, the middle-aged man from the Philippines on an H-1B visa discussed earlier, is legally in the United States, but describes why he prefers living in Central Jersey: "You don't really feel that you are treated different because everyone is different. There is no single majority race and that's why you're just the same as everyone else. Being an immigrant, being a transplant from another country that looks different from those that are in the majority of the people that are here. That's a nice thing to be in, to not feel that you are different. To not feel that you are segregated from everyone else." In Patrick's case, living in a racially and ethnically diverse community (that isn't necessarily dominated by Filipinos) makes him feel connected with others.

Those who don't live in immigrant spaces have a hard time engaging in even everyday activities. Luz, the Colombian immigrant discussed earlier, explained, "Well, because I am Hispanic and I do not know how to speak perfect English, people hate when they speak to me and I do not understand. That is one of the reasons why I do not go out so much, to avoid trouble or any embarrassment. My sons always protect me and guide me but they're not always going to be there." Luz not only describes her confinement to her home but also reveals how her sons, both Colombian-born but raised in the United States, help her to negotiate life in American society.

Ambivalent Americans

Given the kinds of exclusions immigrants experience on a day-to-day basis, perhaps it not surprising that immigrants are ambivalent about U.S. citizenship. When asked if he ever felt proud to be an American, Jin, an immigrant from South Korea, responded, "I mean, I don't feel ashamed to be an American, but I wouldn't say I would boast about it. No. I would say having American citizenship is more of a convenience than splat-out [*sic*] pride."

Aziz, the young Indian Muslim man who came to the United States as a child with his parents, describes what U.S. citizenship means to him, particularly possessing a U.S. passport: "Indian citizenship is a piece of sh@#. It holds a lot of value, power, and status to have a U.S. passport." When queried about the right to vote, an important right granted only to U.S. citizens, he responded, "Voting is a useless right but having the right to not get deported for any criminal offense is good. Better jail than deportation." Indeed, deportation is not just an abstraction for Aziz. When asked if he had knowledge of family members or friends who had been deported he answered with an emphatic, "Hell yeah!" As mentioned above, a close friend of the family was purportedly "ambushed" by ICE agents and deported.

For Patrick the Filipino H-1B visa holder, American citizenship is racialized. Possessing American citizenship, he believes, does not necessarily guarantee that he will actually be an American. In other words, belonging to America is an elusive prospect. He explains: "For me, my being Filipino doesn't stop when I become an American citizen. I am Filipino and I cannot deny it. My hair doesn't change to blond [laughs]. My skin color doesn't change. It's still me and I'm the same person. Same everything. It's just a paper that says I am American."

Like Patrick, an immigrant from China believes that citizenship is more about having entitlements to economic benefits and less an issue of belonging. When asked whether she would become a U.S. citizen and whether she saw any advantages to becoming a citizen of the United States, she responded, "Well, there's definitely advantage in terms of . . . benefits after you become a citizen to work. But um, yeah, I don't know how the economy is going to be in the future for both China and the U.S. Whichever side is better of course is the side I'm going to choose-choose [*sic*]."

Rachel, the white immigrant from England quoted earlier, was in her twenties at the time of the interview. She arrived in the United States as a child with her parents. When asked about the advantages and disadvantages of obtaining U.S. citizenship, she responded, "A big [disadvantage of not having U.S. citizenship] is I can't vote. My dad really wants to be able to vote. And then, in the back of my mind, I mean I know this isn't really going to happen, but I still think about it sometimes, I wonder what if there's a fallout [*sic*] between the U.S. and England. Then would I have the INS watching out for me?" This is a poignant example of how much national security and immigration have become conjoined in the minds of immigrants, even those racialized as white. Immigrants have a keen sense that their loyalties may be questioned.

The United States claims to be a multicultural "nation of immigrants," yet when immigrants are asked to what extent they believe that to be true, many are dubious. Luz, the Colombian native and naturalized U.S. citizen, observes,

> I personally do not think that this is [a multicultural society] or will ever be. The reason why I say that is because in this country, there is too much hatred and too much racism. People discriminate against each other like it was something normal that was done every day. In order for a more fair multicultural society to happen, this country would need to suspend all borders, get rid of all its laws in which discriminates against people and allow cultures to be treated equal. But we all know that is never going to happen. It just isn't.

Being "White"

It is important to underscore that when differences are drawn between immigrants and citizens in national discourse, it is often specifically the differences between immigrants and color and white citizens. Sociopsychological research confirms that these differences deeply shape individuals' unconscious cognitive assessments of one another in the United States: "When perceptions are assessed at a level that escapes conscious control or awareness, a robust American = White effect emerges."[40] Both whites and nonwhites draw those distinctions.[41] In this section, I will examine how European immigrants (and others who may be racialized as "white") draw distinctions between themselves and immigrants of color when asked about the impact of immigration debates and post-9/11 immigration policies on their daily lives.

Nick arrived in the United States from Greece in the 1970s on a student visa. He became a legal permanent resident through the sponsorship of his wife ("I get [*sic*] married here in order to stay") and acquired citizenship. He was sixty-one at the time of his interview. In response to a query about whether he felt as if he were treated differently as an immigrant when he's out in public, Nick replied, "No, I don't . . . I'm not considered a minority. I am considered white. Europeans are considered white so there is not a big difference from the Americans. Many people, they don't even recognize that I am an immigrant except when I'm speaking and I [mis]pronounce words. I have [an] accent and people don't understand me sometimes but it's fine. It doesn't bother me." When asked what his sense of the public's perceptions of people with his background was, Nick responded, "Oh they love it. We have a very good welcome because the Greeks are good. My background is good. We don't bother people. We try to educate the kids. We are very hardworking and not too many troublemakers. Not too many criminals. Always there are a few, some here and there but in general we are very welcomed in the American society, all the Greeks."

As whiteness scholars remind us, however, Greeks were not always considered "white." Nick's claim to whiteness and Americanness would have been questioned by the broader American public and the U.S. state a century ago. According to historian and American Studies scholar Matthew Frye Jacobson, "As races are invented categories—designations coined for the sake of grouping and separating peoples along lines of presumed difference—Caucasians are made and not born. White privilege in various forms has been a constant in American political culture since colonial times, but whiteness itself has been subject to all kinds of contests and has gone through a series of historical vicissitudes."[42] Among its "vicissitudes" have been debates over whether Southern Europeans like Greeks were authentically Caucasian (white). At the same time, Nick's claim to whiteness is also class-inflected. As anthropologist Susan Ortner argues in her research exploring race and class identity among Jews from the Weequahic section of Newark, "Race and ethnicity categories almost always carry a hidden class referent."[43] To be (or to claim) whiteness is also to claim a higher class status. Nick, for instance, makes clear that not only are Greeks white, but they are hardworking and strive to educationally advance themselves. Recall the narratives by immigrants of color in an earlier section of this chapter: they described how they believed that in public discourse immigrants are stereotyped not only in racialized ways but in classed ways as well. It is assumed they are uneducated, low-wage workers or lazy people who illegally take advantage of public goods and services.

White immigrants vacillate when it comes to identifying as whites and/or immigrants. Polina, an immigrant from Russia, is a case in point. Polina was interviewed in the fall of 2007 when George W. Bush was president of the United States. In the spring of 2007, he had proposed comprehensive immigration reform, including a pathway for legalization for undocumented immigrants. His plan failed to garner sufficient support.[44] When Polina was asked about what she thought about the national immigration debate, she responds in this way:

POLINA: I would say that right now, I guess, we don't like Bush's politics, that how many thousands he wanted to make legal people, or whatever. Nobody likes immigrants. I don't know. But at the same time, who works here? Like say Mexicans mowing the lawns and they get paid five bucks per hour, we're not going to do that. I mean no one is going to work those hours for so much money. Americans, they don't want to do that. I feel that yeah, there is some kind of people that look at you that you're immigrants that you come to take our jobs, some kind of attention like that I think.

INTERVIEWER: Do you feel you are affected by those perceptions in any way?

POLINA: I guess I try to be fair with everyone. 'Cause I know what it is to be kind of illegal, I remember to be illegal and now I am legal, I could do whatever I want to do. So I can understand them.

In her narrative, Polina slips between identifying as American as when she claims, "we don't like Bush's politics," to identifying as an immigrant, as when she says, "there is some kind of people that look at you that you're immigrants that you come to take our jobs." Moreover, she demonstrates a certain empathy with undocumented immigrants because indeed, she was once "illegal" herself.

Immigrants are acutely aware of the ways in which whiteness offers passage to full membership to the polity and a sense of safety and security from the prospects of detention and deportation, which is increasingly a palpable risk that all noncitizens face in the post-9/11 immigration enforcement context. Some even try to claim whiteness for protection. In an interview with a young Coptic Egyptian woman from Jersey City, I was struck by her insistence that the state had mistakenly apprehended, detained, and deported one of her close friends by not recognizing that she was in fact "Caucasian." In the wake of 9/11, Jersey City residents were subject to intensive surveillance and policing.[45] Members of the Egyptian community, Christian and Muslim alike, shared experiences of being surveilled. One of the Coptic priests there was commissioned by local DHS authorities to work as a kind of "cultural ambassador" to help agents better distinguish between people in the Egyptian community who might have terrorist links and those who do not in response to complaints by the Coptic community that they were being unfairly targeted. Nevertheless, Coptic Egyptians were caught in the immigration enforcement dragnet.

White immigrants are aware, moreover, of the privileges they enjoy as whites. When a young Israeli woman was asked what her sense of the public's perceptions of immigrants was, she stated "Usually I think it is bad. Citizens of the United States don't want more people coming to this country and stealing jobs. The public seems to have a difficult time integrating and accepting the immigrants into the society. But I also believe that it also has to do with the type of immigrants that comes. For instance, I think Hispanics are treated poorly while those coming from Europe are treated better." When further queried about whether she is affected by these public perceptions, Ayala responds, "No because I look American and I don't have an accent so people generally don't know that I have immigrated here . . . because when you look at me you really cannot tell that I am Middle Eastern." Generally speaking, Ayala does not experience much hostility or negativity despite her immigrant status. She states, "I think I am treated better since I am Caucasian and look like your average American."

European immigrants' identity as *immigrants* is just as salient as their identities as whites. Boris, a Russian immigrant, expresses this in his interview:

INTERVIEWER: Now can you see yourself getting along with someone who has immigrated faster than someone who has lived here their entire life?

BORIS: Yes. A lot of immigrants have common experience because they experienced common difficulties, you know, coming to the country not knowing how things work. It didn't matter if you spoke Russian or Polish or you speak an African language. If you don't speak English you experience similar issues. I would say that people with immigrant backgrounds get along better because they kinda have walked in each other's shoes. In other words, they know how difficult things were. If you were born here it's not that you are bad. You just never experienced it so it's a little harder to relate. Just to say you understand how they feel doesn't mean you do because often times you really have to experience it.

Immigrant Detention in New Jersey

Thus far, I have shared the experiences of immigrants living in different communities across New Jersey in the post-9/11 context. I turn now to a discussion of the immigrant detainee experience. What does it feel like when the Homeland Security State apparatus has branded you a problem and has excised you from your home and locked you up?

Immigration enforcement has been heightened in many communities, particularly suburban communities, across New Jersey. It should not be surprising that heavy surveillance of immigrant communities was put into place in New Jersey's cities in the immediate post-9/11 period. Jersey City, for example, was a site of aggressive surveillance by the federal government as mentioned earlier.[46]

As a result of both local and federal officers' immigration enforcement work in suburbs and cities, there has been a tremendous increase in immigrant apprehensions, detentions, and deportations. In just over a decade since the passage of the 1996 IIRIRA, immigration detention tripled.[47] In the state of New Jersey, deportations (which are preceded by a period of detention) increased steadily after 2001. In 2009, in only seven months, deportations from New Jersey totaled 4,103, almost as many deportations as all of 2008.[48] Moreover, although the Supreme Court ruled in 2001 that the government could not detain undocumented immigrants indefinitely if there was no country willing to take them, immigrant detainees may nevertheless spend months and even years in detention as they await removal proceedings.[49] Furthermore, even though there was a time when immigrants (including asylum seekers) were only being detained if they posed a danger to society immigration policy has come to assume, over the last thirty years, that immigrants "do present a threat, and only releasing migrants who can prove otherwise."[50] This has led to a bloated federal detention system.[51] Hence, since 2001 the DHS has increasingly had to contract out the detention of immigrants to county jails. Approximately 67 percent of immigrant detainees are held in state and county jails across the United States.[52] As of 2016, four of New Jersey's county jails have contracts (Bergen, Essex, Hudson, and Monmouth) with the federal government to house immigrant detainees.[53] However, other county jails have had contracts with ICE in the past including Middlesex, Suffolk and Passaic.[54] Immigration detention has been a money-making scheme for local municipalities. Counties have turned to immigrant detention as a form of revenue.[55] White suburbanites may claim that immigrants residing in their towns are a drain on public resources, but they can be considered a source of public "income" if they are residents of county jails.

Everyday Life in Detention

After pressure from immigrant rights' groups, the Department of Homeland Security's Office of the Inspector General (OIG) was forced to conduct an audit of five immigrant detention centers nationally in 2006. Notably, of the five centers that were investigated, two were in New Jersey: the Hudson and Passaic County Jails. Although the New Jersey Civil Rights Defense Committee (NJCRDC) considers the report a "whitewash" and produced an alternative report that brought immigrant detainees' voices to the fore, the OIG's audit nevertheless confirmed what the NJCRDC and other activists had long known: a wide range of abuses were taking place at the Passaic County Jail in particular.[56] The NJCRDC's "shadow report" notes, moreover, that more than 50 percent of the requests for nonemergency medical assistance at the facility were not responded to in a timely manner.

The OIG's report omits the voices of detainees themselves, but I read numerous letters from immigrants at the Passaic County Jail while working with the NJCRDC. The letters provide a stark picture of life in detention. R.E. writes, for instance, "We cannot all fit into the day room unless we are shoulder to shoulder. . . . There are mice bite holes in our commissary, leaky roofs, cockroaches, and we're being housed in a jail built to house 800 inmates, where today, it houses over 2,200 inmates." In a 2005 petition signed by detainees from three different units in Passaic, one detainee describes how he "literally poured milk into the cereal in the tray and grease was floating on top of the milk due to the spaghetti with tomato sauce we had for dinner the night before." In other words, their food trays were dirty.

Only two New Jersey county facilities were inspected by the OIG; however, immigrant detainees from many other jails wrote to the NJCRDC describing conditions no different from those in the Passaic County facility. A January 2006 petition signed by thirteen detainees from diverse backgrounds including Latin America, the Caribbean, Africa, and the Middle East describes conditions in the Bergen County jail: "The housing

TAORIO Gwah #150586
Passaic county Jail
11 sheriff's plaza Patterson N/J 07501

New Jersey civil Right Deffence
P.O Box 353
Piscataway N/J 08855 - 0353

Dear Ms, Gabriel,

How are you and the rest of your staff? Hope everyone is fine. I am writing to you guys to let you know I am still at passaic county Jail and barely alive. I recently fell down and seriously hurt myself when I slipped on the water coming down the wall right in front of my room. Even though I have been complaining about the water and they know I can't walk around without a walker they still refused to take any action. since the heart - surgery I have been very sick and, should I be sent to my native country in Africa I would'nt be able to get proper care for my heart implant and medication. I know the law is on my side based on the nature of my crime relatively minor fraud at my Job long - time ago, the length of my residing in the U.S.A. and my status: 28 years as a permanent resident, and both my wife and daughter are born in this country. Also being working as a limousine driver for a long time.

P.T.O.

PHOTO 6. Letter from immigrant detainee (From "Voices of the Disappeared" by the New Jersey Civil Rights Defense Committee)

conditions are deplorable. Mice are running all over the living area. This has been brought to the officers' attention on duty. The response was that there is nothing they could do about it." By June 2006, six months later, detainees describe worsening conditions. A short, hurriedly written letter in broken English that demonstrates the urgency of their situation states,

"We . . . have filed many grievance forms concerning major health violations. We have rain coming in unit an electrical problem of major concern a fire hazard." A year after they filed the initial petition, Bergen County's detainees continued to suffer and were compelled to filed yet another one in 2007 to protest inhumane living conditions. There were forty-four signatories.[57]

Writing from the Monmouth County jail in 2005, a detainee describes being forced to sleep on the floor because his cell is overcrowded. As a result, a preexisting problem with his vertebral column was exacerbated. He has a short right leg but was denied use of orthopedic shoes that were prescribed by a jail doctor. This not only caused him great pain but also injury. His multiple complaints to Monmouth County authorities fell on deaf ears.[58] Also in 2005, another detainee hastily wrote a letter by hand pleading that the NJCRDC investigate the death of a fellow detainee. He reports that his fellow detainee had complained of chest pains but was ignored until it was too late. Both local and federal officials failed to respond to queries from our group about the death. As a *New York Times* article describes it, the case "underscores the secrecy and lack of legal accountability that continue to shield the system from independent oversight. . . it is a patchwork . . . of county jails, profit-making prisons and federal detention centers."[59] Detainees in at least six county jails (Bergen, Camden, Hudson, and Middlesex in addition to Monmouth and Passaic) faced medical abuse. A Cuban immigrant detained in the Camden County Jail in early 2002 wrote about his untreated hernia. Authorities rebuffed all his attempts to seek medical care until he was released three years later in 2005.[60] Hudson County Correctional, one of the facilities audited by the OIG, denied medical care to a diabetic, hypertensive Pakistani detainee in his early sixties who also suffered from a heart condition and was confined to a wheelchair. He was forced to pay his fellow detainees to assist him in daily tasks like getting in and out of bed and bathing.

Media attention has often focused on the experiences of the children of undocumented immigrants who have been apprehended by immigration enforcement; there has been much less attention given to immigrant parents who are in detention. Detainees are practically isolated from their family members. A Barbadian detainee writing to the NJCRDC from the Passaic County Jail writes, "The visiting schedule is too short and our families are traveling long distance and we only get to talk to them for about fifteen minutes in front of a big glass and unable to touch our kids, nieces, nephews, etc. . . . The phone system is not helping us, it is too expensive and we have to buy phone cards from the jail and there are many times inmates lose time on calling cards because the phones are having problems which we won't get reimbursed for."

A Dominican detainee who first arrived in the United States at the age of five also writes in a letter to the NJCRDC about how his U.S.-citizen family members are likely to be impacted by his detention:

> Please see if you can help me in any way possible I have no legal representation because I can't afford a lawyer. Please don't let them break the Molina family apart. My wife is left all alone to work and care for three small children. It is very hard for her. She is suffering the loss of her husband very much and the children miss their father very much. . . . I am totally devoted to my family and trying to raise my children the best way possibly but now I am about to lost my family.

A detainee from Pakistan similarly describes the negative impact his detention has on his family: "My wife is in a very fragile and serious health condition as a cancer patient and she and my kids really need me now the most. I have five kids and my youngest child is five years old."[61]

Suffering what is often illegal neglect, immigrant detainees also face the prospect of physical abuse. Almost immediately upon admission into the Hudson County Jail, P.S. describes in his 2005 letter to NJCRDC how "Officer X slammed me into the block wall, slammed my head into the wall repeatedly as several other officers came out from behind the counter to assist in the first part of the attack." His offense: when he was asked to spit out his gum, P.S. missed the trash can but was unable to pick it up from the floor because he was in handcuffs. After initially beating him, the officers released P.S. from his handcuffs so he could properly dispose of the gum. He says that after doing so, "I was dragged . . . to the back and was then . . . pummeled. I was hit repeatedly in my back, my rib, punched in the face, in the back of my knees as my head then bounced off the metal benches. The whole time the second part of the beating took place I was violently being restrained with officers holding both my arms very hard and up behind my neck. . . . My head finally broke open and blood squirted everywhere." Hudson County jailers' abuse made it to the national media, though curiously enough, it was completely absent in the OIG report. Both the *New York Times* and National Public Radio reported on the case of Egyptian detainee Sadek Awaed, who was severely beaten by guards. The beating occurred after guards had beaten another detainee with whom they were arguing. The guards ordered the other detainees back to their cells. Though Awaed complied, a knee surgery made it difficult for him to move. Guards then beat him for supposedly "faking" injury and not complying with their order to return to his cell.[62]

Also missing from the OIG's audit was thorough investigations of allegations of physical abuse in the Passaic County Jail. Indeed, human rights activists documented allegations of physical abuse in the facility as early as 2002. Detainees claimed that guards used police dogs to intimidate them.[63] In 2005, P.A. wrote to the NJCRDC, "I was punch into my side of my neck [*sic*] by Sgt. X then he grab me by my shirt and slam me by my chest into the jail bars." It took four years after the initial reports of abuse before Passaic County's sheriff at the time, Jerry Speziale, would be forced to end the jail's contract with the federal government to house immigrant detainees.

Conclusion

Drawing from the title of Du Bois's classic text, this chapter is similarly inspired to lift up the voices of New Jersey's immigrant suburbanites as they negotiate life under the regime of the Homeland Security State. We hear from a range of immigrants in this chapter. They come from all corners of the world and very different walks of life. Some have lived in the United States for extended periods. Others are new arrivals. I talked to legal immigrants, other foreign-born migrants, the undocumented, and naturalized citizens. There are striking similarities, particularly between immigrants of color. They share similar experiences of racialization and can attribute many of their experiences to the changes wrought by post-9/11 immigration policy.

Not all immigrants necessarily share a collective identity, however. Some draw very firm distinctions between themselves and others on the basis of religion, ethnicity, race, and legal status. These distinctions are even crafted through discourses usually associated with xenophobic, nativism. Others recognize they share common cause with other immigrants. As I will discuss in the next chapter, these are the sort of immigrants who often take the next step to participate collectively in social justice formations as activists. Even as this chapter's main aim has been to give voice to immigrants' everyday experiences, I draw the title of this chapter from Du Bois for another reason. I think it is important to highlight how the "color line" very much organizes American life despite claims that we live in a post-racial society. Immigrants themselves make this point painfully clear.

This chapter, moreover, has aimed to lift up the voices of immigrant detainees, the voices of the "disappeared." The fact is that many immigrants have vanished from communities as a result of the immigrant enforcement dragnet imposed by both local and federal authorities. I offer only a small glimpse into immigrants' lives in detention, but over the course of my years as both a scholar and activist, I have learned that detainees are literally a disappeared population. There have been cases where immigrants who cannot speak English or do not have sufficient economic means are unable to contact loved ones. Immigrants' friends and families can go for months without knowing that they have been detained. This chapter's intent is not only to shed light on detainees' horrific and heartbreaking experiences behind bars but also to point to the crucial work being done by immigrant rights activists and advocates, whose creative and valiant organizing efforts I discuss in the next chapter.

5

Fighting on the Home Front

Lovely, spacious Victorians, the former homes of well-to-do locals when Bridgeton, located in Cumberland County, was an industrial and commercial center at the turn of the twentieth century, share space with strings of smaller "gingerbread" worker homes along tree-lined street after tree-lined street of the town. It was once one of the wealthiest communities in New Jersey, and it is difficult not to be impressed by the distinctiveness of Bridgeton's landscape compared to the relative blandness of the McMansions that dot the landscapes of other New Jersey suburbs.[1] Indeed, Bridgeton's officially defined historic district encompasses two thousand properties and is the largest such district in the state.[2] Bridgeton is an historic preservationists dream . . . or nightmare. Many of the buildings, though still beautiful, are in severe disrepair with dilapidated roofs and peeling paint.

The community of Bridgeton, like many of New Jersey's suburbs, has been dramatically transformed as a consequence of recent immigration. The foreign-born population of Bridgeton is 24 percent, compared to the state average of 21 percent; 41 percent of the population in Bridgeton speaks a language other than English compared to the state average of close

PHOTO 7. Historic home in Bridgeton, New Jersey (Photo credit: Robyn Rodriguez)

to 30 percent. In terms of ethnic-racial breakdown, almost 44 percent of Bridgeton's population is Hispanic/Latino compared to the state average of about 18 percent.[3]

At the same time, Bridgeton has largely lost the economic base from which its earlier residents drew their wealth. Straddling the Cohansey River, it was an industrial and commercial center and home to glass factories, sewing factories, metal and machine works, and other manufacturers in the late nineteenth and early twentieth centuries. However, when water-based transport routes lost their centrality in favor of land transport (the mode of transportation that also fueled suburbanization), and roads replaced rails, Bridgeton became an out-of-the way place. The town narrates its official history this way on its website: "The city suffered an economic downturn in the 1980s with the loss of its remaining manufacturing sector jobs in glass and textiles. Agricultural employment, however, has continued to attract immigrant workers largely from Mexico, creating new challenges and opportunities for revitalization. A significant minority of Bridgeton residents speak Zapoteco. Immigrants work primarily in nurseries and in agricultural processing occupations near the city, which are among some of the most productive in New Jersey."[4]

Bridgeton's contemporary racial and ethnic landscape, at least based on the local government's own reckoning in this official history, is largely shaped by suburban demands. Its economic base in agriculture, particularly in nurseries and thus the production of ornamental plants, is likely due to suburbanites' investments in the adornment of their homes as well as the corporate campuses where they work. Not surprisingly, Latino immigrants work in those nurseries even as they work to maintain suburban gardens in Bridgeton and towns across the state.[5]

Many suburban communities have dug in their heels to secure their towns against the perceived threat of immigrant outsiders. They often work to preserve some imagined idyllic, white middle-class suburban past. In addition to passing local ordinances restricting immigrants' settlement, efforts at historic preservation have also become a mechanism for excluding immigrants through the celebration of and investment in a built environment that is bereft of minority immigrants' histories, experiences, and aesthetics. Yet something very different is happening in Bridgeton. The town's Center for Historic American Building Arts (which prefers to be known by its acronym, CHABA) represents a novel intervention not only in historic preservation but also in immigrant inclusion. Offering new ways that immigrants can participate not just in historic preservation but perhaps more crucially in place making, it offers immigrants a means by which to make New Jersey their home. According to Flavia Alaya, a highly energetic, Italian American, long-time immigrant rights activist in New Jersey and the creative force behind the organization, CHABA works together with old families and new to "script the landscape," by highlighting narratives within the built environment that elaborate the stories of "striving" workers and entrepreneurs, as well as to lay down new narrative tracks that embrace the lives and dreams of Latino immigrants. Indeed, CHABA's entire project is constructed on the principle that the same built environment that has the potential to create and perpetuate exclusion can also be a site for the formation of identity and belonging.[6]

This chapter highlights the various ways immigrants have tried to (re) claim a sense of "home" in New Jersey after 9/11, a process I think of as "home-making." During a historical moment of heightened national security fears, fears incited by the presence of those perceived to be Others (simply because they are nonwhite, foreign-born people), fears that have led to policies and practices meant to expel and exclude these Others, the

PHOTO 8. Mural by Cesar Viveros-Herrera in Bridgeton, New Jersey (Photo credit: Robyn Rodriguez)

work of CHABA and many other groups imagines new visions of and open new opportunities for immigrants' belonging beyond the exclusive and exclusionary notions of citizenship that have always defined and delimited membership in America's suburbs, and indeed in America more broadly.[7]

Immigrants' activism at the municipal level has been increasing around the country due to what some scholars describe as "the multi-scalar policies criminalizing immigrants."[8] The complex web of federal, state, county, and local policies aimed at excluding and expelling immigrants that I have discussed throughout this book is what these scholars mean by "multi-scalar policies" and is a phenomenon taking place across the United States.

Immigrants are responding to these policies in kind, however. Chicano Studies scholar Genevieve Carpio and colleagues argue that the immigrant activism taking place in the Los Angeles suburbs they study offers a more expansive definition of citizenship for immigrants, including "the right to self-governance without citizenship, the right to political participation beyond the electoral and the right to be agents of political, economic and cultural change."[9] The resistance to anti-immigration politics and the home-making practices I track in this chapter can similarly be thought of from this framework.

Immigrant activism in New Jersey is necessarily multi-scalar. In this chapter, I start first with a discussion of the ways New Jersey's immigrant activists have localized national immigrant rights campaigns. I then turn my attention to the unique ways that New Jerseyans have organized for immigrant rights more locally. I look at how New Jerseysans draw on different frames to make claims for immigrants' rights in different communities. In some cases, activists articulate their advocacy in terms of "workers' rights" or "civil rights." In other cases, activists invoke immigrants' "human rights" but in very unexpected ways. I then turn to an extended discussion of spatial practices of resistance and home-making. By spatial practices, I am talking about things like the work CHABA does, such as transforming neighborhood landscapes to ensure that immigrants' membership in the local community is reflected in the built form; however, I am also referring to practices that are not necessarily fully elaborated and intentional kinds of spatial practices like CHABA's. I find geographer Steve Pile's definition of these other sorts of spatial practices useful here. He argues that "thinking through what people do, it can be seen that [subject] positionings are not necessarily articulated or articulable. They are better witnessed, better understood in the ways in which people produce or turn places and spaces for their own uses."[10]

The National Immigrant Rights Movement in New Jersey

New Jersey's immigrants and immigrant rights advocates have responded to legislative battles taking place at the national level and have organized protests of federal anti-immigrant policies as well as support for federal immigrant-friendly reforms. Like hundreds of thousands of others across the country, New Jerseyans took to the streets in late 2005 and the first half of 2006 to protest the passage by the U.S. House of Representatives of the Border Protection, Anti-terrorism, and Illegal Immigration Control Act of 2005 (H.R. 4437, also referred to as the Sensenbrenner Bill), a law that many in the immigrant rights community considered to be an especially draconian piece of legislation. The law would have made undocumented status a criminal offense and it would have made it illegal for advocates to provide assistance and support to undocumented people. Scholars and activists alike have characterized these mobilizations as truly historic and among the largest since the civil rights demonstrations of the 1960s.[11] It is estimated that 3.7 to 5 million immigrants and their supporters mobilized in more than 160 cities across the country between February and May 2006.[12] Throughout the state, New Jerseyans participated in demonstrations during that period of time. In March, a thousand immigrant rights' supporters rallied in Trenton, the state capital.[13] In April 2006, a reported three thousand protesters participated in the March for Peace and Liberty for Immigrants in Newark organized by the Immigrant Rights Defense Committee of New Jersey.[14]

New Jersey's immigrant rights' groups have consistently and persistently held local actions in support of federal immigration reform or to contest the aggressive enforcement of existing immigration policies in their communities. Groups like the Unidad Latina in Action from Hightstown, continuing what is now a tradition of standing up for immigrant rights on May 1, mobilized on May 1, 2013, in favor of comprehensive immigration reform, joining other groups across the nation.[15] Later that year as part of the ninth annual Latino Festival of Monmouth County, activists continued their call for reform. Cultural events become an opportunity to raise political issues.[16] More recently, in February 2016, dozens of New Jersey activists protested new rounds of ICE raids in the state.[17]

In response to anti-immigrant federal legislation or failed immigration reform, immigrant rights' advocates in New Jersey have focused on state legislation. For example, the Latino Leadership Alliance, along with other groups, led efforts to get state legislation passed that would make it legal for the undocumented to apply for a driver's license. The campaign was prompted, in part, by the passage of the REAL ID Act in 2005, which establishes federal standards for the issuance of driver's licenses, including a requirement that applicants provide proof of their legal status in the United States.[18] The struggle for driver's licenses continued for a decade, with activists (re)forming a statewide coalition in 2015 under the banner "New Jersey for All."[19] Owing to activists' sustained work, by late 2015, the Homeland Security and State Preparedness committee of the New Jersey State Assembly voted to approve a measure in support of state driver's licenses for undocumented immigrants. [20] Although Republican governor Chris Christie vowed to oppose such legislation, immigrant rights advocates were able to secure support from both state and local legislators.[21]

As much of the recent scholarship has documented, immigrant youth and students as well as immigrant workers have been among the main actors leading the national immigrant rights movement.[22] One of the most sustained and perhaps most visible national campaigns for immigration reform has been the movement in support of the Development, Relief, and Education for Alien Minors, or DREAM Act, led by undocumented youth and students. Indeed, what is notable about the struggle for the DREAM Act is that it has been led and championed by both Latino and Asian undocumented young people.[23] The act was first introduced in Congress in 2001 and aimed to provide a pathway for the undocumented children of immigrants to adjust their status.[24] The struggle for the passage of the DREAM Act has prompted activists to push through versions of the act at the state level. Alongside national DREAM efforts, immigrant youth and student activists in New Jersey together with statewide organizations like the New Jersey Regional Coalition, a coalition of religious leaders, the New Jersey Catholic Conference, and the New Jersey Immigrant Policy Network (NJIPN) have fought for the In-State Tuition Act, which would allow undocumented students to pay in-state tuition rates in New Jersey's colleges and universities.[25] Students on specific campuses worked to get university policies similar to the In-State Tuition Act implemented. This was the case at Rutgers University in 2010, for example, where students of the Latino Student Council led efforts to get the university president, Richard L. McCormick, to enact university policy to grant in-state tuition to undocumented students who had completed high school in the state.[26] By 2014, immigrant rights' activists were getting the New Jersey Dream Act signed into law by Republican governor Chris Christie.[27]

Immigrant Workers' Rights

Immigrant workers of color have also taken a leading role in national immigration reform efforts in recent decades. First of all, the mainstream trade union movement, represented by the AFL-CIO (American Federation of Labor and Congress of Industrial Organizations) despite its history in leading the fight for racist immigration exclusion in the late nineteenth and early twentieth centuries, has made concerted efforts since the 1980s and 1990s to organize Latino and Asian immigrant workers and has become increasingly involved in leading the fight for immigration reform.[28] Secondly, there has been growth in nonprofit, community-based workers' centers that advocate for immigrant workers' rights, particularly targeting those in industries where more traditional trade unions are absent.[29] Thirdly, immigrant rights activists have often highlighted immigrants' economic contributions to the United States in order to garner support from the broader public.[30] This strategy aims to counter nativists' representations of immigrants, especially the undocumented, as being an economic burden on taxpayers. Finally, many immigrant rights organizations are made up of individuals who have been involved in or influenced by Marxist and other left formations based either in the United States or abroad. These activists' focus on immigrants' status as exploited workers in a capitalist society, as opposed to focusing merely on their status as racialized minorities or foreigners without legal status, is meant to draw out their common cause with white as well as African American workers.

On May 1, 2006, workers and immigrant rights' organizations throughout the United States called for a "Day Without an Immigrant" and encouraged immigrant workers' to boycott work for the day to demonstrate their economic power and therefore their necessity to the U.S. economy.[31] That immigrant rights organizations nationally chose May 1 as a day for joint mobilizations is significant. Around the world, in many immigrants' countries of origins, May 1 is International Workers' Day and is typically celebrated by trade unionists with mass rallies. Ironically, although May 1 earned its distinction as International Workers' Day worldwide because it marks a moment in American history when tens of thousands of workers in Chicago walked off the job to demand an eight-hour workday in 1886, it is generally not celebrated in the United States.[32] That changed in 2006 as immigrant rights organizations made labor issues a central issue around which to mobilize.[33] Since 2006, immigrant rights groups around the country including New Jersey have tried to mobilize regularly on May 1.[34]

For the May 1, 2006 boycott, there was much debate among the leadership of immigrant rights groups nationally about whether it was wise to encourage immigrants, especially the undocumented, to boycott work. Moreover, immigrants themselves were fearful of the negative repercussions of participating in a work boycott. Nevertheless, many did stop work for the day and joined in mass mobilizations in support of comprehensive immigration reform. Those who did not boycott work joined in the protests in other ways.

One news report suggests that some of the business districts in New Jersey's smaller towns virtually shut down.[35] Many immigrant rights activists and advocates engaged in mobilizations across the state, then made their way to New York City. I was able to observe and participate in the New York City demonstration organized by the May First Coalition for Worker and Immigrant Rights. It was awe-inspiring. The streets were packed with people and the march to the designated rallying site where a program was to take place proceeded at a snail's pace because of the volume of people on the streets. Streams of people ascended from the city's subways making the march swell with even greater numbers.

Buoyed by the excitement of the 2006 mobilizations, a critical mass of grassroots activists formed the New Jersey May First Coalition (NJMFC) to begin planning activities for a major statewide mobilization on May 1, 2007, as well as to create a venue through which to share information about and coordinate support for local organizing efforts. Activists were keen on building on the energy and inspiration of the May 1, 2006, national boycott and demonstrations. Although many participated in the New York City mobilization, many from New Jersey believed that their organizing efforts should be concentrated at the state and local level. Several dozen individuals and groups made up the NJMFC, including members of labor unions like the United Food and Commercial Workers, but more significantly, it included representatives from labor and workers' rights organizations not formally affiliated with the trade union movement, such as the United Day Laborers based in Freehold, the Gilberto Soto Workers Center based in Elizabeth, and the statewide group New Jersey Fight Human Trafficking. It also included the immigrant ministries of different churches, groups working against immigrant detention, ethnic organizations (both Asian and Latino), and leftist formations. Notably, it also included the People's Organization for Progress (POP), based in Newark, which has traditionally focused on African Americans' issues and concerns.

Nationally, activists hoped to sustain immigrants' engagement in advocating for comprehensive immigration reform. In early 2007, organizations from across the country gathered in Los Angeles and unanimously agreed to hold a Great American Boycott II on May 1, 2007. Their demands included: full legalization for all undocumented immigrants living in the United States; an end to detention and deportation; an end to the expansion of the U.S.-Mexico border wall, the militarization of the border, and the criminalization of immigrants; equal rights for all workers regardless of foreign-born or native-born status; and more jobs offering a living wage, starting in Katrina-damaged New Orleans and along the Gulf Coast. The organizations declared, "No human being should ever be illegal."[36] Sixty-three organizations with influence in seventy-five cities across sixteen states called for the 2007 boycott.[37]

Members of the NJMFC agreed to support the national boycott by mobilizing immigrants to attend a mass meeting in Elizabeth, New Jersey. After much discussion, it was decided that it would be important to try to enlist prospective attendees to engage in local organizing efforts in a sustained way as opposed to having them participate in a singular event. As many scholars and activists have observed, despite the overwhelming success of the May 1, 2006 mobilizations, in the sense that they drew many immigrants "out of the shadows" and led to the defeat of major anti-immigrant policy proposals at the federal level, their shortcoming was that they seemed to be a one-time affair for many participants. The hope was that the 2007 action would lead to increased involvement by immigrants in their communities. Hence organizers of the NJMFC called for a "mass meeting" as opposed to a "mass mobilization" to encourage attendees to think of themselves not as simply attendees but actual participants in a longer-term project. Elizabeth was chosen as the site for the mass meeting because it has a sizable immigrant population that could be most readily mobilized. At the time, Elizabeth also had a Latino mayor who many believed would support permits and other related bureaucratic requirements needed for such an event. Perhaps most importantly, Elizabeth was chosen because it is home to a major port.

The leading proponent for holding New Jersey's May 1, 2007 demonstration in Elizabeth was a Latino organizer for the Gilberto Soto Workers Center. At a NJMFC meeting he argued that "anyone who controls the ports controls significant power." In his view, a successful shutdown of the Elizabeth port by immigrant workers as well as the holding of a mass meeting would be an especially strong show of immigrant workers' power. This was a perspective shared unanimously by members of the NJMFC. Indeed, one of the most significant actions taken by immigrant workers in support of the May 1, 2006, national boycott was the one-day cession of work by truckers at the Los Angeles and Long Beach ports in California. According to one report, 90 percent of the twelve thousand truckers employed at those two ports did not work that day, virtually halting the flow of goods.[38] NJMFC members believed that immigrant workers at the Elizabeth port could have the same impact. Through a show of collective strength, the NJMFC believed that immigrant workers could demonstrate how truly indispensable they are to the state and national economy. The NJMFC shared sociologist William Robinson's conclusion that immigrant workers' organizing efforts challenge "the class relations that are at the very core of global capitalism."[39]

What was also important for members of the NJMFC, moreover, was building bridges across racial and citizenship divides to highlight New Jersey citizens' shared struggles as working people. This reflected the sentiment in the national movement as well. In the build-up activities for the May 1, 2007 boycott and demonstration, the NJMFC highlighted the "unity" between immigrants and the native-born as workers. In a flyer for a Statewide Speak Out and Unity Meeting, it stated, "Attacks on migrants are attacks on *all of us*—by maintaining a working sector too afraid to assert their rights to decent pay and working conditions." The theme of unity was repeated throughout the flyer, which described the event as a "speak out for the rights of all."

Although the NJMFC often championed immigrants' rights on the basis of their contribution to American society as workers (some flyers for their events would state, for instance, "Immigrants Make This Nation Strong"), members of NJMFC were very careful not to bolster the "good immigrant" narrative. Distinctions are often made between "good" and "bad" immigrants in public discourse and even among immigrants themselves. As sociologists Nazli Kibria and colleagues put it, "The 'good immigrant' is one who is fit to become American, whereas the 'bad immigrant' is not only unfit but a threat to the social and political fabric of America."[40] At times, the "good immigrant" is figured as the legal immigrant while the "bad immigrant" is the undocumented or "illegal" immigrant. At other times, the "good immigrant" is figured as the white ethnic immigrant whereas the "bad immigrant" the immigrant of color. At the same time, the "good immigrant" narrative is often deployed against African Americans. This narrative suggests that immigrants of all kinds are more deserving of rights than African Americans because they work and African Americans presumably do not. This latter construction of the "good immigrant" is one that members of the NJMFC and the broader national movement with which it identified rejected. To reflect their commitment to interracial alliances, the coalition worked closely with African American groups like POP that were invited to play a leadership role in coordinating activities. Later, the NJMFC changed its name to New Jersey Immigrant and Worker Rights Coalition (NJIWRC), reflecting its interracial class-based vision.

It is important to note that the class politics that the NJMFC championed were not without critics. During a March 15, 2007, NJMFC meeting I attended, there was discussion about how the NJMFC was being critiqued by some Latino immigrant rights organizations. One criticism raised by the Latino Leadership Alliance was that they believed that the NJMFC spokespeople should be Latino, not white. In fact, the NJMFC had a range of spokespeople; moreover, it was a Latino immigrant worker who spearheaded the organizing of the May 1, 2007, event in Elizabeth. Yet it was true that the primary contact for the NJMFC on press releases was a white male. He also managed the groups e-mail listserv. It was also true that those who participated in NJMFC meetings tended to be English-speaking. Many were, however, bilingual (generally in English and Spanish). A good number of meeting participants were white, but the members of the organizations they represented were working-class immigrants of color whose English-language skills were limited. Yet there were also a good number of immigrants and people of color in attendance as well.

Questions of leadership, race, and class have plagued the immigrant rights movement in different regions of the United States. Laura Pulido, a scholar of American studies and ethnicity, found in her research of the immigrant rights movement in Los Angeles, for example, that there were tensions between working-class grassroots Latino immigrants and their mainstream, moderate, and middle-class counterparts. Grassroots Latino immigrant workers supported the May 1, 2006, boycott of work, school, and stores and called for amnesty for the undocumented. Meanwhile, mainstream middle-class Latinos organized a separate mobilization after school and work for those who did not boycott. They did not articulate support for amnesty. As Pulido puts it, "As often happens, the middle-class leadership, in this case, Chicano and Latino politicians, are repackaging the demands of the working class into a form that they feel will be acceptable to the establishment—and in the process, selling out the people. No elected official is demanding amnesty."[41]

NJMFC members interpreted the Latino Leadership Alliance's critiques as fundamentally based in class politics, not race politics. In other words, members of the NJMFC believed that the Latino Leadership Alliance took issue with the role of whites as a means of masking their anti-working-class politics. The NJMFC's Latinos believed that the Alliance represented the interests of long-established, relatively elite Puerto Ricans and Cubans and not recent working-class immigrants from Mexico or Central America. According to the Latino Leadership Alliance's website, it is a "dynamic group of mature Latino professionals and emerging leaders."[42] The Alliance did not send representatives to NJMFC meetings, although they were fairly visible in meetings called by other formations, including the New Jersey Immigrant Policy Network (NJIPN), which is a more traditional nonprofit organization (whose executive director at the time, ironically enough, was white). Meanwhile, grassroots groups representing working-class immigrants like day laborers participated in both spaces.

Struggles for State Reform

Even as immigrant rights activists in New Jersey participated in national campaigns either to oppose anti-immigrant federal legislation or support comprehensive immigration reform, New Jersey immigrant rights activists have engaged in struggles for immigrant-friendly state policies. For example, organizations like the NJIPN engaged in legislative advocacy in early 2006 calling for the then newly elected governor of New Jersey, Jon Corzine, to create an office of immigrant affairs at the state level.[43] Corzine responded positively to these demands and launched a Blue Ribbon Advisory Panel on Immigrant Policy the following year.[44] The panel was composed of immigration rights advocates, scholars, and legislators who held conferences and hearings across the state to gauge the most pressing issues facing immigrants in different communities. In March 2009, the panel submitted its policy recommendations, which included a recommendation for driver's licenses for undocumented immigrants, in-state tuition for undocumented students, and the establishment of a Commission on New Americans. Governor Corzine created the commission through an executive order signed in 2010, and there has been much progress toward the issuance of driver's licenses for undocumented immigrants and in-state tuition for undocumented students was signed into law by Corzine's Republican successor, Governor Chris Christie in 2013.[45]

Many of the struggles for immigrant rights in New Jersey take place at the level of the municipality if not the neighborhood. Significantly, these struggles are taking place in suburbs. Some of these struggles include, for instance, fights for or against municipal (or county) legislation affecting immigrants. These struggles also take the form of what I call spatialized home-making practices. CHABA activists, for instance, work to rebuild and revitalize their houses in ways that reflect immigrants' distinctive experiences, aesthetics, and identities and as a way to signal immigrants' belonging to a changing Bridgeton through infusing the built environment with both new character and continuity. Other activists work to make their immigrant neighbors feel safe and secure, in effect, to make them feel at home in the communities they have chosen to settle.

The dominant constituencies leading the national immigrant rights movement have been undocumented youth and immigrant workers. Undocumented youth have framed their claim to rights on the basis of both their cultural citizenship and their "innocence." They have argued that having been raised in the United States for most of their lives, they are practically American even if they lack American citizenship. Moreover, they argue that their undocumented status is not by choice but is rather a consequence of choices made by their parents. Immigrant workers, on the other hand, have often framed their claim to rights on the basis of their economic contributions to the United States. New Jerseyans have framed their struggles for immigrant rights in these ways, but also on other bases. Some have fought for immigrants' civil rights. Others have fought for immigrants' human rights. Still others have asserted that immigrants deserve rights because they are neighbors who have long inhabited New Jersey's communities. In addition to documenting the legislative as well as the spatial home-making practices of New Jersey's immigrant rights activists, I am also interested in the various kinds of claims they are making to expand the scope of immigrant belonging.

Fighting Local Anti-Immigrant Ordinances

Although there has been a localization and interiorization of border enforcement, as I illustrate throughout this book, there are community members in nearly every place I discuss who have worked diligently and persistently to resist anti-immigrant local ordinances through legal and legislative struggles. By legal struggles, I am referring to lawsuits brought against local governments that have passed anti-immigrant legislation. By legislative struggles, I am referring to the different forms of protest that immigrant rights' groups engaged in to oppose anti-immigrant legislation or, alternatively, to support pro-immigrant legislation. This includes attending town or borough council meetings and speaking for or against specific laws, policies, and practices, holding pickets, mobilizing support or opposition through the traditional media as well as social media, and the like.

In Riverside, New Jersey, local community members filed two lawsuits (one included business owners as well as property owners as plaintiffs) against the municipality after it passed its Illegal Immigration Relief Act in 2006, which made hiring or renting property to an undocumented immigrant punishable by a $2,000 fine and jail time.[46] With the passage of the law, nearly a third of the population fled and local businesses suffered, but the lawsuits hampered the town from actually enforcing the law.[47] At the same time, groups like the National Coalition of Latino Clergy and Christian Leaders (known as CONLAMIC) put pressure on Riverside's school district to ensure that regardless of the ordinance, the children of immigrants could still register to attend local schools. CONLAMIC succeeded in securing school superintendent Robert Goldschmidt's assurances, even getting him to appear on a Spanish-language radio show to affirm that all children registered in the district could attend school regardless of their parents' immigration status.[48] Moreover, residents voted the mayor, Republican Charles Hilton, who took a lead on the passage of the local ordinance, out of office later that year.[49]

In Freehold, residents also used legal strategies to contest anti-immigrant policies. When the borough closed the "muster zone" for day laborers in 2003, some of Freehold's Latino community members filed suit against the municipality. The suit was settled with the borough council agreeing to pay $245,000 in legal fees to individual plaintiffs three years later. The council also agreed to establish a $33,000 fund to reimburse day laborers for fines assessed against them.[50] According to the executive director of the New Jersey Appleseed Public Interest Law Center, which represented the day laborers, the settlement "has ramifications beyond Freehold as to the rights of people, regardless of their documentation status. It's sort of setting the parameters for the other debates about immigration."[51] Indeed, Freehold became the symbolic center of the immigration debate in New Jersey for both opponents and supporters of immigration. The United Patriots, a national anti-immigration organization linked to the Minutemen Project, a group that recruited civilians to patrol the U.S.-Mexico border, attempted to hold a meeting in Freehold in 2005. Its efforts were thwarted. Steve Lonegan, the Bogota mayor who led the fight to ban Spanish-language signs in his town, was slated to be the group's keynote speaker until the Freehold event was canceled. Responding to pressure from immigrant rights advocates, the local veterans' hall denied the United Patriots access to the space. According to a Veterans of Foreign Wars (VFW) official, "I was in the military and we fought for the rights of the Constitution and the freedom of speech and the right of assembly. But we got more than fifty calls from people telling me we should not let [the United Patriots of America] meet here. We did not want to be in the middle of this thing."[52]

As I have discussed in earlier chapters, in March 2007 Morristown was the first and only municipality in New Jersey where the mayor took the initiative to apply to have local police deputized as immigration enforcement agents through the federal 287(g) program[53] Morristown-based immigrant rights advocates, led by Wind of the Spirit, organized very vocal protests of the mayor's actions at town council meetings. Wind of the Spirit not only organized Morristown residents to oppose the 287(g) application, it also brought together immigrant rights advocates from across the state and even national immigrant rights groups to support their cause. In a press conference announcing their plan to formally present the town council with a petition opposing the mayor's proposal, Wind of the Spirit was joined by the Spanish Alliance Church, also based in Morristown, as well as the Newark branch of the American Friends Service Committee, the Morris County Organization for Hispanic Affairs, and groups from out of state, including the Florida Minority Community Investment Coalition and the United States Hispanic Advocacy Association.[54] Immigrant rights activists even made appeals directly to President Obama.[55]

When Monmouth County began applying to the 287(g) program under the leadership of Republican Kim Guadagno after she took office as county sheriff in late 2007, different groups across the county and the state, including the Wind of the Spirit (though they are based in Morris County), began to strategize about how to stop the process. Freehold's (it is located in Monmouth County) church halls, notably African American churches, were among the sites where these strategy sessions were held. African American community members expressed opposition to the 287(g) program because they believed it would lead to racial profiling, as one resident commented in a town hall meeting about the issue, "I don't know how many times I've been pulled over. It's sad. This is America. I'm black."[56]

If Freehold was considered a hotbed of anti-immigrant organizing, it was also considered a hotbed for the immigrant rights movement in New Jersey. Groups like Casa Freehold and the United Day Laborers of Freehold had earned the admiration of immigrant rights activists around the state for their valiant efforts in fighting the various initiatives aimed at preventing immigrant settlement in the borough. Among the key strategies activists agreed on was the mobilization of residents in the county to publicly oppose 287(g) proposal at Monmouth County freeholder meetings. Monmouth County's participation in the 287(g) program was formalized in 2009.[57] Although the activists were not successful in averting the county's participation in the 287(g) program, immigrant rights' activists have been successful in many other struggles. The networks and relationships created between activists while working to stop 287(g) have been instrumental in sustaining the immigrant rights movement across the state.

Citizens' Obligations and Rights

As I've discussed thus far in this chapter, immigrant activists in New Jersey have engaged in struggles on multiple scales. They've participated in the broader immigrant rights movement for reform at the national level while also coordinating efforts to advocate for state and local level reforms as extensions of the national movement. They have also been involved in directly contesting anti-immigrant local ordinances. What's interesting in immigrant rights activism in New Jersey is the explicit attempt to engage citizens in the fight for immigrant rights. Many activists believe citizens, specifically whites, have a duty and responsibility to fight on behalf of and in partnership with immigrants because when the rights of immigrants are compromised, so too are the rights of citizens. We see this in the work of the NJCRDC and the NJMFC /NJ Immigrant and Worker Rights Coalition.

Organizations like the NJCRDC, for example, framed their advocacy for immigrant rights as a concern for "civil rights." In describing its work the group's website states that it "acts to protect the Bill of Rights."[58] Its invocation of "civil rights" was aimed at mobilizing citizens to play an advocacy role in the fight for immigrants. In remarks made at a public forum on detention, a white NJCRDC organizer noted, "Since the terrorist attacks, many Americans seem to have forgotten that all people living in the United States have civil rights." This was a dominant narrative through which members of the organization, almost all of whom were white, native-born Americans, described their work. Citizenship for them came with particular responsibilities. They called for a practice of citizenship that includes taking up the mantle of rights for those who might lack the political (and legal) status to do so themselves. Among the NJCRDC's chief campaigns was the effort to end the incarceration of undocumented immigrants in local and county jails.

If NJCRDC's members attempted to galvanize citizens to fight for immigrants' civil rights, detainees themselves would assert their civil rights in the thousands of letters they wrote to the group. In a press release supporting immigrant detainees' petition following the death of Arturo Alvarez, a detainee in the Middlesex County Jail, NJCRDC activists describe how the petition "made appeals to the guarantees of the Bill of Rights" and decried "the unconstitutional and inhuman conditions under which the petitioners are held." Moreover, detainees, called "for an end to immigration detention as a violation of both constitutional and human rights."[59]

The group's framing of immigrant rights as civil rights also connects it to a specific activist genealogy: namely the civil rights movement, particularly whites' participation in the civil rights movement. Members of the NJCRDC made concerted efforts to work closely with African American groups, including POP. POP had long been involved in fighting the racial profiling of and police violence against blacks throughout the state. NJCRDC situated the experience of immigrant detainees within a longer history of police violence against men of color. NJCRDC organizers were concerned about steering away from the "good immigrant" trope that seemed to run through other immigrant activists' work. That is, organizers in other activist spaces would often make the argument that undocumented immigrants did not deserve to be in jail because they were hardworking, family-oriented individuals who were not criminals. Yet this construction of the "good immigrant" is about claiming a kind of worthiness to American citizenship (and therefore a proximity to white, neoliberal citizenship) that runs dangerously close to a position of antiblackness. This was a position NJCRDC organizers were staunchly against.

Immigrant rights advocates also drew attention to the fact that anti-immigrant policies and programs do not solely affect individual immigrants but also affect the families in which immigrants are embedded. "Mixed status" families are commonplace among immigrants. Many of the detainees NJCRDC worked with had U.S.-citizen children and spouses; hence the group highlighted the ways immigrants' detention was an infringement of the rights of their U.S.-citizen family members. Similarly, one of the campaigns launched by the NJIWRC was to support a class-action suit led by Maria DaSilva, a U.S. citizen married to an undocumented immigrant facing the possibility of deportation, with whom she has a child. In a press conference on the suit, the NJIWRC claims that DaSilva "is now being denied her rights to the pursuit of happiness and her rights to a trial by jury."[60]

Home-Making Struggles

Much of the organizing in New Jersey I've described so far has been defensive in the sense that activists were responding to anti-immigrant legislation. Activists have also, however, been proactively involved in trying to make their communities immigrant friendly in a number of ways. One response to proactively resist cooperation between local and federal authorities as well as to defy anti-immigrant trends in different municipalities has been for communities to define themselves as "sanctuary cities." The "sanctuary city" movement traces its roots to the 1980s. It was a response to anti-immigrant U.S. nativism during that period, when there was opposition to the granting of asylum to Central American refugees who were fleeing the violence of their homelands. Supporters of asylum attributed the violence to U.S. intervention in the region as part of its Cold War policy of containment. Members of the clergy supporting refugees' asylum claims heavily championed the movement.[61] In New Jersey, as in other communities across the United States, immigrant rights advocates drew from the success of these earlier campaigns to introduce sanctuary policies in their towns.

Sanctuary city campaigns, however, did not only aim at defying anti-immigration currents nationally and locally; they aimed to reassure immigrants that they had a place they could call home. The campaigns were, more than anything else, community-building efforts. As legal scholar Hiroshi Motomura suggests, sanctuary city campaigns "should be interpreted not just as skepticism or resistance to enforcement, but also as efforts to establish safe zones in which public and private initiatives can foster integration."[62] If anti-immigrant legislation was framed as necessary to better secure suburbs against the threat of immigrants as an extension of national security fears stoked by nativist and xenophobic forces, those supporting sanctuary city policies constructed alternative notions of safety and security.

The total number of sanctuary cities in New Jersey is difficult to ascertain, however Hightstown has been a highly celebrated case among immigrant rights activists in the state. It passed its sanctuary city resolution in 2005. What made Hightstown stand out was the fact that the town's mayor at the time, a white Republican, Robert Patten, supported the policy. In fact, he was more than a mere supporter but an active promoter of the sanctuary city policy and expressed great pride in his town's citizens for their stance on immigration. He often accepted invitations to address audiences of immigrants and immigrant rights advocates who were more aligned with the Democratic Party. According to Patten, "It's not our responsibility as local police to implement these Nazi-style actions in the United States and just go around taking people off the street who may be undocumented."[63] Moreover, he stated, "We look at people from other countries as a positive who make our community better. We enjoy our differences and celebrate them."[64] In another media interview Patten stated that he defines sanctuary "not as where criminals can be immune from the law. But, a sanctuary would be a place of comfort where you are treated fairly, equally, respectively. And we do have a sanctuary in that definition."[65] In contrast to other suburbs, the borough Hightstown was dubbed "Paradise City" by some Spanish-language media outlets.[66] Interestingly, Hightstown was once home to the KKK and the site of race riots in the 1970s.[67]

In 2011, six years after it was adopted, the sanctuary city resolution became a major campaign issue for Republican candidates for borough council seats in Hightstown. As in other municipalities, these candidates characterized the undocumented Latino population as a threat to the community. According to Councilwoman Skye Gilmartin, the resolution "has severely affected the safety, quality of life, property values, and economic stability" of the community. Part of the Republicans' campaign to discredit the resolution included phone surveys to residents. Residents were told that Hightstown shared the same status as the city of Newark as a sanctuary and then asked if the status had a negative effect on Hightstown. The survey clearly played on suburbanites' fears of the city by likening Hightstown to Newark. Local community members who attended a borough council meeting and raised their concerns during the public comment section, however, met the candidate's fear tactics with outrage.[68]

Although Hightstown garnered much attention for its sanctuary city policy, in large part because of its seemingly unlikely spokesperson—a white, male, Republican mayor—in other cities, such policies were the result of cross-racial coalitions. This is true, for instance, in Prospect Park. Prospect Park elected Mohamed Khairullah, an Arab Muslim whose candidacy was met with racist opposition. In 2007, after being elected despite fears of his "terrorist" links, Mayor Khairullah and Councilman Richard Esquiche, a Latino, took the lead in securing the passage of an ordinance to name Prospect Park a "sanctuary city." The Latino Leadership Alliance Passaic County Chapter played an active role in promoting the ordinance in Prospect Park. The group sought to promote the adoption of similar ordinances in other New Jersey municipalities.

Leaders in the African American community have been avid supporters of sanctuary policies in their communities. At a 2007 community dialogue on immigration that focused on the rise of anti-immigrant vigilantism at the U.S.-Mexico border led by the likes of the Minutemen Project, a paramilitary group that tries to apprehend immigrants crossing from Mexico into the United States, then-Newark Councilmember-at-Large Donald Payne Jr. related his experiences of growing up in New Jersey during the civil rights era. He connected his experiences of discrimination as an African American youth with the discrimination being experienced by immigrants in contemporary New Jersey and vowed that he would ensure the enforcement of Newark's sanctuary policy.

A recent attempt at securing sanctuary city status took place in Princeton, New Jersey, in 2013. Princeton's mayor reaffirmed her community's sanctuary city status in a public statement in 2015.[69] Those officials initially crafting the policy insisted that theirs was not quite a sanctuary city resolution, but one official did declare, "[The resolution] is good for public safety, and it's good for human rights."[70] Here, ensuring the "safety" of Princeton's community members is raised as a primary concern for the resolution's supporters. This is in stark contrast to the ways the Hightstown Republican contenders characterized their town's sanctuary city policy. The suburb has often been figured in the popular imagination as a sanctuary, that is, a safe haven from the city and its associated populations for whites. In their struggles for sanctuary city resolutions, immigrant rights activists and advocates envision a more inclusive notion of sanctuary.

Some municipalities have done more than simply declare themselves to be sanctuaries for undocumented immigrants; they have introduced measures that effectively extend what Monica Varsanyi calls "urban citizenship." This includes offering migrants local forms of identification. As of this writing, three New Jersey municipalities—Newark, Roselle, and Dover—had introduced municipal identification to immigrant residents.[71]

Spatialized Practices

Immigrant rights activists not only struggle at the level of the municipality, but right in their neighborhoods. For example, in response to immigration raids in the town of Avenel, the organization POP Central Jersey distributed flyers appealing to local residents to come together to resist further raids. POP called on people to mobilize as neighbors. The flyer it produced was titled, "Your Neighbors' Homes Were Invaded Last Week by Armed Men from the INS," and urged, "Those of us who can, must speak out against these abuses of power. One thing you can do is help to contact your local officials and let them know that you are concerned if your neighbors are being unjustly treated or unfairly targeted. Tell everyone you know, family, friends, the media, that this is happening. Join protests with your neighbors who are being targeted."[72] Similarly, in a bid for support in its fund-raising campaign to advance its advocacy of immigrant detainees, the group First Friends issued the following statement: "Do you know what is happening to your immigrant neighbor? First Friends, a private charitable organization, has been visiting and providing non-legal services to detainees for over eight years. We have received permission to contact the 350 immigrant detainees held at the Hudson County Correctional Center in Kearny and need volunteer visitors and pen pals for these unfortunate, confined neighbors in our midst."[73]

In their protests against the detention of undocumented immigrants, activists organized in a highly localized way. Mobilizations were done as close to detention facilities as possible. Members of the NJCRDC, for example, frequently picketed the entrance of the Passaic County Jail throughout the early 2000s when the group received numerous letters from immigrant detainees detailing horrific treatment at the hands of jailers under the leadership of former Sheriff Jerry Speziale. The jail is located in a predominantly immigrant neighborhood in the city of Paterson. NJCRDC used the jail's location to its advantage and mobilized locals to join its demonstrations. Indeed, local organizing work in Paterson prompted the OIG to conduct an internal investigation of the county jail as well as other New Jersey facilities. The group was successful in terminating the Passaic County Jail's contract with the DHS in 2006.[74]

In the case of antidetention work in Middlesex County, organizers attempted to actively engage the communities directly surrounding New Brunswick, which is the county seat and is where Rutgers University is centered, as well as the neighboring town of Highland Park. Not only were many sympathetic Rutgers University faculty and students living in Highland Park but it was also where localized responses to the detention of Indonesian immigrants had taken place. Activists wanted to literally bring the issue of immigrant detention home to people and have them understand the goings on right in their neighborhoods.

Neighborhood organizing was done specifically to protest the conditions suffered by immigrant detainees at the Middlesex County Jail. When Arturo Alvarez, an immigrant detainee, died in detention in March 2008, activists attributed his death to medical neglect. Letters from Alvarez's fellow detainees led activists to this conclusion. Activists attended county freeholder meetings and staged silent protest actions before and during meetings. One meeting was preceded by a march that began in Highland Park, across the bridge from New Brunswick where the freeholders' meetings are held. Protesters dressed in prison garb and holding signs with the names of detainees silently marched from Highland Park to New Brunswick. They then entered the freeholder meeting room, lined themselves along the walls, and selected Middlesex County residents among them stepped up to voice their opposition to the county's treatment of immigrant detainees during the meeting's open-forum session. Protest organizers were especially mindful of assigning residents of the county to participate in the open-forum session so that they could claim their rights as local citizens who are entitled to responses from their elected representatives.

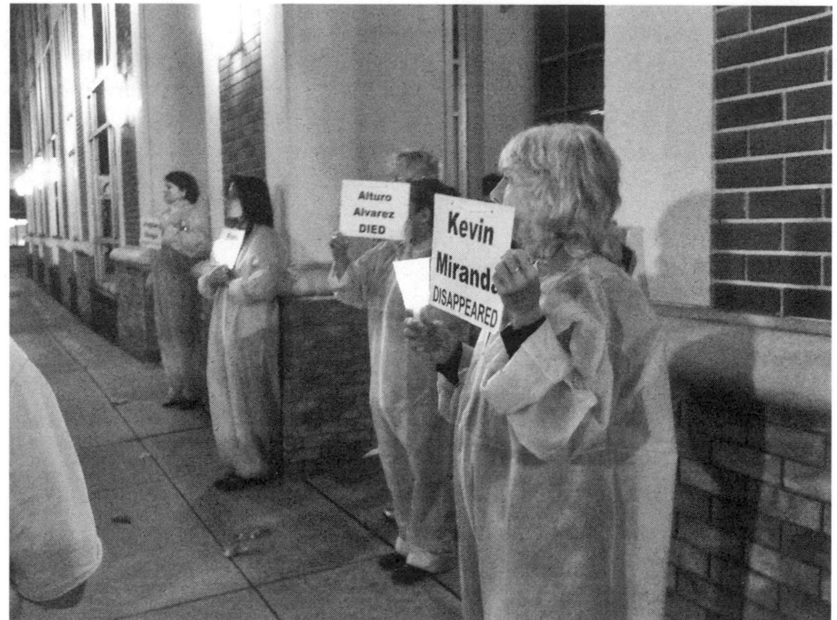

PHOTO 9. Anti-immigration detention march from Highland Park to New Brunswick (Photo credit: Robyn Rodriguez)

If residents invoked "neighborliness" to appeal for the protection of immigrants from immigration enforcement, others attempted to craft neighborhood-based responses to immigration enforcement. Organizations like the Latin American Legal Defense and Education Fund (LALDEF) and NJMFC attempted to craft localized responses to protect immigrants from detention and deportation. Activists from LALDEF, for instance, would arrive at the scene of a reported deportation raid by federal immigrant enforcement agents to monitor their activities and ensure that immigrants' rights were not violated in the process. In many cases, immigration agents looking for a specific individual in a specific worksite or apartment complex will apprehend the targeted individual's coworkers and neighbors. According to members of the group, as a result of LALDEF's efforts, immigration agents have been less likely to apprehend large groups of immigrants and focus only on the individuals they were tasked to pick up. Among the ideas NJMFC put forward was identifying work sites with large Latino immigrant workforces and distributing "know your rights" brochures. Another idea the NJMFC launched on May 1, 2007, was the

Rapid Response Network (RRN), envisioned as a neighborhood-based strategy akin to a neighborhood watch. The idea is that immigrants' allies would immediately mobilize at workplaces or housing complexes in their local areas in the event of an impending raid to directly interrupt and stop enforcement actions either through direct negotiation, public shaming, distraction techniques, or even bodily intervention.

Although the RRN was difficult to organize and activate, there were other kinds of highly localized responses to impending deportation. Immigrants and immigrant rights advocates frequently posted on listservs with news of individuals or families in particular communities who were being slated for "removal." They would call on listserv members to call local ICE offices and members of Congress who represented the individual's or family's district to demand stays of removal.

The RRN depended on the mobilization of citizens to engage in bodily resistance against local immigration enforcement efforts, but undocumented migrants themselves have also engaged in bodily expressions of resistance. In the statewide, municipal, and neighborhood struggles I have discussed throughout this chapter, undocumented immigrants have taken to the streets in a highly visible manner to participate in pickets and other kinds of public protests in spite of the enhanced powers of local police. Although their public displays of protest put them at risk for apprehension, detention, and ultimately deportation, they insist on claiming a place in their communities. Nicholas De Genova calls this a "corporeal and spatial form of subjectivity."[75] He argues that "even apart from the precise content of their words," immigrants enunciate "through their actions the urgency of substantial needs and demands that had been previously unspeakable or at least coercively muted by their 'unauthorised' status."[76]

Spatial Practices in New Jersey's Neighborhoods

Ned Kaufman, a historic preservationist, asks in his book, "How should preservationists balance the competing claims of disparate sites and divergent values recognized by culturally diverse groups? How do historical narratives, traditions and memories define sense of place? Is the persistent whiteness of the profession a problem in a society becoming ever more diverse?"[77]

CHABA's answer to these questions has been to include and engage Bridgeton's Latino residents in historic preservation efforts by facilitating the translation of New Jersey's historic preservation guidelines into Spanish. Its translation efforts aimed at helping immigrants in the community to understand and appreciate local town histories (histories of labor and agriculture, for example) as their very own. In weaving recent immigrants' histories into the broader historical fabric of Bridgeton, CHABA embeds Latinos into the community's future in meaningful ways. The translation of the guidelines or *guias* was a major undertaking for the group. Because historic preservationists have not necessarily included non-English-speaking populations, CHABA members were forced to look at historic preservation documents from Puerto Rico to ensure that the *guias* used the most appropriate translations of architectural terms. Architect Maria Cerda-Moreno, a first generation Latino immigrant, led the translation effort with the assistance of Bridgeton-raised, CHABA intern, Jaime Bustos-DeHaro. Cerda-Moreno (along with CHABA) earned a Preservation Education Award from Preservation New Jersey in 2015 and Bustos-DeHaro received the Ada Louise Huxtable scholarship from Boston Architectural College for their work on the *guias*.

According to Flavia Alaya, an activist I met while doing antidetention work and whom I interviewed several times, CHABA's mission is to support "preservation without gentrification," and "people-centered preservation." This sentiment is clearly stated in CHABA's organizational material: "Why shouldn't working families in these communities enjoy the same benefits of beautiful streetscapes as folks in Montclair and Haddonfield? Historic preservation doesn't have to be gentrifying, and it isn't just for the rich. It preserves our collective community memory, and that is no small thing. But it can also help create new jobs, develop and preserve artisan skills, and help assure quality of life across whole neighborhoods now and for the future. ¡Adelante!"[78] The *guias* (along with videos and workshops on restoration techniques offered by CHABA) encourage first, second and third-generation Latino families to consider investing in the still-useful (as well as beautiful) and sustainable historic houses of Bridgeton. Because the depressed Bridgeton housing market has made home ownership highly affordable, this is a very real possibility for many of them. Thus these communities can actually enjoy the potential appreciation long associated with home buying in historic (and highly gentrified) urban enclaves. Alaya adds that homes, particularly those in Bridgeton, were a kind of "Facebook of another generation," a platform through which people constructed their identities and through which communities were formed. Immigrants' participation in historic preservation work allows them, following this logic, to connect with previous generations of townspeople.

Bustos-DeHaro's involvement in CHABA was motivated by his sense that local officials and native-born community members in his town have the mistaken idea that the Mexican community has no stake in Bridgeton because its members are more interested in remitting money to Mexico and sustaining their transnational families. He suggests that the municipality can and should support the community-building efforts of the Mexican community as is being done through CHABA. Bridgeton has lacked a town center for many years, and Mexican business-owners have become the de facto "center" for town residents; they, in Bustos-DeHaro's view, should be provided the tools to be able to at once participate in preservation efforts and work on building the community on their own terms.

A local Catholic priest, Father David Rivera of the parish of the Holy Cross at Bridgeton, also sees CHABA as offering immigrants the opportunity to feel connected to the community. History, he suggests, can become a means by which people can make connections to a place. "When you find out about the history of a place, it allows you to plant roots." Moreover, for Father Rivera, history becomes important to identity formation. In speaking to the role of the church in community formation, Father Rivera notes that "the church cannot ignore the town in which its congregation lives. Congregation building requires an investment in a place. . . . The church faces the practical challenge of bridging cultures as its congregation has changed over the years. The church can play a role of facilitator in bridge building not only within the church but between the secular community and communities of faith. It can do so because the church has resources including space and communications mechanisms." He says that "it is tempting to blame the newcomers," but the church's role is to help change perceptions. He notes that historic preservation might be said to be a "first-world problem" for which immigrants have little money or time, but he sees CHABA's work as a way to get immigrants to "bridge build" and change the perceptions of residents who have lived in the community longer. Moreover, because many Mexicans work as landscapers and in construction, historic preservation can become an opportunity for new forms of entrepreneurship.[79]

"HomeFronts" is a set of bilingual workshops on historic preservation that CHABA has instituted for Latino residents to engage the local community in novel ways.[80] Indeed, "HomeFronts" is an interesting title for these workshops as the term has multiple sets of meanings. On a basic level the workshops are about "home fronts" that is, the façades of buildings (as one of the key components of historic preservation) and thus involve going over the *guias*. Yet, home front also conjures up images of "war," particularly when we think of "the front." CHABA's use of the term signifies a particular kind of engagement in the "domestic front" of the immigration "fight" while also signifying a possibility for inclusion and the expansion of who can be considered a member of this society. In its organizational literature, for example, CHABA describes the workshop as an "initiative, to assure that everyone who lives in the historic district now, especially those who own or are thinking about owning a home, realize how their personal investment is also an investment in a community, and how much the proven economic value of that investment is tied to the district's long, rich historic character." Furthermore, CHABA literature states, "The whole idea of CHABA is to maintain the character of the Historic District without forcing anybody to make unrealistic business decisions. Let's demystify this process together . . . or recreate it if we need to! Here's a chance."[81]

The HomeFronts initative is aimed at inclusion. It is aimed at redefining the terms of community and belonging through the work of historic preservation and shaping the built environment. Just as importantly, the histories that CHABA aims to preserve are precisely those that resonate with the experiences of its current residents. According to Alaya, what is perhaps the most distinctive feature of the town's historic district is "its interconnected, industrial era, working-class neighborhoods." She states, "These neighborhoods . . . saw many waves of immigrants through the process of making the so-called American Dream real, in a community tradition of mutual support as well as upward mobility."[82]

CHABA engages in specific practices of collective memory making. This is evidenced in its "Obie" awards named after what CHABA describes as "a remarkable Bridgetonian—New Jerseyan—American—world-class genius and working-class hero, Oberlin Smith."[83] The purpose of the award is to promote a particular sort of remembering for the community and among its youngest members. The 2015 recipient (who was also the very first to get this award) was a local Latina Bridgetonian, Maribel Juarez. Of importance to CHABA in giving out the award is not just remembering the industrial and commercial elite of the past but "working class heroes." CHABA also attempts to narrate the history of Bridgeton as one that has long been characterized by racial inclusion. In her recounting of Bridgeton history during a conference on historic preservation in 2014, Flavia Alaya notes that Bridgeton is also home to the free black settlement, Gouldtown, which was established in 1700.[84]

In addition to efforts to translate existing preservation code, there is also interest in changing it. The code itself "encodes" particular kinds of aesthetics and styles that are narrow, what urban historians Becky M. Nicolaides and James Zarsadiaz call "design assimilation."[85] Among the questions that CHABA has pondered is how to incorporate Mexican aesthetics and cultural practices, including muralism, an art movement led by the likes of Diego Rivera in Mexico in the 1920s. CHABA even helped bring a muralist from Mexico to town to complete a piece (and commissioned him to do a second) because public art, according to Alaya, "is a wonderful way to reimagine places." CHABA members have even discussed how they can create a Mexican-styled plaza in the center of the town.

The work done by CHABA is an exercise in what Kaufman calls "storyscape" preservation, yet it is also about creating opportunities for "scripting" (as Alaya describes it) new stories. It is a way of not simply preserving houses but also cultivating home and belonging through place making. The built form becomes a canvas not only for preservation but for new imaginings. "Anyone who lives deeply in a place is likely to become attached to it through these local and personal stories and sites. And being attached to place, if being aware of and dedicated to inhabiting a particular place, can bolster citizenship in the twenty-first century, then cultivating a rich storyscape will be an enterprise of the greatest social value."[86]

"Scale-Jumping": Translocal and Supranational Organizing

While New Jersey's immigrant rights activists worked in very local ways, they also engaged in what some scholars call "scale jumping." That is, they have been involved in activism on multiple scales. For instance, activists have participated in translocal organizing. Local activists in New Jersey connected with and supported those in Texas and Connecticut who were similarly struggling with anti-immigrant local ordinances. New Jerseyans mobilized in 2009 to commemorate immigration enforcement raids that took place in Postville, Iowa, in 2008. The Postville raids alarmed many in the immigrant rights community around the country. Agents apprehended four hundred immigrants, mainly Latinos, working at the Agriprocessors meatpacking plant. More than half were eventually deported. Those not swept up in the raids have since left the town. It was "the largest single site operation of its kind ever in the United States," according to ICE spokesman Tim Counts.[87]

Organizers working specifically against 287(g) adoptions in local communities coordinated efforts. This was partly facilitated through national formations like the National Day Laborer Organizing Network. If Morristown's Mayor Cresitello attracted national attention for being the first mayor to apply to the 287(g) program, it was perhaps Arizona sheriff Joseph Arpaio's implementation of the 287(g) program in Maricopa County that drew the most sustained attention nationally. Raids under Arpaio's command were large and far-reaching. There were reports of raids taking place over the course of several days and involving hundreds of sheriff's deputies and volunteers. Immigrant rights activists in New Jersey networked with activists struggling against 287(g) in other parts of the country and circulated breaking news from Maricopa County regularly. They also participated in petition campaigns calling for the termination of the 287(g) in Maricopa County.

Organizing against 287(g) took place not only on a translocal level but on a supranational level. Immigrant rights advocates submitted a report to the United Nations Committee to End Racial Discrimination in which they exhorted the committee to examine "the dramatic rise in discrimination on account of race, national origin and ethnicity that directly result from 287(g) agreements." Indeed, both detainees and advocates like NJCRDC also invoked human rights law as defined by the United Nations in making their appeals to U.S. citizens to support detainees' demands. In a press release, NJCRDC quotes United Nations Human Rights Inspector Jorge Bustamente, who made a public statement that mandatory immigrant detention in the United States "violates the spirit of international laws and conventions and in many cases also violates the actual letter of those instruments."[88] Human rights discourses seemed to be especially prevalent in 2008 as that year was also the sixtieth anniversary of the United Nations' Universal Declaration of Human Rights. Many immigrant rights groups around the state, as well as around the country, used the anniversary as an opportunity to throw a spotlight on immigrant rights. The ACLU and the American Friends Service Committee's New Jersey chapters for example, released a report titled "The Rights of Immigrants in New Jersey" on December 10, 2008.

Conclusion

Anti-immigrant local ordinances, although alarmingly widespread in New Jersey and across the United States, do not get introduced without major contestation. Immigrant rights activists and their allies have, in many cases, been able to stop the implementation of anti-immigrant ordinances in their communities. They have drawn on numerous strategies to do so, ranging from court challenges to street protests. New Jersey immigrant rights activists, however, work on multiple scales. They have been just as invested in organizing at the national, supranational, and translocal levels even as they organize in their local neighborhoods.

Much of the work activists do might be characterized as "reactive," that is, they are reacting to initiatives of anti-immigrant forces who are often very well-resourced financially and in some cases, enjoy the power of local political office, to push through their objectives However, activists also engage in very proactive, creative strategies of immigrant inclusion. At the state level, American-raised undocumented immigrant youth have successfully fought to open up educational opportunities for themselves and their peers. The New Jersey Dream Act allows them to pay in-state tuition at state colleges and universities. "Sanctuary city" ordinances, a tool immigrant advocates first developed in the 1980s, are being passed in as many municipalities as are anti-immigrant ordinances. Other communities have gone so far as offering municipal identification cards to the undocumented.

Immigrant rights activists have asserted immigrants rights as workers, and they have stood up for immigrants' civil and human rights. At the same time, they have called on U.S. citizens to play a role in supporting immigrants in their communities. In all their invocations of rights, however, activists are not necessarily wedded to the notion of "citizenship." In other words, activists do not necessarily see the answer to immigrant exclusion as a "pathway to citizenship." Legalizing undocumented immigrants and giving them the chance to become naturalized American citizens is not always what activists aspire to, though many do. Many of the activist organizers I have encountered in different New Jersey neighborhoods recognize full well the limitations of U.S. citizenship. They recognize that it has, from its inception, depended on racialized, classed, and gendered exclusions. They offer alternative visions and notions of community, collectivity, and belonging through highly localized, spatialized practices. Perhaps the most novel strategy I have come across has been the work of CHABA in "rescripting" historic preservation. CHABA ensures that even as older histories are restored and preserved in Bridgeton's local landscapes, it is not at the cost of displacing or excluding the community's newest settlers. CHABA strives to make the built form of its community signify diversity and inclusiveness.

6

Conclusion

In this book, I have tried to make sense of anti-immigrant local ordinances in a place where they don't make sense. New Jersey has always been a state of immigration. Immigration is part and parcel of the state's identity. New Jersey even claims the national immigration landmark, Ellis Island, as its very own. Yet this state of tremendous ethnic and racial diversity that so many immigrants call home is also a state in which anti-immigrant local ordinances have been introduced by local politicians and citizens alike and in many cases passed by local governments. Some places have not necessarily introduced explicitly anti-immigrant ordinances, but have used other formal and informal mechanisms to exclude and ultimately expel immigrants. I estimate that at least twelve of New Jersey's twenty-one counties have communities that are anti-immigrant in these various ways. It would be unfair and inaccurate to say that the state of New Jersey is entirely anti-immigrant. Yet that anti-immigrant politics and policies are present in a majority of its counties makes New Jersey not completely different from states bordering Mexico like Arizona or southern states like Alabama, Mississippi, or even North Carolina where anti-immigrant politics might not be surprising and where anti-immigrant policies have in fact been introduced and passed at the state, county, and local levels.

Many scholars have been paying closer attention to anti-immigrant local ordinances and have offered a variety of explanations to make sense of them though not all can quite explain what's happening in New Jersey. Most of us agree that the rise of anti-immigrant local ordinances is in large part due to post-9/11 immigration enforcement policies, which have become more interiorized and localized. I find that this holds true to a great extent for New Jersey. New Jersey's local police cooperate both formally and informally with ICE, for example. Some counties have contracts with ICE to hold immigrant detainees in county jails. Others go so far as having 287(g) agreements with ICE so that county law enforcement officers can also serve as immigration agents. Even in communities where contracts with ICE do not exist, local police have taken the initiative to hand individuals they suspect to be undocumented over to ICE. A routine traffic stop in some neighborhoods can end in an immigrant being whisked away, uprooted from their homes and their families and put into detention.

Other scholars also attribute the rise of anti-immigrant local ordinances in different parts of the country to the fact that some communities are "new destinations" for immigrants, particularly immigrants of color. This does not quite apply to New Jersey since the state is hardly a new immigrant destination and indeed, many of the municipalities where I have tracked anti-immigrant politics and policies have been home to different immigrant groups for decades. Still others attribute the rise of anti-immigrant local ordinances to partisan politics, that is, whether a place is "blue" (largely Democratic) or "red" (largely Republican). But this explanation also doesn't quite apply to New Jersey. Party affiliation is not the best indicator of whether a government official or citizen supports or opposes immigration in this state. In the cases I've overviewed in this book, I've found a Democratic mayor (Cresitello of Morristown) calling for more immigration enforcement in his town and a Republican mayor (Patterson of Hightstown) insisting on making his town an immigrant "sanctuary." Similarly, New Jersey citizens, even those who might be affiliated with the Democratic Party or may think of themselves as receptive to immigration, harbor sentiments that feed into anti-immigrant policies.

As an alternative explanation, I believe that to understand what's happening in New Jersey, you have to understand the history, economy, political structure, and perhaps most important, the culture of American suburban life. Suburbs in New Jersey, indeed, across the nation do not all look and feel the same. However, the suburb, as an ideology has a form and structure that is shared by many in this country. A home in the suburbs has come to represent the accomplishment of economic (upward) mobility for many if not most people in the United States. It epitomizes having achieved the American Dream. Yet many white suburbanites feel that this is an illusory dream and blame immigrants for making that dream difficult to accomplish. Neoliberalism has made suburban life increasingly precarious, yet rather than blaming the "one percent," whose interests are protected and promoted by the neoliberal state, these suburban citizens blame their newest neighbors. To keep them out, those working-class and middle-class white suburbanites who see immigrants as a problem have turned to their municipal governments and taken local control over their communities' immigrant populations. New Jersey is an especially rich site from which to study race, immigration, and suburbia because not only is it a state of immigration, it is a quintessentially suburban state.

I have found that in numerous white suburbs, New Jerseyans have introduced a plethora of policies meant to stop immigrants, particularly undocumented, working-class Latinos, from settling in their communities. Often, they have drawn on racist discourses to justify these policies. Some of these discourses are the tried and true discourses that have been used against immigrants for generations: They steal our jobs! They rape our women! They're dirty and diseased! They threaten our culture and way of life! They're criminals! This was true in Freehold, for example. Some of the discourses used to justify anti-immigrant local ordinances are distinctively a consequence of the post-9/11 world we now live in: They are terrorists! Of course, immigrants have been accused of being the purveyors of dangerous ideas in the past (think Emma Goldman or Sacco and Vanzetti), but the idea of immigrants as terrorists has been especially heightened since the attacks on New York City's World Trade Center.[1] In Morristown, immigrants were figured as potential terrorist threats. In fact, those opposed to immigrant settlement in that community deployed the entire arsenal of anti-immigrant discourses and policies. Immigrants were simultaneously figured as illegals, criminals, and terrorists. When the strict enforcement of housing ordinances didn't work to eliminate the immigrant population, the town tried to deputize its police as immigration enforcement agents.

Just as often, however, the discourses that white suburbanites use to introduce and justify different municipal policies do not draw from explicitly racist or racializing discourses. In fact, these supposedly colorblind policies may not even appear to have anything to do with immigrants at all.

In Freehold, for instance, residents led "historic preservation" or "quality of life" campaigns. Indeed, campaigns like these can even be considered "anti-suburban" as they are sometimes meant to resist large-scale building of suburban tract housing. Yet closely examining both the history of Freehold Borough and the areas of the borough that these campaigns targeted, it becomes clear that they are meant to oust immigrants from the town.

In so-called ethnoburbs, I have found that the existence of a numerical majority of immigrants of color has not necessarily led to the fundamental transformation of local governance or a radical shift in the political terrain. Even when the majority of immigrants come from a highly valorized, widely celebrated "model minority," like Asian Americans, the same sorts of anti-immigrant discourses are deployed. Immigrant "mom and pop" shops do not represent American entrepreneurship, in places like Edison or Palisades Park, but are said to pose both an economic and a cultural threat. Even big-box retailers like Walmart are more welcome (provided that they don't invite unsavory immigrant clientele) than immigrant-owned businesses. Nativist sentiment even extends to immigrants' second-generation children who are always figured as outsiders, as was the case for Edison's former mayor Jun Choi. Indians have borne the brunt of xenophobia in that community, however. Their neighbors have used local ordinances to limit their ability to exercise their religious and cultural practices publicly. These ordinances may not be aimed at driving immigrants out of town, but they certainly aim at making immigrants feel as if they don't belong. In extreme cases Indians have been subjected to violent hate crimes.

Whether we are talking about white suburbs or ethnoburbs, suburban municipal governance has been antiblack from its inception. It is here where I draw the connections between suburban governance historically prohibiting the settlement of African American in the suburbs with anti-immigrant ordinances targeting Latinos and other immigrants today. The logics and technologies of antiblackness have been used, sometimes unevenly, against different groups of people of color. It is through the securing of racialized, classed, and gendered spaces for themselves, particularly the securing of the suburb, that middle-class (and middle-class aspiring) whites and their families can achieve the American Dream and thereby authentically exercise American citizenship. Another way of thinking about it is that the rights and privileges of American citizenship, which are ultimately reserved for middle-class whites and their families, can best be enjoyed in the suburbs. Understanding the racial politics of suburban community and identity formation is crucial for making sense of why anti-immigrant local ordinances have been introduced in places like Freehold, Morristown, and Edison, the New Jersey communities I focus on here, as well places like Hazelton, Pennsylvania, Farmer's Branch, Texas, and Maricopa County, Arizona.

Many scholars have long considered New Jersey a bellwether state.[2] To reflect, therefore, on the race and immigration politics that characterize New Jersey's suburbs and cities is necessarily to reflect on suburban living in the United States more broadly. Suburban living is at the core of the American "way of life." As of 2000, more Americans were living in the suburbs than in cities and the countryside combined.[3] New Jersey, not surprisingly, had the distinction of being one of the most suburbanized states in the country at the turn of the twenty-first century and suburbanization has not abated.[4]

Given the significance New Jersey has had in shaping suburban development and governance across the country, it's important to see the potential consequences these localized struggles over immigration have. Over the course of the last century, subnational political struggles have had broader national impacts. As historian Erika Lee illustrates, San Francisco's anti-Chinese policies in the late nineteenth century would later come to inform federal immigration policy with the eventual consolidation of immigration agencies and the passage of the Chinese Exclusion Act.[5] Proposition 187's passage by the citizens of California critically shaped the 1996 IIRIRA law and served as a template for Arizona's SB1070 in 2010. Policies do not emerge in a vacuum and have effects beyond their intended constituencies.

I have attempted to draw connections across the experiences of very different sets of racialized groups—African Americans, Latinos, Asian Americans—because I am invested in both an analytics and a politics that foregrounds commonalities shared by peoples of color in the United States. I am aware that it is problematic and even dangerous to engage in a form of comparativism that simply parallels the experiences of racialized communities. We are not all the same. Even though we have all been subjected to racializing processes, those processes are highly uneven and have very divergent consequences, consequences that can literally mean life for some and death for others. The caution that scholars like Danika Medak-Saltzman and Antonio T. Tiongson Jr. call for in their 2015 article "Racial Comparativism Reconsidered" is something I take seriously here.[6] I am inspired by the direction in comparative research mapped out by Grace

Kyungwon Hong and Roderick A. Ferguson in their anthology, *Strange Affinities: The Gender and Sexual Politics of Comparative Racialization*.[7]

At the same time, my impulse toward a kind of comparativism comes from my experiences as a social justice activist. I have seen how simplistic, ahistorical attempts at interracial connection produce fragile coalitions on the ground. Yet I've also seen how connections built through sometimes painful confrontations and recognitions of the ways racializing processes historically privilege some of us even as they disadvantage others of us can, nevertheless, lead to enduring solidarities. On a basic level, activist/organizer/comrades from backgrounds other than my own have enriched me not just as a scholar-activist but also as a person. Breaking bread with people who have had life experiences different from mine and struggling against the structures of power that dominate our lives has shaped me in indelible and deeply meaningful ways. I am who I am because of these affectionate affinities.

Although I have drawn links between contemporary, twenty-first century and mid-twentieth-century suburban New Jersey politics, it is important to situate the racialized spatial practices that have become commonplace in the state's suburbs within an even longer historical timeframe. Arguably, the precedent for various forms of black exclusion is New Jersey's history, particularly that of South Jersey, as a site for slavery. The Dutch brought slavery into New Jersey, and the "peculiar institution" persisted from 1662 to the early 1700s. Some of the worst pro-slavery laws were passed in southern New Jersey. New Jersey did not abolish slavery until 1808. Although New Jersey's was the first state constitution to extend suffrage to all men (including blacks), by 1820 the state's legislators rescinded black voting rights. The Colonization Society, established in Newark in 1817, had aims similar to those of anti-immigration groups today: to expel or deport, in this case, black citizens. During Reconstruction, the state refused to ratify the Fourteenth and Fifteenth Amendments.[8]

Suburban logics can even be linked to American imperialism and settler colonialism. I mention this in different moments in this book, but here at its close, I think it is especially important to underscore this fact. Because immigration policies today are a consequence of the rise of the Homeland Security State after 9/11, links to the United States' more recent imperial ambitions should be fairly clear. However, the racialized spatial practices of imperialism and settler colonialism historically undergird the logics of the suburbs. These practices include population displacement and the sequestration of racialized bodies within and without specifically defined spaces. In this way, I build on the scholarly work of the likes of Sunaina Maira, and others who, like me, examine the consequences of post-9/11 immigration policy yet historicize it over the *longue durée* of racial formation in this country.

It is important not to forget, moreover, that suburbs have been formed very explicitly against other kinds of spaces—notably urban spaces. The city is the Other to the suburb. The suburban imaginary cannot be formed without an Other against which it is contrasted; the city represents everything that the suburb is not. You can't have a "good" place without differentiating it from a "bad" place. The city is disorganized, filthy, and dangerous. The suburb is orderly, clean, and safe. The city is black. The suburb is white. If suburbs have been fenced (literally and figuratively), cities have been locked down (again, literally and figuratively). As economic and political elites have progressively cut back on social and economic protections in favor of trickle down white supremacist, neoliberal policies, they attempt to secure support from white suburban citizens by guaranteeing, if not their social and economic security, then at least their sense of personal security. What has emerged is a "double regulation of poverty by the joint action of punitive welfare-turned-workfare and an aggressive penal bureaucracy."[9] Policing becomes an easy way to manage the poor and the increasingly disenfranchised working classes who are confined to urban areas. When policing is not sufficient, then incarceration and in many cases, death, become the final solution as proven by the indiscriminate killing of African Americans in cities (and suburbs) across the country, a fact all African Americans have known to be true for generations although it has only garnered the attention of the broader public with the spread of photos and videos of antiblack state violence through social media in recent years. At the same time, U.S. suburban imaginaries are often juxtaposed against representations of the Third World. As Robert Beauregard notes, "the suburb figured prominently in U.S. global projections that were designed to create a 'better world abroad and a happier society at home'" at the height of the Cold War.[10] Suburban life continues to fuel the ongoing U.S. imperialist project.

This book is, at its core, a study of U.S. racial formation within the broader context of global neoliberal racialized capitalism. It is important not to lose sight of this fact. Neoliberal globalization has unleashed unprecedented economic dislocations. The sociologist Saskia Sassen calls these dislocations processes of expulsion. She argues, "The notion of expulsions takes us beyond the more familiar idea of growing inequality as a way of capturing the pathologies of today's global capitalism."[11] Among these "expulsions" is international migration as people are forced to seek a living far from the places they call home. Meanwhile, the rights that American citizenship once guaranteed, at least for whites of relative economic privilege, are dwindling fast. Americans themselves are experiencing a form of "expulsion." Nativist and xenophobic reactions like those we find in New Jersey and other parts of the United States are not unique to this country but are a global phenomenon and are a response, however misplaced, to the various expulsions caused by neoliberal globalization. Municipalities and their suburban residents have policed the borders of their communities against outsiders to bolster whatever remains of their increasingly bankrupt citizenship. Indeed, around the world today, citizenship is "a hegemonic mechanism of sociopolitical power and control, discipline and normative regulation" that works in service of the advancement and triumph of global capitalist interest even as it privileges different social groups.[12] Race and racism are central to neoliberalism and by extension, citizenship. Cultural studies scholar Jodi Melamed argues, "Race continues to permeate capitalism's economic and social processes, organizing the hyperextraction of surplus value from racialized bodies and naturalizing a system of capital accumulation."[13] Yet ideas that characterize the United States as at best "multicultural" or at worst "postracial" create "a situation where official antiracisms themselves deflect and limit awareness of the logics of exploitation and domination in global capitalism."[14]

If this book is about centering understandings of race and neoliberalism, it is just as importantly a book aimed at lifting up stories of resistance. New Jersey's immigrant communities have mobilized to resist anti-immigrant local ordinances on multiple scales and with a variety of strategies. For example, whereas historic preservation and quality of life campaigns can be used in some towns to drive immigrants out, in other towns it is being used to draw them in. In Bridgeton, CHABA's work stands out for its creative and intentional efforts to interpret and apply historic preservation principles in ways that are inclusive of immigrants' histories, contributions, and aesthetics; as means of improving their quality of life as it were. CHABA's aim is to transform and rescript the civic landscape.

I don't want readers of this book to over-romanticize immigrant activism. In fact, this is book is also aimed at addressing some of the shortcomings and limits of different forms of activism as I encountered them as a scholar-activist. Too often, I've heard activists deploy what are essentially neoliberal, antiblack discourses to make their claims on behalf of immigrants. I've been guilty of it to some extent myself. When I first started doing antideportation work, I helped to support the Cuevas family, an undocumented Filipino family, based in a city neighboring the town where I grew up. In attempting to galvanize support of this family, my colleagues and I projected the "good immigrant" narrative by highlighting the family's middle-class status (they shouldn't be deported because they are economically productive!). I've seen some of my colleagues in the immigrant rights movement assert that undocumented immigrants are "not criminals," and therefore shouldn't be deported. Yet, from a different view that statement can be interpreted as coded to mean that undocumented immigrants are "not black" and that blacks, unlike the undocumented, are in fact deserving of imprisonment. It is my hope that by historicizing anti-immigrant local ordinances in the way I have here, we can sharpen our understandings of the workings of race and immigration to create enduring alliances.

Although our work has sometimes been seriously flawed, New Jersey's social justice activists and organizers offer an important glimpse into what kinds of change can be possible.[15] We show how "community," "belonging," and "home" can be infused with new kinds of meanings and practices and that these terms can be unmoored from the spatial racial politics to which they have been attached.

Epilogue

As I finished writing the first full draft of this book, the country was debating how to manage the aftermath of what has been labeled a terrorist attack: the mass shooting in San Bernardino, California which took place in December 2015. As the media and political pundits dissected the case, a key fact that became a central point of discussion was that one of the shooters was an immigrant. Within hours, as investigations of the full facts of the shooting were still underway, news commentators looked in detail into the process by which he arrived in the United States. Underlying the analysis implicitly (and often explicitly) was the notion that it was too easy for him to come in, that our borders are simply too porous to threating people. Alongside the analysis of the immigration process was an analysis of how a seemingly integrated, second-generation immigrant could be radicalized. Moreover, racist analyses have ensued. It is as if to be born Muslim is to be necessarily inassimilable and hostile to the United States. The shooting occurred at the height of the presidential primary race. Donald Trump, a contender for the Republican nomination at the time, called for no less than the outright ban of Muslim immigrants as well as the building of a U.S.-Mexico border wall. In just days after his inauguration, he has tried to make good on these campaign pledges.

Meanwhile, debates about the criminal justice system, triggered in large part by the mass mobilizations across the country in response to police and vigilante/citizen violence against African Americans as well as court verdicts exonerating them from such charges, are ongoing. Beginning with widespread protests led by African Americans of Trayvon Martin's 2012 shooting in a Florida suburb by Mark Zimmerman and Zimmerman's not-guilty verdict, whites in this country are forced to confront what many African Americans and other people have color intimately understand about the criminal justice system. For the first time in a long time, presidential primary candidates on both sides were forced to address how they would make "black lives matter."

America today is literally up in arms with respect to race and immigration. On the surface it might seem that the San Bernardino shootings and the Trayvon Martin shooting are two disconnected issues: one is an "international" or "foreign" issue, the other is a domestic issue, yet this book points out that they are deeply, inextricably related. Despite claims that the United States, especially with the election of an African American president in 2008 is a "postracial" society, "race" has and continues to be "a central principle of social organization" in American life.[16] The very essence of anti-immigrant local ordinances (whether immigrants are figured as outsiders, criminals, or terrorists), like their antiblack precedents, is containment and expulsion. Even as neoliberalism is an ideology that favors the retreat of the state in the provision of social goods and in the regulation of markets, it requires the disciplining of the population. In other words, if some of the functions of the state are diminished under neoliberalism, its policing functions are enhanced.

As I write on these issues plaguing this country, I am beset by a deeply personal loss. In the last year, my mother had to sell our house in suburban San Ramon, California. Although I didn't spend my growing up years in that house (my parents moved there when I was a junior in high school), and although I have very little affection for the city (I recall anti-immigrant editorials being written by my brother's high school newspaper in the 1990s, racist antiblack graffiti was found scrawled in the bathroom stalls most recently), the house was the center of our family lives into my adulthood. Both of my children lived for a time in that house. All the Christmases of my adult life were celebrated there. It was the house where my father took his very last breath. As I critique suburban living and suburban identities, I still recognize how meaningful houses are and the immense sense of loss we feel when we lose them. Nevertheless, I want to believe that it can be possible for everyone in this country, indeed, in this world, to have some place, a home, to call their own. Neoliberalism threatens to make that impossible, but even in the face of loss, I remain ever hopeful.

Notes

Preface and Acknowledgments

1 Jerry Cheslow, "If You're Thinking of Living In/Highland Park, N.J.; Small in Size but Large in Diversity," *New York Times*, October 7, 2000, accessed July 10, 2016, http://www.nytimes.com/2000/10/08/realestate/if-you-re-thinking-living-highland-park-nj-small-size-but-large-diversity.html?pagewanted=all.

2 Saskia Sassen, *Expulsions: Brutality and Complexity in the Global Economy* (Cambridge, MA: Harvard University Press, 2014), 1.

Chapter 1 The Politics of Race and Immigration in the "Garden State"

1 Nancy Foner, *From Ellis Island to JFK: New York's Two Great Waves of Immigration* (New York: Russell Sage Foundation, 2000), 1.

2 Linda Greenhouse, "The Ellis Island Verdict: The Ruling; High Court Gives New Jersey Most of Ellis Island," *New York Times*, May 27, 1998, accessed July 20, 2016, http://www.nytimes.com/1998/05/27/nyregion/ellis-island-verdict-ruling-high-court-gives-new-jersey-most-ellis-island.html.

3 From John Truslow Adams, *The Epic of America* (Boston: Little, Brown, 1931). The Library of Congress cites it as a teaching resource on the topic of the "American Dream," accessed July 10, 2016, http://www.loc.gov/teachers/classroommaterials/lessons/american-dream/students/thedream.html.

4 See Liberty State Park brochure from the State of New Jersey, Department of Environmental Protection, Division of Parks and Forestry, State Park Service.

5 Jens Manuel Krogstad and Michael Keegan, "15 States with the Highest Share of Immigrants in Their Population," Pew Research Center, May 14, 2014, accessed October 9, 2015, http://www.pewresearch.org/fact-tank/2014/05/14/15-states-with-the-highest-share-of-immigrants-in-their-population/.

6 "New Americans in New Jersey," Immigration Policy Center, January 1, 2015, accessed October 9, 2015, http://www.immigrationpolicy.org/just-facts/new-americans-new-jersey.

7 "Facts About Immigrant NJ," Eagleton Program on Immigration and Democracy Rutgers University, n.d., accessed July 12, 2016, http://epid.rutgers.edu/gallery/facts-about-immigrant-nj/.

8 By "post-1965" immigration, I'm referring to the dynamics of immigration following the passage of the 1965 Immigration Act. Among the most important shifts that occurred with that act is that all racially based immigration exclusions were dropped from immigration law. I'll discuss this more in future chapters, but suffice it to say, immigration law up until that point was explicitly racist and included language that prohibited the immigration of specific racial (mostly Asian) groups. Another important provision of the law is that it allowed family reunification, that is, it allowed legal permanent residents the chance to sponsor their overseas family members to join them as permanent residents in the United States. Many scholars believe that these changes in the 1965 Immigration Act are what led to the exponential growth of both the Latino and Asian populations in this country.

9 "Map the Impact of Immigration Across the Nation," Partnership for a New American Economy, n.d., accessed July 12 2016, http://www.maptheimpact.org/state/new-jersey/.

10 "New Americans in New Jersey," *Immigration Policy Center*.

11 "Facts About Immigrant NJ," *Eagleton Program*.

12 Jens Manuel Krogstad and Jeffrey S. Passel, "5 Facts about Illegal Immigration in the U.S.," Pew Research Center, November 19, 2015, accessed July 12, 2016, http://www.pewresearch.org/fact-tank/2015/07/24/5-facts-about-illegal-immigration-in-the-u-s/.

13 Elizabeth M. Grieco et al., "The Size, Place of Birth, and Geographic Distribution of the Foreign-Born Population in the United States: 1960 to 2010," United States Census Bureau, Population Division, October 2012, accessed July 26, 2016, https://www.census.gov/population/foreign/files/WorkingPaper96.pdf.

14 Randal C. Archibold, "Arizona Enacts Stringent Law on Immigration," *New York Times*, April 23, 2010, accessed July 26, 2016, http://www.nytimes.com/2010/04/24/us/politics/24immig.html?_r=0.

15 Associated Press, "U.S. Judge Dismisses Challenge of Arizona's SB 1070 Immigration Law," *Los Angeles Times*, September 9, 2015, accessed July 26, 2016, http://www.latimes.com/nation/immigration/la-na-nn-arizona-immigration-law-20150905-story.html.

16 Ian Gordon and Tasneem Raja, "164 Anti-Immigration Laws Passed Since 2010? A MoJo Analysis," *Mother Jones*, March-April 2012, accessed July 26, 2016, http://www.motherjones.com/politics/2012/03/anti-immigration-law-database.

17 According to the National Conference of State Legislatures (NCSL), from 2014 to 2015, there was a 26 percent increase in immigration-related legislation enacted by state governments, from 171 laws in 2014 to 216 by the end of 2015. Although they do not provide a breakdown of anti- versus pro-immigrant legislation, that states are increasingly engaged in address immigration is important to note. See National Conference of State Legislatures, "Report on 2015 State Immigration Laws," National Conference of State Legislatures, February 16, 2016, accessed July 26, 2016, http://www.ncsl.org/research/immigration/report-on-2015-state-immigration-laws.aspx.

18 See Kevin S. O'Neil, "Challenging Change: Local Policies and the New Geography of American Immigration" (PhD diss., Princeton University, 2011).

19 Caroline B. Brettell and Faith G. Nibbs, "Immigrant Suburban Settlement and the 'Threat' to Middle Class Status and Identity: The Case of Farmers Branch, Texas," *International Migration* 49, no. 1 (2010): 8; Rigel C. Oliveri, "Between a Rock and a Hard Place: Landlords, Latinos, Anti-illegal Immigrant Ordinances, and Housing Discrimination," *Vanderbilt Law Review* 62 (2009): 53.

20 Monica W. Varsanyi, "Immigration Policing Through the Backdoor: City Ordinances, the 'Right to the City,' and the Exclusion of Undocumented Day Laborers," *Urban Geography* 29, no. 1 (2008): 29.

21 See Steven W. Bender, "Old Hate in New Bottles: Privatizing, Localizing, and Bundling Anti-Spanish and Anti-Immigrant Sentiment in the 21st Century," *Nevada Law Journal* 7 (2006): 883–894, for an analysis of English-only or English-language regulations being passed at the local level alongside anti-immigrant ordinances.

22 Kyle E. Walker and Helga Leitner, "The Variegated Landscape of Local Immigration Policies in the United States," *Urban Geography* 32, no. 2 (2011): 158. Today some people might think of California as the "Left Coast" (not only referring to its geography but also to its culture and politics, which is typically thought of as liberal, or left of center), but California has also been the site for major anti-immigrant policies, with Proposition 187, passed in the mid-1990s, as a significant example. It has been over two decades since Proposition 187, yet many immigration experts agree that it helped to shape the form that anti-immigration and anti-immigrant policies take at the national and local level in the present day. It is also important to note that states and municipalities have not only been engaged in passing anti-immigrant policies. Many have also been engaged in passing pro-immigrant policies, sometimes in active defiance of what they believe to be anti-immigrant policies at the state and federal level. Different municipalities, for example, have passed "sanctuary city" policies in recent years. Through these policies, city governments take a stand against mobilizing their resources to support federal immigration enforcement efforts, which have become more aggressive since 9/11. Whether subnational government units are passing anti- or pro-immigrant policies, it is clear that immigration is an issue that is of local significance in different communities across the country.

23 Walker and Leitner, "The Variegated Landscape of Local Immigration Policies in the United States," 159.

24 The interiorization and localization of immigration enforcement is not entirely new. Nayan Shah's study of the role of public health bureaucracies and their role in regulating the lives of Chinese immigrants in the city of San Francisco is illustrative of early forms of interior and localized immigration enforcement. See Nayan Shah, *Contagious Divides: Epidemics and Race in San Francisco's Chinatown* (Berkeley: University of California Press, 2001).

25 Tanya Golash-Boza, "Targeting Latino Men: Mass Deportation in the USA, 1998–2012," *Ethnic and Racial Studies* 38, no. 8 (2015): 1223.

26 Gretchen Gavett, "Map: The U.S. Immigration Detention Boom," PBS, October 18, 2011, accessed February 2, 2015, http://www.pbs.org/wgbh/frontline/article/map-the-u-s-immigration-detention-boom/.

27 Ana Gonzalez-Barrera and Jens Manuel Krogstad, "U.S. Deportations of Immigrants Reach Record High in 2013," Pew Research Center RSS, October 2, 2014, accessed July 29, 2016, http://www.pewresearch.org/fact-tank/2014/10/02/u-s-deportations-of-immigrants-reach-record-high-in-2013.
28 See http://www.pewhispanic.org/files/reports/133.pdf#page=24, accessed November 5, 2016.
29 Rudy Larini, "Migrants Deported in Record Numbers in N.J.," *Star-Ledger*, November 7, 2008.
30 See the elaboration on the "securitization of migration" in Thomas Faist, "'Extension du Domiane de la Lutte': International Migration and Security Before and After September 11, 2001," *International Migration Review* 36 (2002): 2.
31 Nicholas De Genova, "The Production of Culprits: From Deportability to Detainability in the Aftermath of 'Homeland Security,'" *Citizenship Studies* 11, no .5 (2007): 422.
32 Ibid., 424.
33 Louise Cainkar, "Post-9/11 Domestic Policies Affecting U. S. Arabs and Muslims: A Brief Review," *Comparative Studies of South Asia, Africa and the Middle East* 24, no. 1 (2004): 245. Of course, even immigrants who are racialized as "white" have been caught in the immigration enforcement dragnet. For example, a Little Falls, New Jersey, Ukrainian family was detained under the Homeland Security State. A local newspaper columnist declared, "This is no way to treat a family. Not here. Not in America. At least not in the America I thought I knew." See the article by Bob Braun, "Give Us Your Tired, Poor and Gullible," *Star-Ledger*, February 9, 2006.
34 Golash-Boza, "Targeting Latino Men," 1221.
35 See Solana Larsen, "The Anti-Immigration Movement: From Shovels to Suits," *NACLA Report on the Americas* 40, no. 3 (2007): 14–18, for a discussion of the Minutemen. However Larsen points out that they are but a small fraction of a much larger anti-immigrant movement.
36 Julie A. Dowling and Jonathan Xavier Inda, "Introduction: Governing Migrant Illegality," in *Governing Immigration through Crime: A Reader*, ed. Julie A. Dowling and Jonathan Xavier Inda (Stanford, CA: Stanford University Press, 2013), 2.
37 Tom K. Wong, "287(g) and the Politics of Interior Immigration Control in the United States: Explaining Local Cooperation with Federal Immigration Authorities," *Journal of Ethnic and Migration Studies* 38, no. 5 (2012): 739.
38 "Nativists" is another term used to describe anti-immigrant individuals and groups. "Nativist" derives from "nativism," which is the notion that the United States can only be home to those who are native-born. For a study on the relationship between immigrant population growth and anti-immigrant local ordinances, see Jill Esbenshade and Barbara Obzurt, "Local Immigration Regulation: A Problematic Trend in Public Policy," *Harvard Journal of Hispanic Politics* 20 (2007–2008): 42–43. For a regional focus on suburban Washington, DC, see Jill H. Wilson, Andrey Singer, and Brooke DeRenzis, "Growing Pains: Local Response to Recent Immigrant Settlement in Suburban Washington D.C.," in *Taking Local Control: Immigration Policy Activism in U.S. Cities and States*, ed. Monica Varsanyi (Stanford, CA: Stanford University Press, 2010), 193–215. Legal scholars studying an anti-immigrant local ordinance in Nebraska attribute it to demographic changes, see Ashleigh Bausch Varley and Mary C. Snow, "Don't You Dare Live Here: The Constitutionality of the Anti-Immigrant Employment and Housing Ordinances

at Issue in Keller v. City of Fremont," *Creighton Law Review* 45 (2011): 507. For a national study that gauges anti-immigrant opposition (that is, anti-immigrant attitudes that have not necessarily led to the introduction of anti-immigrant local ordinances) on a local scale, see Daniel J. Hopkins, "Politicized Places: Explaining Where and When Immigrants Provoke Local Opposition," *American Political Science Review* 104, no. 1 (2010): 40–60. Hopkins finds that a sudden demographic change in a locality coupled with highly politicized anti-immigration rhetoric leads to hostility toward immigrants on a local level. Local residents' concerns that the undocumented population drains public services or due to their fears that the undocumented have a greater propensity to commit crimes have driven them to introduce anti-immigrant ordinances on a the subnational level. I'll discuss this in relation to California's Proposition 187 from the mid-1990s later in this chapter. For a study of mid-2000s anti-immigrant local ordinances that attributes them to these reasons as well see, John Ryan Syllaios, "The Future of Discriminatory Local Ordinances Aimed at Regulating Illegal Immigration," *Washington and Lee Journal of Civil Rights and Justice* 16 (2010): 639–670. Note that there has been quite a lot of focus on the cases of Hazelton, PA, and Farmer's Branch, TX, in the legal scholarship that I haven't cited here but these and other citations throughout this book do reference these particular cases.

39 Karthick S. Ramakrishnan and Tom (Tak) Wong, "Partisanship, Not Spanish: Explaining Municipal Ordinances Affecting Undocumented Immigrants," in *Taking Local Control: Immigration Policy Activism in U.S. Cities and States*, ed. Monica Varsanyi (Stanford, CA: Stanford University Press, 2010), 89.

40 Walker and Leitner, "The Variegated Landscape of Local Immigration Policies," 161.

41 "Cultural citizenship" is distinct from "legal citizenship." When scholars refer to legal citizenship, they are talking about laws that determine how citizenship is achieved or conferred by the state. A simple example of "legal citizenship" in the United States is that one is automatically a U.S. citizen if one is born on U.S. territory. In other countries, citizenship is not granted in this way. "Cultural citizenship" on the other hand, is more subjective. It is about ideas of belonging that are shaped by a country's norms and values as well as individuals' sense of connection or inclusion in a society. For example, people who have not been born in the United States may have been brought to the United States by their parents as young children. They may have spent their entire lives in the United States (gone to American schools and speak only English). People might think of them as "American" from the way they comport themselves; they may even think of themselves as "American," yet they are not legally American because they do not possess legal citizenship.

42 Brettell and Nibbs, "Immigrant Suburban Settlement," 10.

43 See the New Jersey state government's website for an account of the history of the state's nickname http://www.state.nj.us/nj/about/facts/nickname/. It is important to note that many of the suburban plans crafted in New Jersey borrowed heavily from the planning ideals of Ebenezer Howard's "Garden Cities of Tomorrow." Howard, a British urban planner and social reformer, wrote his treatise on how to address the ills of urban life in 1902. His book envisioned concepts that suburban planners incorporated into their approaches and indeed, though difficult to pin down, may be what explains New Jersey's nickname, "The Garden State." See

Ebenezer Howard and Frederic J. Osborn, *Garden Cities of To-morrow* (Cambridge, MA: MIT Press, 1965).

44 Kenneth T. Jackson, *Crabgrass Frontier: The Suburbanization of the United States* (New York: Oxford University Press, 1985), 33. Also see Barbara G. Salmore and Stephen A. Salmore, *New Jersey Politics and Government: The Suburbs Comes of Age*, 4th ed. (New Brunswick, NJ: Rutgers University Press, 2013), 240.

45 Jon C. Teaford, *The American Suburb: The Basics* (New York: Routledge, 2008), 3.

46 Jackson, *Crabgrass Frontier*, 33.

47 Ibid.

48 Lizbeth Cohen, *A Consumers' Republic: The Politics of Mass Consumption in Postwar America* (New York: Knopf, 2003), 197.

49 Jackson, *Crabgrass Frontier*, 85.

50 Ali Modarres and Andrew Kirby, "The Suburban Question: Notes for a Research Program," *Cities* 27, no. 2 (2010): 116.

51 Jackson, *Crabgrass Frontier*, 98.

52 Gwendolyn Wright, *Building the Dream: A Social History of Housing in America* (New York: Pantheon, 1981).

53 Ibid.

54 Richard Lacayo, "Suburban Legend: William Levitt," *Time*, July 3, 1950, n.p. Notably, high-profile personalities like the novelist, Pearl S. Buck criticized the uniformity of Levittown's housing tracts as well as its racial covenant policies as being too dangerously similar to Chinese Communist-planned communities. As quoted in David Kushner's book, *Levittown: Two Families, One Tycoon, and the Fight for Civil Rights in America's Legendary Suburb* (New York: Walker and Company, 2009), 70: "When I walked through Levittown one day and saw hundreds of houses being built, all for white families and not one for Negroes, I saw a straight line of connection between those houses and that Communism won China away from us."

55 Robert A. Beauregard, *When America Became Suburban* (Minneapolis: University of Minnesota Press, 2006), xi.

56 Dolores Hayden, "Building the American Way: Public Subsidy, Private Space," in *The Suburb Reader*, ed. Becky M. Nicolaides and Andrew Wiese (New York: Routledge, 2006), 273.

57 Ira Katznelson, *When Affirmative Action Was White: An Untold History of Racial Inequality in Twentieth-Century America* (New York: W. W. Norton, 2005), 25–52.

58 George Lipsitz, *The Possessive Investment in Whiteness: How White People Profit from Identity Politics* (Philadelphia: Temple University Press, 1998), 5.

59 Early on, the suburbs were imagined as "an alternative environment where those forced to work in the city could maintain a home life attuned to the tranquility, beauty, and purity of nature and where families could thrive safely removed from the urban ills threatening the health and morals of youth," see Teaford, *American Suburb*, 4.

60 Elijah Anderson, "'The White Space,'" *Sociology of Race and Ethnicity* 1, no. 1 (2015): 10.

61 Cohen, *Consumers' Republic*, 171.

62 Leah Platt Boustan, "Was Postwar Suburbanization 'White Flight'? Evidence from the Black Migration," *Quarterly Journal of Economics* (2010): 418.

63 Lipsitz, *Investment in Whiteness*, 7.

64 David R. Roediger, *Working toward Whiteness: How America's Immigrants Became White* (New York: Basic Books, 2005), 158.
65 See Roediger's discussion of James in *Working toward Whiteness*, 5.
66 W. E. B. Du Bois, *Black Reconstruction in America; an Essay toward a History of the Part Which Black Folk Played in the Attempt to Reconstruct Democracy in America, 1860–1880* (New York: Russell & Russell, 1966), 700.
67 Lipsitz, *Investment in Whiteness*, 8.
68 According to Jones-Correa, a racial restrictive covenant is a private agreement barring non-Caucasians from occupying or owning property. See Michael Jones-Correa, "The Origins and Diffusion of Racial Restrictive Covenants," *Political Science Quarterly* 115, no. 4 (2001): 541.
69 Teaford, *The American Suburb*, 32.
70 Roediger, *Working toward Whiteness*, 174.
71 Jones-Correa, "Racial Restrictive Covenants," 544.
72 Ibid.
73 Restrictive covenants were also used to keep out Jews, Italians, and Russians. See Garrett Power, *Generations* (Fall 1996): 5–7. Accessed October 24, 2016, http://digitalcommons.law.umaryland.edu/cgi/viewcontent.cgi?article=1252&context=fac_pubs, for a discussion on Jewish exclusion in suburban Baltimore. Interestingly, racial covenants are still attached to the original deeds of many homes. See Jessica Garrison, "Living with a Reminder of Segregation" *Los Angeles Times*, July 27, 2008. Accessed October 24, 2016, http://articles.latimes.com/2008/jul/27/local/me-covenant27.
74 Jones-Correa, "Racial Restrictive Covenants," 563.
75 James W. Loewen, *Sundown Towns: A Hidden Dimension of American Racism* (New York: New Press, 2005), 5.
76 George Lipsitz, "The Racialization of Space and the Spatialization of Race: Theorizing the Hidden Architecture of Landscape," *Landscape Journal* 26, no. 1 (2007): 11.
77 Teaford, *The American Suburb*, 13.
78 Salmore and Salmore, *New Jersey Politics*, 242.
79 Teaford, *The American Suburb*, 13.
80 Salmore and Salmore, *New Jersey Politics*, 242.
81 Ibid., 241.
82 Ibid., 239.
83 Teaford, *The American Suburb*, 167.
84 Ibid., 169.
85 David L. Kirp, John P. Dwyer, and Larry A. Rosenthal, *Our Town: Race, Housing, and the Soul of Suburbia* (New Brunswick, NJ: Rutgers University Press, 1995), 2.
86 Teaford, *The American Suburb*, 174.
87 Kirp, Dwyer, and Rosenthal, *Our Town*, 7.
88 Brad R. Tuttle, *How Newark Became Newark: The Rise, Fall, and Rebirth of an American City* (New Brunswick, NJ: Rutgers University Press, 2009), xix.
89 I use the term "riots" in quotes to reject dominant portrayals of African Americans' participation in urban upheavals as disruptive or even immoral. I prefer to refer to these episodes as race rebellions. They continue to be a means by which African Americans collectively express their outrage at different forms of white supremacy when all other options to express dissent are cut off or denied.

90 The Kerner Report was produced by the National Advisory Commission on Civil Disorders, which was established by President Lyndon B. Johnson to investigate the causes of urban unrest around the country and to offer policy recommendations based on its findings. For a full text copy of the report, see https://www.ncjrs.gov/pdffiles1/Digitization/8073NCJRS.pdf, accessed November 5, 2016.

91 Health Beth Johnson, *The American Dream and the Power of Wealth: Choosing Schools and Inheriting Inequality in the Land of Opportunity* (New York: Routledge, 2006), 6.

92 Ibid., 8.

93 Lipsitz, *Investment in Whiteness*, 34.

94 Gary Oldfield, "School Desegregation after Two Generations: Race, Schools, and Opportunity in Urban Society," in *Race in America: The Struggle for Equality*, ed. Herbert Hill and James E. Jones (Madison: University of Wisconsin Press, 1993), 240.

95 Salmore and Salmore, *New Jersey Politics*, 310.

96 Educational policy, particularly issues related to school funding, have historically been a point of major contention in the state of New Jersey. It is beyond the scope of this chapter to provide an overview of these struggles. See Salmore and Salmore, *New Jersey Politics*, chapter 15, for this information.

97 See https://www.civilrightsproject.ucla.edu/news/press-releases/2013-press-releases/urban-suburban-divide-widens-in-new-jersey-schools-levels-of-racial-isolation-contradicts-state-constitution.

98 Johnson, *The Power of Wealth*, 59.

99 Ibid. See also Camille L. Zubrinsky and Lawrence Bobo, "Prismatic Metropolis: Race and Residential Segregation in the City of the Angels," *Social Science Research* 25, no. 4 (1996): 335–374; Douglas S. Massey and Nancy A. Denton, "Hypersegregation in U.S. Metropolitan Areas: Black and Hispanic Segregation along Five Dimensions," *Demography* 26, no. 3 (1989): 373. A 2016 report from the National Center for Education Statistics finds, "Between fall 2003 and fall 2013, the number of White students enrolled in public elementary and secondary schools decreased from 28.4 million to 25.2 million, and the percentage who were White decreased from 59 to 50 percent," (see http://nces.ed.gov/programs/coe/indicator_cge.asp, accessed November 18, 2016). This data supports what sociologists have been finding over the last two decades. Tom Romero suggests that anti-immigrant local ordinances, because they drive Latinos to relocate from communities and thus leads to increased population concentration and segregation, is likely to mean that Latino children's educational opportunities will be severely constrained. See Tom I. Romero, "No Brown Towns: Anti-Immigrant Ordinances and Equality of Educational Opportunity for Latina/os," *Journal of Gender, Race and Justice* 12 (2008): 13.

100 Teaford, *The American Suburb*, 82.

101 Jones-Correa, "Racially Restrictive Covenants," 563.

102 Evan McKenzie, "Privatopia: Homeowner Associations and the Rise of Residential Private Government," in *The Suburb Reader*, ed. Becky M. Nicolaides and Andrew Wiese (New York: Taylor and Francis Group, 2006), 455–459.

103 Setha Low, "Behind the Gates: Life Security, and the Pursuit of Happiness in Fortress America," in *The Suburb Reader*, ed. Becky M. Nicolaides and Andrew Wiese (New York: Taylor and Francis Group, 2006), 462.

104 Zaire Zenit Dinzey Flores, *Locked In, Locked Out: Gated Communities in a Puerto Rican City* (Philadelphia: University of Pennsylvania Press, 2013), 22.

105 By "recent" I'm referring to the police shootings of unarmed African American men like Michael Brown (Ferguson, MO), Eric Garner (Staten Island, New York City), and countless others.

106 Loewen, *Sundown Towns*, 4. Loewen takes "sundown" from the signs that used to demarcate these towns' boundaries. They would often read, "Nigger, Don't Let the Sun Go Down on You in [name of town]." In fact, he starts his book with a description of Anna, Illinois. Anna is actually an acronym for "Ain't No Niggers Allowed."

107 In 1998 state troopers fired eleven shots at a vanload of African American men on their way to a basketball clinic. Although the troopers attempted to justify their actions by claiming that they believed the men were in possession of drugs, further investigations revealed that the van only contained sporting equipment and Bibles. See Alejandro Del Carmen, "Profiling, Racial: Historical and Contemporary Perspectives," in *Encyclopedia of Race and Crime*, compiled by Helen Taylor Greene and Shaun L. Gabbidon (Los Angeles: Sage, 2009), 666–668. Also see, Phil W. Petrie, "Newark Branch Still Battling Discrimination," *The New Crisis*, March/April 2003.

108 Boishampayan Chatterjee, "Did Suburbanization Cause Residential Segregation? Evidence from U.S. Metropolitan Areas," May 15, 2012, Available at SSRN: http://ssrn.com/abstract=2250579 orhttp://dx.doi.org/10.2139/ssrn.2250579, accessed November 18, 2016.

109 Charles E. Jacob, "Reaganomics: The Revolution in American Political Economy," *Law and Contemporary Problems* 48, no. 4 (1985): 7.

110 Because Reagan is affiliated with the Republican Party, which is generally described as "conservative" compared with the Democratic Party, which is thought of as "liberal," it sometimes confusing to then think of his approach as "neoliberal." "Neoliberalism" refers to a specific economic and political ideology that Republicans and Democrats alike have supported.

111 Matt Taibbi, *The Divide: American Injustice in the Age of the Wealth Gap* (New York: Spiegel and Grau, 2014), 325.

112 Inda and Dowling, "Migrant Illegality," 4.

113 Mike Davis, *Prisoners of the American Dream: Politics and Economy in the History of the US Working Class* (London: Verso, 1999), 227.

114 Lisa McGirr, *Suburban Warriors: The Origins of the New American Right* (Princeton, NJ: Princeton University Press, 2001), 2.

115 Ruth Wilson Gilmore, "Fatal Couplings of Power and Difference: Notes on Racism and Geography," *The Professional Geographer* 54, no. 1 (2002): 19.

116 Davis, *Prisoners of the American Dream*, 160.

117 Michelle Alexander, *The New Jim Crow: Mass Incarceration in the Age of Colorblindness* (New York: New Press, 2012), 2; 54.

118 Ibid., 48.

119 Inda and Dowling, "Migrant Illegality," 4.

120 Alexander, *New Jim Crow*, 7.

121 McGirr, *Suburban Warriors*, 204.

122 Martin Gottlieb, "Successes and Strains in Drive to Fix Statue of Liberty," *New York Times*, November 3, 1985, accessed August 4. 2016, http://www.nytimes.

com/1985/11/04/nyregion/successes-and-strains-in-drive-to-fix-statue-of-liberty.html?pagewanted=all.

123 Mike Wallace, "Hijacking History: Ronald Reagan and the Statue of Liberty," *Radical History Review* 37 (1987): 121.

124 Ali Behdad, *A Forgetful Nation: On Immigration and Cultural Identity in the United States* (Durham, NC: Duke University Press, 2005), 77.

125 "Horatio Alger narrative" refers to the narrative structure that characterizes the novels of Horatio Alger whose main protagonist was often a young shoeshine boy who rises out of poverty and achieves great wealth. See Juan F. Perea, "The Statue of Liberty: Notes from Behind the Gilded Door," in *Immigrants Out!: The New Nativism and the Anti-immigrant Impulse in the United States*, ed. Juan F. Perea (New York: New York University Press, 1997), 44–58, and Luke Desforges and Joanne Maddern, "Front Doors to Freedom, Portal to the Past: History at the Ellis Island Immigration Museum, New York," *Social & Cultural Geography* 5, no. 3 (2004): 437–457, for critical reflections on the symbolism of Lady Liberty as well as Ellis Island. Though Lady Liberty is often thought of symbolizing America's embrace of immigrants, a closer examination of the historical context of its official reception when it was first gifted to the United States from France in 1884 and later its declaration as a national monument in 1924 reveal a much darker side. If Emma Lazarus's poem at the Statue's base depicts her as a "Mother of Exiles," a poem by Thomas Bailey Aldrich, written in 1895, reflects the racist anti-immigrant sentiment of the country, which had just a little over a decade earlier passed the Chinese Exclusion Act. Notably, the same year that the Statue of Liberty was declared a national monument, President Calvin Coolidge had penned the National Origins Act of 1924, an immigration restriction law that extended previous restrictions against Asian immigrants to those from southern Europe.

126 Clinton made the following statement while on the campaign trail on October 23, 1991: "The new covenant can break the cycle of welfare. Welfare should be a second chance, not a way of life. In my administration we're going to put an end to welfare as we have come to know it. I want to erase the stigma of welfare for good by restoring a simple, dignified principle: No one who can work can stay on welfare forever." See https://www.c-span.org/video/?23518–1/clinton-campaign-speech, accessed November 18, 2016.

127 Lynn Fujiwara, *Mothers without Citizenship: Asian Immigrant Families and the Consequences of Welfare Reform* (Minneapolis: University of Minnesota Press, 2008), 35. Emphasis in original.

128 Robin Dale Jacobson, *The New Nativism: Proposition 187 and the Debate over Immigration* (Minneapolis: University of Minnesota Press, 2008), 125.

129 Fujiwara, *Mothers without Citizenship*, 38. Note: neither of these laws has been rescinded. They continue to be in force as of this writing.

130 Indeed, antiblack and anti-immigrant policies are also connected to antiradicalism. In her study of the deportation case of black communist, Claudia Jones, Carole Boyce Davies makes the case that anti-immigrant (or more specifically deportation) policies are also ideologically and politically motivated. That is, the state has used deportation as a means of quelling radicalism, particularly among blacks. In her study, Davies quotes Michael Hanchard, who argues that "immigration, racial politics and political repression are not so separate and discrete" as, she adds, "U.S. African Americans are often wont to make them." See Carole Boyce

Davies, "Deportable Subjects: U.S. Immigration Laws and the Criminalizing of Communism," *South Atlantic Quarterly* 100, no. 4 (2001): 955.

131 In his study of the antiblack and anti-immigrant propositions passed by the California electorate in the 1990s, political science and ethnic studies professor Daniel HoSang raises the following sets of questions: "Could it be possible instead that white supremacy as an ideological formation has been nourished, rather than attenuated, by notions of progress and political development? What if we imagine racism as a dynamic and evolving force, progressive rather than anachronistic, generative and fluid rather than conservative or static? What if we understand racial hierarchies to be sustained by a broad array of political actors, liberal as well as conservative, and even, at times, by those placed outside the fictive bounds of whiteness?" See Daniel HoSang, *Racial Propositions: Ballot Initiatives and the Making of Postwar California* (Berkeley: University of California Press, 2010), 2. These are questions that my book has also been framed by. HoSang encourages us to query how white supremacy might be sustained by political actors we do not ordinarily think of as being driven by white supremacist agendas (like the Democrats or even non-whites). I explore the latter point in chapter 4.

132 Alexander, *The New Jim Crow*, 57.

133 Coleman argues that the construction of the undocumented immigrant as criminal and terrorist can actually be traced to the immigration debates of the 1980s and 1990s. Mathew Coleman, "Between Public Policy and Foreign Policy: U.S. Immigration Law Reform and the Undocumented Migrant," *Urban Geography* 29, no. 1 (2008): 18.

134 Mary K. Bloodsworth-Lugo and Carmen R. Lugo-Lugo, "Citizenship and the Browning of Terror," *Peace Review* 20, no. 3 (2008): 276.

135 "Anchor babies" is a term that has been used, mainly by conservative political pundits, to describe the U.S.-born children of immigrants. It is believed that immigrants, particularly the undocumented, strategically give birth on U.S. soil to ensure that their children are U.S. citizens and thus serve as "anchors" who will eventually be able to help their parents adjust their immigration status. During the 2016 Republican primary race, Donald Trump made headlines when he claimed that the U.S. born children of undocumented immigrants are not American citizens. See Donald Trump: "'Anchor Babies' Aren't American Citizens," CBS News. Accessed October 24, 2016. http://www.cbsnews.com/news/donald-trump-anchor-babies-arent-american-citizens/. Birthright citizenship is guaranteed by the Fourteenth Amendment of the Constitution.

136 Latinas' sexuality has been a source of public debate even prior to attempts at curbing the birth of "anchor babies." Many conservatives have long worried about high fertility rates among Latina immigrants fearing that their children would exhaust American jobs in addition to deplete social services. See Leo R. Chavez, *The Latino Threat: Constructing Immigrants, Citizens, and the Nation* (Stanford, CA: Stanford University Press, 2008), 70–95.

137 See "8 U.S. Code § 1227—Deportable Aliens," *LII / Legal Information Institute*, Cornell University Law School, n.d., accessed August 5, 2016, https://www.law.cornell.edu/uscode/text/8/1227.

138 It is far beyond the scope of this chapter and indeed this book for me to fully theorize these connections. I have barely scratched the surface, but I do think work by African American and Black Studies scholars is productive and necessary here.

Although they do not necessarily connect immigrant detention and black imprisonment, Jared Sexton and Elizabeth Lee's essay has been especially provocative for me. See Jared Sexton and Elizabeth Lee, "Figuring the Prison: Prerequisites of Torture at Abu Ghraib," *Antipode* 38, no. 5 (2006): 1005–1022.

139 I think Mike Davis makes this point very clear in *Prisoners of the American Dream.*

140 This one of the central arguments in the book by Ronald L. Mize and Alicia C. S. Swords, *Consuming Mexican Labor: From the Bracero Program to NAFTA* (Toronto: University of Toronto Press, 2010).

141 Matthew W. Hughey, "White Backlash in the 'Post-Racial' United States," *Ethnic and Racial Studies* 37, no. 5 (2014): 721–722.

142 Andrew L. Barlow, *Between Fear and Hope: Globalization and Race in the United States* (Lanham, MD: Rowman & Littlefield, 2003). 84.

143 Patricia Zavella, "The Tables Are Turned: Immigration, Poverty, and Social Conflict in California Communities," in *Immigrants Out! The New Nativism and the Anti-Immigrant Impulse in the United States*, ed. Juan F. Perea (New York: New York University Press, 1997), 143.

144 Jacobson, *New Nativism*, xxvii.

145 Hughey, "White Backlash," 725.

146 Monica W. Varsanyi, "Neoliberalism and Nativism: Local Anti-Immigrant Policy Activism and an Emerging Politics of Scale," *International Journal of Urban and Regional Research* 35, no. 2 (2010).

147 To clarify, I am using an expanded notion of citizenship here. Bloemraad, Korteweg, and Yurdakul offer a useful definition: "Citizenship is usually defined as a form of membership in a political and geographic community. It can be disaggregated into four dimensions: legal status, rights, political and other forms of participation in a society, and a sense of belonging." See Irene Bloemraad, Anna Korteweg, and Gökçe Yurdakul, "Citizenship and Immigration: Multiculturalism, Assimilation, and Challenges to the Nation-State," *Annual Review of Sociology* 34, no. 1 (2008): 154. From its inception the suburb was imagined as a site for the exercise of citizenship. As Llewellyn Park's developer Llewellyn S. Haskell put it, the suburb was to serve as "a retreat for a man to exercise his own rights and privileges." See Jackson, *Crabgrass Frontier*, 77.

148 Cohen, *Consumers Republic*, 197.

149 Dianne Harris, "Race, Space, and the Destabilization of Practice." *Landscape Journal* 26, no. 1 (2007): 1.

150 Londoño and Davila make the following observation about contestations over neoliberalism and space in their article, "Race and the Cultural Spaces of Neoliberalism," that is very relevant here: "The organization of space and mapping of difference onto space are central to its privatization and to the dominance of market-driven logics in urban development. However, space is also central to popular interventions and debates over citizenship and belonging. These issues become especially salient in twenty-first century American cities and suburban neighborhoods, where the outnumbering of whites by former 'minorities' poses challenges to normative neoliberal logics and modes of belonging that seek to domesticate and subordinate difference from the mainstream American landscape." See Johana Londoño and Arlene Davila, "Race and the Cultural Spaces of Neoliberalism: Introduction," *Identities* 17, no. 5 (2010): 455.

151 On Asian settlement in the suburbs, see Iver Peterson, "Newest Immigrants Head Straight to New Jersey's Suburbs," *New York Times*, March 9, 2001, accessed August 5, 2016, http://www.nytimes.com/2001/03/10/nyregion/newest-immigrants-head-straight-to-new-jersey-s-suburbs.html. On the significance of the Hispanic population, see Rohan Mascarenhas, "Census Data Shows Hispanics as the Largest Minority in N.J.," nj.com, February 3, 2011, accessed August 5, 2016, http://www.nj.com/news/index.ssf/2011/02/census_data_shows_hispanics_as.html.

152 Although today uprisings in response to police violence against African Americans might popularly be associated with Ferguson, Missouri, or Baltimore, Maryland, images from the uprising in Newark, New Jersey, in response not only to police violence but also to the growing disenfranchisement of African Americans in the city were widely circulated in national magazines like *Time* and *Life* in the summer of 1967.

153 See http://www.nytimes.com/2001/10/28/nyregion/fear-and-loathing.html?_r=0. Accessed November 18, 2016.

154 See http://www.theatlantic.com/politics/archive/2016/09/dissecting-donald-trumps-support/499739/. Accessed November 18, 2016.

155 Evan Osnos, "The Fearful and the Frustrated," *New Yorker*, August 24, 2015, accessed August 5, 2016, http://www.newyorker.com/magazine/2015/08/31/the-fearful-and-the-frustrated.

156 I do not get into an extensive discussion of how I approach my understanding of the concept of race, but suffice it to say, I am critically informed by sociological and critical ethnic studies understandings of race and racism that go beyond the more individualist and psychosocial approaches to race that seem to dominate in American society. That is, most people in the United States, especially whites, think of "racism" as a quality of backward-thinking, uneducated individuals. Whites have a difficult time recognizing that even if they do not harbor consciously, prejudicial ideas about non-whites, they nevertheless benefit from a white supremacist and antiblack social order and that they may even engage in actions that have racially discriminatory outcomes. The anti-immigrant forces I discuss in this book are not necessarily rock-throwing segregationists or white-hood wearing white supremacists, yet that doesn't mean that they aren't engaged in practices that have the effect of keeping their communities white. I can't provide an extensive set of citations here, but here is just a small sampling of the sociologists of race that inform my thinking: Michael Omi, and Howard Winant, *Racial Formation in the United States*, 3rd ed. (New York: Routledge, 2015); Eduardo Bonilla-Silva, "The Essential Social Fact of Race," *American Sociological Review* 64, no. 6 (1999): 899. doi:10.2307/2657410; Evelyn Nakano Glenn, *Unequal Freedom: How Race and Gender Shaped American Citizenship and Labor* (Cambridge, MA: Harvard University Press, 2009); Patricia Hill Collins, *Black Feminist Thought: Knowledge, Consciousness, and the Politics of Empowerment* (New York: Routledge, 2000).

157 Alfonso Gonzales, *Reform without Justice: Latino Migrant Politics and the Homeland Security State* (New York: Oxford University Press, 2014), 5.

158 William Walters, "Secure Borders, Safe Haven, Domopolitics," *Citizenship Studies* 8, no. 3 (2004): 241.

159 The *New York Times* offers a useful chronology of its coverage of what has come to be known as SB 1070, the Arizona Immigration Law, which sparked national debates about the role of states versus the federal government in regulating

immigration. See http://topics.nytimes.com/top/reference/timestopics/subjects/i/immigration-and-emigration/arizona-immigration-law-sb-1070/index.html. Accessed November 18, 2016.

160 Suburbs are much more complex than I am presenting it here. It's not as if there are only two types: white suburbs versus ethnoburbs. I do contrast them here, but there are in fact a great variety of suburbs. See, for a useful typology, Bernadette Hanlon, "A Typology of Inner-Ring Suburbs: Class, Race, and Ethnicity in U.S. Suburbia," *City & Community* 8, no. 3 (2009): 221–246.

Chapter 2 My Hometown: Immigration and Suburban Imaginaries

1 "'My Hometown'—100 Greatest Bruce Springsteen Songs of All Time," *Rolling Stone*, January 16, 2014, accessed February 2, 2015, http://www.rollingstone.com/music/lists/100-greatest-bruce-springsteen-songs-of-all-time-20140116/my-hometown-19691231.

2 Jim Zarolli, "New Jersey's Freehold Draws Undocumented Labor," NPR, August 2, 2005, accessed February 2, 2015, http://www.npr.org/templates/story/story.php?storyId=4782702.

3 See http://newjersey.news12.com/news/freehold-hispanic-community-fearful-as-immigration-raid-rumors-spread-1.11319482. Also see http://www.dailyrecord.com/story/news/2015/09/17/latinos-protest-cartel-signs-morristown-home/32536975/, accessed November 8, 2016.

4 Karen Humes, Nicholas A. Jones, and Roberto R. Ramirez, *Overview of Race and Hispanic Origin, 2010*, Washington, DC: U.S. Dept. of Commerce, Economics and Statistics Administration, U.S. Census Bureau, 2011, accessed August 11, 2016, http://www.census.gov/prod/cen2010/briefs/c2010br-02.pdf.

5 See http://www.pewhispanic.org/files/states/pdf/NJ_11.pdf.

6 "Third World" is a term used to describe formally colonized countries. Sometimes the term "global south" is also used to describe these countries.

7 It is important to note that Puerto Ricans really should not be thought of as immigrants. Since Puerto Rico continues to be U.S. territory and Puerto Ricans carry U.S. passports, they are not technically "foreigners" to the United States. What marks them as "other" or different is the racialization of many as black and the fact that they speak Spanish.

8 See JoAnna Poblete, *Islanders in the Empire: Filipino and Puerto Rican Laborers in Hawai'i* (Urbana: University of Illinois Press, 2014).

9 Though they were allowed entry into the United States and its territories and possessions, it must be pointed out that the Puerto Rican people could not and still cannot exercise U.S. citizenship fully.

10 Ramón Grosfoguel, *Colonial Subjects: Puerto Ricans in a Global Perspective* (Berkeley: University of California Press, 2003), 53–58.

11 José Itzigsohn, *Encountering American Faultlines: Race, Class, and the Dominican Experience in Providence* (New York: Russell Sage Foundation, 2009), 23.

12 This is true, for example, in the Philippines. See Robyn Rodriguez, *Migrants for Export: How the Philippine State Brokers Labor to the World* (Minneapolis: University of Minnesota Press: 2010), 11.

13 Ramona Hernández, *The Mobility of Workers under Advanced Capitalism: Dominican Migration to the United States* (New York: Columbia University Press, 2002), 24–26.

14 Tanya Maria Golash-Boza, *Immigration Nation: Raids, Detentions, and Deportations in Post-9/11 America* (Boulder, CO: Paradigm Publishers, 2012), 35.

15 Alejandro Portes and Rubén G. Rumbaut, *Immigrant America: A Portrait* (Berkeley: University of California Press, 1990), 18.

16 As Chicano historian Rudy Acuña reminds us, "The Border Crossed Us," that is, the borders that currently divide the United States and Mexico have not always been fixed. The United States' history of colonialism and imperialism has shaped what that border would ultimately demarcate. It is beyond the scope of this chapter to speak to this history, but I think it is crucial note it here. See Rodolfo F. Acuña, *Occupied America: A History of Chicanos* (San Francisco: Longman Press, 2011).

17 Joon K. Kim, "California's Agribusiness and the Farm Labor Question: The Transition from Asian to Mexican Labor, 1919–1939," *Aztlán: A Journal of Chicano Studies* 37, no. 2 (2012): 66.

18 Ronald L Mize and Alicia C. S. Swords, *Consuming Mexican Labor: From the Bracero Program to NAFTA* (Toronto: University of Toronto Press, 2010), 3.

19 Ibid., 205. Also see, Rubén Hernández-León, *Metropolitan Migrants: The Migration of Urban Mexicans to the United States* (Berkeley: University of California Press, 2008), 15–16.

20 Audrey Singer, "Twenty-First-Century Gateways: An Introduction," in *Twenty-First-Century Gateways: Immigrant Incorporation in Suburban America*, ed. Audrey Singer, Susan Wiley Hardwick, and Caroline Brettell (Washington, DC: Brookings Institution Press, 2008), 3–30.

21 Elizabth Llorente, "Illegal Immigrants in N.J.: 350,000 and Counting," *Record* (Bergen County, New Jersey), March 22, 2005. See Robert C. Smith, *Mexican New York: Transnational Lives of New Immigrants* (Berkeley: University of California Press, 2006), 20, for some information on Mexicans in New Jersey.

22 David W. Chen and Kareem Fahim, "Immigration Checks Ordered in New Jersey," *New York Times*, August 22, 2007, accessed February 2, 2015, http://www.nytimes.com/2007/08/23/nyregion/23immig.html?_r=0. See also Department of Law and Public Safety, Office of the Attorney General (Anne Milgrim), *Attorney General Law Enforcement Directive 2007–03* (Newark: Office of the Attorney General, 2007).

23 Kareem Fahim, "Immigration Referrals by Police Draw Scrutiny," *New York Times*, March 22, 2008, accessed August 11, 2016, http://www.nytimes.com/2008/03/23/nyregion/23immig.html?pagewanted=all.

24 "Homeland Security," 287(g) Program: A Law Enforcement Partnership (ICE), accessed February 2, 2015, http://www.dhs.gov/external/287g-program-law-enforcement-partnership-ice.

25 https://www.ice.gov/news/releases/ice-new-jersey-recognizes-local-law-enforcement-continued-support; see also http://www.nj.com/hudson/index.ssf/2016/07/hudson_county_extends_immigration_program_advocate.html, accessed November 8, 2016.

26 Claire Marie Celano, "Sheriff's Hopeful Proposes Inmate Immigration," *Tri-Town News*, July 5, 2007, accessed February 2, 2015, http://tri.gmnews.com/news/2007-07-05/Front_page/066.html.

27 Elizabeth Llorente and Miguel Perez, "Policing Illegal Immigration: Dilemma Can Turn American Dream into Nightmare," *Record* (Bergen County, New Jersey), June 26, 2005.
28 Minhaj Hassan, "Morris Detained 600 People for Immigration in 18 Months," *Daily Record* (Morristown, New Jersey), November 30, 2008.
29 Rachel H. Adler, "'But They Claimed to Be Police, Not La Migra': The Interaction of Residency Status, Class, and Ethnicity in a (Post-Patriot Act) New Jersey Neighborhood," *American Behavioral Scientist* 50, no. 1 (2006): 59–60. A news report about a raid in Woodbury describes a similar scenario. See Jim Six, "Agents Arrest 9 Illegal Immigrants in City," *Gloucester Times* (Woodbury, New Jersey), August 17, 2006.
30 David Holthouse, "How Illegal Immigration Is Dividing a Town's Business Owners," *CNN Money*, April 18, 2008, accessed February 23, 2015, http://money.cnn.com/2008/04/17/smbusiness/illegal_immigration_dividing.fsb/.
31 "Rental Overcrowding," *New Jersey Real Estate Report*, June 28, 2006, accessed February 2, 2015, http://njrereport.com/index.php/2006/06/28/rental-overcrowding/.
32 http://www.freeholdboro.org/did-you-know/.
33 See Sofia D. Martos, "Coded Codes: Discriminatory Intent, Modern Political Mobilization, and Local Immigration Ordinances," *NYU Law Review* 85 (2010): 2099.
34 Clare Marie Celano, "Recommendation for Rental ID Check off Council's Table," Nt.gmnews.com, March 7, 2007, accessed February 7, 2015. http://nt.gmnews.com/news/2007–03–07/Front_Page/094.html.
35 Marc Levine, "Your Turn," Nt.gmnews.com, September 10, 2003, accessed February 7, 2015, http://nt.gmnews.com/news/2003–09–10/Editorials/023.html.
36 Carlos Sandoval García, *Shattering Myths on Immigration and Emigration in Costa Rica* (Lanham, MD: Lexington Books, 2011), 162.
37 Joshua Brunstein, "Immigration Stirs Up Bound Brook, Again," *New York Times*, August 8, 2008, accessed May 14, 2013, http://www.nytimes.com/2008/08/10/nyregion/nyregionspecia12/10boundnj.html.
38 Kara Richardson, "MyCentralJersey.com News—Section," MyCentralJersey.com, July 7, 2008, accessed February 7, 2015, http://www.mycentraljersey.com/apps/pbcs.dll/article?AID=%2F20080707%2FNEWS%2F80707036.
39 USA, Department of Justice, Housing and Civil Enforcement, *Consent Decree—U.S. v. Borough of Bound Brook, New Jersey (D.N.J)*, March 12, 2004, accessed February 7, 2015, http://www.justice.gov/crt/about/hce/documents/boundbrooksettle.php.
40 Richardson, "MyCentralJersey.com News—Section," 2008.
41 Maria Newman, "School District Blocks 5 Children of Illegal Immigrants from Classes," *New York Times*, September 20, 2002, accessed February 22, 2015, http://www.nytimes.com/2002/09/21/nyregion/school-district-blocks-5-children-of-illegal-immigrants-from-classes.html.
42 Howard Sutherland, "America Educating the World–At Taxpayer Expense," *VDARECOM*, February 10, 2003, accessed February 7, 2015, http://www.vdare.com/articles/america-educating-the-world-at-taxpayer-expense.
43 For information about immigrants' tax contributions, see Andrew Soergel, "'Undocumented' Immigrants Pay Billions in Taxes: A New Report Suggests

Immigrants in the Country Illegally Provide Local Economies Billions of Dollars in Tax Revenue," *U.S. News & World Report*, March 1, 2016, accessed August 5, 2016, http://www.usnews.com/news/articles/2016–03–01/study-undocumented-immigrants-pay-billions-in-taxes. Linda Newton describes how politicians deploy an "ideology of undeserving" to justify laws that limit immigrants' access to different social services. According to this ideology, "taxpayers" are pitted against "freeloaders" with immigrants assumed to be people who unfairly consume public goods that they should not be entitled to because it is assumed that they do not pay taxes. See Linda Newton, *Illegal, Alien, or Immigrant: The Politics of Immigration Reform* (New York: New York University Press, 2008), 106–107.

44 Peggy McGlone, "ACLU Demands 138 NJ School Districts Change Discriminatory Enrollment Policies," nj.com, April 2, 2014, accessed March 2, 2016, http://www.nj.com/education/2014/04/aclu_demands_138_nj_school_districts_to_change_discriminatory_enrollment_policies.html.

45 See Tom I. Romero, "No Brown Towns: Anti-Immigrant Ordinances and Equality of Educational Opportunity for Latina/os." *Journal of Gender Race and Justice* 12 (2008): 13–56, for a legal analysis of the potential impact of anti-immigrant local ordinances in limiting Latino children's access to education.

46 Iver Peterson, "Hispanic Day Laborers Sue Freehold, Claiming Right to Gather to Seek Work," *New York Times*, December 30, 2003, accessed February 8, 2015, http://www.nytimes.com/2003/12/31/nyregion/hispanic-day-laborers-sue-freehold-claiming-right-to-gather-to-seek-work.html.

47 Andrea Alexander, "Freehold Settles with Day Laborers Soaring Legal Fees Impetus," *Asbury Park Press*, November 14, 2006.

48 Elizabeth Llorente, "Beware of 'Bigots,' Day Laborers Told," *Record* (Bergen County, New Jersey), January 7, 2006.

49 Ibid.

50 Nina Bernstein, "In a New Jersey Town, an Immigration Fight Pits Brother Against Brother," *New York Times*, September 4, 2007, accessed May 14, 2013, http://www.nytimes.com/2007/09/04/nyregion/04brothers.html?pagewanted=all.

51 Paul H. B. Shin, "McD's Ad in Spanish Jolts Burg," *New York Daily News*, July 12, 2006, accessed February 8, 2015, http://www.nydailynews.com/archives/news/mcd-ad-spanish-jolts-burg-article-1.585764. For discussions on the ways "English-only" laws and anti-immigrant nativism historically and through the 1990s, see Raymond Tatalovich, "Official English as Nativist Backlash," in *Immigrants Out! The New Nativism and the Anti-Immigrant Impulse in the United States*, ed. Juan Perea (New York: New York University Press, 1997), 78–102.

52 Natalit Zmuda, "With Home Sales Down, Focus Turns to Upkeep," *Advertising Age Special Report Housing RSS*, July 25, 2011, accessed February 11, 2015, http://adage.com/article/special-report-housing/lowe-s-ikea-emphasize-consumers-eye-home-upkeep/228887/.

53 Richard Harris, *Building a Market: The Rise of the Home Improvement Industry, 1914–1960* (Chicago: University of Chicago Press, 2012), 1.

54 See https://www.nps.gov/history/local-law/arch_stnds_0.htm.

55 See https://savingplaces.org/we-are-saving-places?_ga=1.214396754.452090774.1461544986#.Vx10H5MrJmA.

56 Stacy Denton, "The Rural Past-in-Present and Postwar Sub/urban Progress," *American Studies* 53, no. 2 (2014): 121.

57 Cameron Mccarthy, Alicia P. Rodriguez, Ed Buendia, Shuaib Meacham, Stephen David, Heriberto Godina, K. E. Supriya, and Carrie Wilson-Brown, "Danger in the Safety Zone: Notes on Race, Resentment, and the Discourse of Crime, Violence, and Suburban Security," *Cultural Studies* 11, no. 2 (1997): 278.

58 CMX, *Visioning and Revitalization Plan for the Freehold Center Core Redevelopment Plan Area*, Freehold Borough, 2008, accessed February 11, 2015, http://www.freeholdboro.org/wp-content/uploads/2012/04/Redevelopment-Plan.pdf.

59 Freehold Borough, "Freehold Historic District Area," *Freehold Borough*, n.d., accessed February 11, 2015, http://www.freeholdboro.org.

60 Freehold Borough, *Historic Preservation Advisory Commission*, Freehold Borough, n.d.

61 Freehold Township, *Freehold Township: "Western Monmouth's Family Town"* Community Booklet, Freehold Township, n.d.

62 Barbara Pepe, *Freehold: A Hometown History* (Charleston, SC: Arcadia Publishing, 2003).

63 Fred Richani, "Kevin Coyne Preserves Freehold's Rich History Freehold Borough Is One of the Oldest Towns in the Country, and Kevin Coyne Helps Maintain Its Great History," *Freehold Patch*, February 21, 2011, accessed February 11, 2015, http://patch.com/new-jersey/freehold/kevin-coyne-preserves-freeholds-rich-history.

64 Monmouth County Historical Association, "The Monmouth County Historical Association | Revolutionary History, Landmark Collections | New Jersey," *Monmouth County Historical Association RSS News*, January 29, 2015, accessed February 11, 2015, http://monmouthhistory.org/index.php.

65 Freehold Township, *Freehold Township*, n.d.

66 I think it is important to point out that Freehold Township and other municipalities around the state of New Jersey are fiercely proud of their Revolutionary War pasts. This is not a dynamic that is specific to Freehold Borough. Indeed, that it is not unique to Freehold Borough is important in that it suggests that there is a broader historical and cultural context in New Jersey that shapes the collective memories and identities of different places in the state that can impact the question of who is defined as belonging and not belonging.

67 Leland T. Saito, "From 'Blighted' to 'Historic': Race, Economic Development, and Historic Preservation in San Diego, California," *Urban Affairs Review* 45, no. 166 (November 2009): 168.

68 See http://factfinder.census.gov/faces/tableservices/jsf/pages/productview.xhtml?src=CF (for 2000 data) and http://www.census.gov/quickfacts/table/PST045215/3425200 (for 2010 data).

69 Samantha Henry, "Study Says Day Laborers Often Denied Pay, Abused; Report Paints a Picture of Rampant Exploitation," *Herald News* (Passaic County, NJ), January 26, 2006, Our Towns sec.

70 Roben Farzad, "The Urban Migrants; A Housing Boom Brings Jobs and, Sometimes, Abuse," *New York Times*, July 19, 2005, accessed February 11, 2015, http://www.nytimes.com/2005/07/20/business/20immigrants.html?pagewanted=all.

71 Freehold Borough, "Freehold Historic District Area," n.d.

72 Leo R. Chavez, *The Latino Threat: Constructing Immigrants, Citizens, and the Nation* (Stanford, CA: Stanford University Press, 2008), 3.

73 Bonnie Pfister, "Immigration Advocates Urge New Jersey to Focus on Needs of Immigrant Communities," AP Worldstream, January 23, 2006, accessed March 13, 2015. http://www.highbeam.com/doc/1P1–117688564.html?refid=easy_hf.

74 http://www1.gmnews.com/2004/02/26/federal-agents-nab-nine-sex-offenders/, accessed October 31, 2016.

75 Nick Petruncio, "The Asbury Park Press NJ Ocean County News—Section." *Asbury Park Press*, July 11, 2007, accessed February 7, 2015, http://www.app.com/apps/pbcs.dll/article?AID=%2F20070711%2FNEWS02%2F707110394%2F1004%2FNEWS01.

76 In either case, whether it is the single Latino male or the Latino family both might be considered "queer" in the sense of being non-heteronormative. Though I have focused on the racial politics of anti-immigrant local ordinances, it is crucial to understand the gendered and sexual politics that shape immigration politics and policies. See Eithne Luibheid, "Sexuality, Migration, and the Shifting Line between Legal And Illegal Status," *GLQ: A Journal of Lesbian and Gay Studies* 14, no. 2–3 (2008): 296.

77 Elijah Anderson, "'The White Space'" *Sociology of Race and Ethnicity* 1, no. 1 (2015): 13.

78 See Lisa A. Flores, "Constructing Rhetorical Borders: Peons, Illegal Aliens, and Competing Narratives of Immigration," *Critical Studies in Media Communication* 20, no. 4 (2003): 373.

79 http://www.townofmorristown.org/index.asp?SEC=F638B466–8EA0–41B2–8B4D-E6C51597B2D6&Type=B_LOC.

80 http://www.preservationnation.org/travel-and-sites/distinctive-destinations/dozen-distinctive-destinations.html#.Vu16RZMrLVo.

81 Ibid.

82 https://morristourism.org/history/american-revolution/morristown-national-historical-park.

83 Howard Zinn, "The Massacres of History," *Progressive* 62, no. 8 (1998): 17.

84 http://www.townofmorristown.org/vertical/sites/%7B0813EA2E-B627–4F82-BBB0-DDEE646947B5%7D/uploads/Wallstreet.pdf.

85 http://www.metropolitanat40park.com/.

86 http://www.census.gov/did/www/saipe/data/highlights/2014.html.

87 Morris County, New Jersey, Morris County Visitors Center, *Official County Guide 2006–2007* (Morristown: Morris County Visitors Center, 2006).

88 Dave Caldwell, "Morristown, N.J., Historic with a Lively Downtown," *New York Times*, January 9, 2016, accessed August 17, 2016, http://www.nytimes.com/2016/01/10/realestate/morristown-nj-historic-with-a-lively-downtown.html?_r=1.

89 Michael A. Rockland, "Those People," *New Jersey Monthly*, January 30, 2008, accessed May 10, 2013, http://njmonthly.com/articles/lifestyle/people/those-people.html.

90 Tom Baldwin, "State AG Broadens Officers' Power over Illegal Immigrants," *Courier-Post* (Cherry Hill, New Jersey), August 23, 2007, accessed February 22, 2015, http://www.courierpostonline.com/apps/pbcs.dll/article?AID=%2F20070823%2FNEWS01%2F708230422%2F1006%2Fnews01.

91 See http://www.pbs.org/now/shows/342/.

92 Minhaj Hassan, "Morristown Deputizing Plan Stirs up Outcry: Advocates Oppose Town Cops Serving as Immigration Agents," *Daily Record* (Hanover, New Jersey), March 27, 2007.

93 Ibid.

94 For a historical account of this process, see Khalil Gibran Muhammad, *The Condemnation of Blackness: Race, Crime, and the Making of Modern Urban America* (Cambridge, MA: Harvard University Press, 2010).

95 Hassan, "Morristown Deputizing."

96 David Kocieniewski, "6 Men Arrested in a Terror Plot Against Fort Dix," *New York Times*, May 8, 2007, accessed August 17, 2016, http://www.nytimes.com/2007/05/09/us/09plot.html.

97 http://www.democracynow.org/2015/6/25/did_chris_christie_send_entrapped_innocents.

98 http://www.npr.org/templates/story/story.php?storyId=10254921.

99 Irum Sheikh, "Racializing, Criminalizing, and Silencing 9/11 Deportees," in *Keeping Out the Other: A Critical Introduction to Immigration Enforcement Today*, ed. David Brotherton and Philip Kretsedemas (New York: Columbia University Press, 2008), 81.

100 Amy Kaplan, "Violent Belongings and the Question of Empire Today Presidential Address to the American Studies Association, Hartford, Connecticut, October 17, 2003," *American Quarterly* 56, no. 1 (2004): 10.

101 See Fussell's review of this scholarship: Elizabeth Fussell, "Warmth of the Welcome: Attitudes toward Immigrants and Immigration Policy in the United States," *Annual Review of Sociology* 40, no. 1 (2014): 479–498.

102 Ibid., 486.

103 Hassan, "Morristown Deputizing."

104 Tanya Drobness, "Morristown Immigrants Fearful of New Federal Enforcement Policy," nj.com, July 13, 2009, accessed August 16, 2016, http://www.nj.com/news/index.ssf/2009/07/morristown_immigrants_fearful.html. Also see, Kareem Fahim, "Should Immigration Be a Police Issue?" *New York Times*, April 29, 2007.

105 See Jamie Duffy, "Wind of the Spirit Immigration Forum Brings out Experts on 287(g) in Morristown," nj.com, May 2, 2009, accessed August 16, 2016, http://www.nj.com/morristown/jamieduffy/index.ssf/2009/05/wind_of_the_spirit_forum_bring.html. Also see, Elizabeth Llorente, "Morris Rejects Jail Wing for Illegals," NorthJersey.com, February 22, 2008, accessed May 10, 2013, http://www.northjersery.com/news/immigration/15865522.html.

106 http://www.nytimes.com/2007/07/29/nyregion/29rally.html?_r=0. Also see the blog post by Illegalprotest.com, which describes itself as representing "American citizens who are tired of the illegal alien invasion," which posts information about the rally's agenda. http://illegalprotest.com/2007/07/26/support-morristown-njs-proamerica-rally-this-saturday-july-28th/.

107 http://symsess.blogspot.com/2007/08/morristown-proamerica-rally-peter.html. I cannot fully verify whether this is an accurate transcription of the speech, but this blogger posts photos from the rally on another site he/she manages that seem to attest to his/her attendance. https://americanhumanity.wordpress.com/2008/07/16/a-change-of-heart-one-year-after-the-proamerica-rally/.

108 http://www.nownj.org/njNews/2007/0725%201,000%20expected%20at%20Morristown%20immigration%20rallies%20.htm.

109 http://www.911fsa.org/.

110 See Matthew Coleman, "What Counts as the Politics and Practice of Security, and Where? Devolution and Immigrant Insecurity after 9/11," *Annals of the Association of American Geographers* 99, no. 5 (2009): 904–913. doi:10.1080/00045600903245888, for a critical geographical approach to unpacking security and insecurity with respect to post-9/11 immigration politics and policies.

111 http://www.nj.gov/education/legal/commissioner/2016/aug/291–16.pdf, accessed October 31, 2016. See also, http://www.nj.com/education/2016/08/state_overrules_local_voters_orders_32m_school_exp.html, accessed October 31, 2016.

112 https://voicesofny.org/2015/09/trumps-anti-immigrant-message-resonates-for-one-nj-homeowner/, accessed October 31, 2016.

113 http://www.nj.com/news/index.ssf/2015/03/as_tens_of_thousands_flee_nj_immigrants_are_filling_the_void.html, accessed October 31, 2016.

Chapter 3 The New "Main Street"?: Ethnoburbs and the Complex Politics of Race

1 See http://www.oaktreeroad.us/. Accessed November 19, 2016.

2 Joseph Berger, "A Place Where Indians, Now New Jerseyans, Thrive," *New York Times*, April 26, 2008, accessed February 14, 2015, http://www.nytimes.com/2008/04/27/nyregion/nyregionspecia12/27indianj.html?pagewanted=all&_r=0.

3 Joel Stein, "My Own Private India: How the Jersey Town Named for Thomas Edison Became Home to the All-American Guindian," *Time*, July 5, 2010, accessed June 6, 2014, http://content.time.com/time/magazine/article/0,9171,1999416,00.html#ixzz2j3M2oxEg.

4 Lindsay Gellman, "Indians 'Shocked,' 'Offended' by Joel Stein's TIME Article," *Huffington Post*, July 2, 2010, accessed February 14, 2015, http://www.huffingtonpost.com/2010/07/01/indians-shocked-offended_n_632483.html.

5 Stein, "My Own Private India," 2010.

6 Justine Leigh Abrams, "Big Box Retailer: Harmless Chain or Community Pain?" (undergraduate thesis, Rutgers University, 2011).

7 Mia Tuan, *Forever Foreigners or Honorary Whites?: The Asian Ethnic Experience Today* (New Brunswick, NJ: Rutgers University Press, 1998), 37.

8 Wei Li, *Ethnoburb: The New Ethnic Community in Urban America* (Honolulu: University of Hawai'i Press, 2009), 1.

9 I use the term "natives" here (and in some other places throughout the book) because the fact is many who assume the subjectivity of "native" simply are not. After all, the United States is a settler colonial country.

10 A good book-length study that examines questions of race, immigration, and residential assimilation is John Iceland's *Where We Live Now: Immigration and Race in the United States* (Berkeley: University of California Press, 2009).

11 See http://www.apa.org/monitor/nov01/contact.aspx. Accessed November 19, 2016.

12 "An Age of Transformation." *Economist*, May 31, 2008, 33.

13 See Walter Greason, *Suburban Erasure: How the Suburbs Ended the Civil Rights Movement in New Jersey* (Madison, NJ: Fairleigh Dickinson University Press, 2013), for a discussion of African Americans' establishment of and settlement into

suburban communities, especially in southern New Jersey. Perhaps more important, Greason also explores how the kind of autonomy African Americans achieved in creating these communities, while positive, had the effect of curbing more radical critiques of broader processes of segregation at work across the state that came with mass suburbanization.

14 John R. Logan, Wenquan Zhang, and Richard D. Alba, "Immigrant Enclaves and Ethnic Communities in New York and Los Angeles," *American Sociological Review* 67, no. 2 (2002): 299.

15 Joel Kotkin and Wendell Cox, "The Evolving Geography of Asian America: Suburbs Are New High-Tech Chinatowns," *Forbes*, March 18, 2015, accessed August 18, 2016, http://www.forbes.com/sites/joelkotkin/2015/03/18/the-evolving-geography-of-asian-america-suburbs-are-new-high-tech-chinatowns/#477be5eb7f76.

16 For the reference to "majority minority" suburbs, see Wendy Cheng, "'Diversity' on Main Street? Branding Race and Place in the New 'Majority-Minority' Suburbs," *Identities* 17, no. 5 (2010): 458. Also see Frey, *Melting Pot Suburbs*, 1. For a longitudinal study of neighborhood change, including the rise of relatively affluent suburbs where minorities are living more and more with other minorities as opposed to whites, see Richard D. Alba, John R. Logan, and Brian J. Stults, "The Changing Neighborhood Contexts of the Immigrant Metropolis," *Social Forces* 79, no. 2 (2000): 587–621.

17 William H. Frey, *Melting Pot Suburbs: A Census 2000 Study of Suburban Diversity* (Washington, DC: Brookings Institution Press, 2001), 8.

18 For a study of this process, see Richard D. Alba, Nancy A. Denton, Shu-Yin J. Leung, and John R. Logan, "Neighborhood Change under Conditions of Mass Immigration: The New York City Region, 1970–1990," *International Migration Review* 29, no. 3 (1995): 625–656.

19 Pawan Dhingra, *Life behind the Lobby: Indian American Motel Owners and the American Dream* (Stanford, CA: Stanford University Press, 2012), 5.

20 See https://www.whitehouse.gov/blog/2011/11/22/asian-american-entrepreneurship-asset-nation-s-economy. Accessed November 19, 2016.

21 Ibid.

22 Cheng, "'Diversity' on Main Street?," 459.

23 See http://www.neworleans.me/journal/detail/761/NOLA-Filipino-History-Stretches-for-Centuries. Accessed November 19, 2016.

24 There are certainly other texts out there, but my own introduction to early Asian American immigration came by way of University of California, Santa Barbara, Asian American Studies professor Sucheng Chan. See Sucheng Chan, *Asian Americans: An Interpretive History* (Boston: Twayne, 1991).

25 Ibid.

26 Andrew Hsiao, "The Hidden History of Asian-American Activism in New York City," *Social Policy* 28, no. 4 (1998): 23–31.

27 National Archives, *National Archives and Records Administration*, accessed February 12, 2015, http://www.archives.gov/research/chinese-americans/guide.html.

28 In legal parlance, "alien" refers to a person who is not a citizen of a country.

29 Bill Ong Hing, *Making and Remaking Asian America through Immigration Policy, 1850–1990* (Stanford, CA: Stanford University Press, 1993), 53–60.

See http://encyclopedia.densho.org/Alien_land_laws/ for a list of anti-Asian land laws beyond California. Accessed November 19, 2016.

30 Angelo N. Ancheta, *Race, Rights, and the Asian American Experience* (New Brunswick, NJ: Rutgers University Press, 2006), 29.

31 Catherine Ceniza Choy, *Empire of Care: Nursing and Migration in Filipino American History* (Durham, NC: Duke University Press, 2003), 33.

32 Rick Baldoz, *The Third Asiatic Invasion: Empire and Migration in Filipino America, 1898–1946* (New York: New York University Press, 2011), 114.

33 Bruce LaBrack and Karen Leonard, "Conflict and Compatibility in Punjabi-Mexican Immigrant Families in Rural California, 1915–1965," *Journal of Marriage and Family* 46, no. 3 (1984): 529.

34 Brett H. Melendy, *Asians in America: Filipinos, Koreans, and East Indians* (Boston: Twayne, 1977), 188.

35 Vivek Bald, *Bengali Harlem and the Lost Histories of South Asian America* (Cambridge, MA: Harvard University Press, 2013), 6.

36 Hing, *Making and Remaking Asian America*, 32.

37 Yen Le Espiritu, *Asian American Women and Men: Labor, Laws, and Love* (Thousand Oaks, CA: Sage, 1997), 21.

38 Vijay Prashad, *The Karma of Brown Folk* (Minneapolis: University of Minnesota Press, 2000), 47–68.

39 Ronald Smothers, "A New Chapter for a Village, Once Barracks," *New York Times*, October 3, 2006, accessed August 18, 2016, http://www.nytimes.com/2006/10/04/nyregion/04camp.html?_r=0.

40 Prashad, *The Karma of Brown Folk*, viii.

41 Kirk Semple, "In a Shift, Biggest Wave of Migrants Is Now Asian," *New York Times*, June 18, 2012, accessed February 14, 2015, http://www.nytimes.com/2012/06/19/us/asians-surpass-hispanics-as-biggest-immigrant-wave.html?_r=0.

42 Immigration Policy Center, *New Americans in New Jersey: The Political and Economic Power of Immigrants, Latinos, and Asians in the Garden State* (Washington, DC: Immigration Policy Center, 2013), 2.

43 Brad Parks, "Asian Population Bubble Growing: Trendy Tapioca Tea Drink Mirrors N.J. Census Surge," *Star-Ledger*, August 7, 2008. Also see Brad Parks, "Census Shows Spike N.J. Asian Population," nj.com, August 7, 2008, accessed August 18, 2016, http://www.nj.com/news/index.ssf/2008/08/census_shows_dramatic_jump_in.html.

44 Asian American Federation of New York Census Information Center, *Census Profile: New Jersey's Asian American Population* (New York: Asian American Federation of New York, 2004), 1.

45 Ibid., 2.

46 See http://lwd.dol.state.nj.us/labor/lpa/pub/lmv/lmv_18.pdf. Accessed November 19, 2016.

47 S. Mitra Kalita, *Suburban Sahibs: Three Immigrant Families and Their Passage from India to America* (New Brunswick, NJ: Rutgers University Press, 2003).

48 See Federal Bureau of Investigation: http://www.fbi.gov/about-us/investigate/civilrights/hate_crimes/overview; accessed March 9, 2015.

49 My thinking about race as a "social construction" has been largely shaped by Michael Omi and Howard Winant's work in *Racial Formation in the United States*, 3rd ed. (New York: Routledge, 2015), 105–136.

50 Junaid Akram Rana, *Terrifying Muslims: Race and Labor in the South Asian Diaspora* (Durham, NC: Duke University Press, 2011, 85).
51 See http://www.sikhcoalition.org for more information.
52 Deborah N. Misir, "The Murder of Navroze Mody: Race, Violence, and the Search for Order," in *Contemporary Asian America: A Multidisciplinary Reader*, ed. Min Zhou and James V. Gatewood (New York: New York University Press, 2000) 501–517, 505. Also see Elizabeth Gutierrez, "The 'Dotbuster' Attacks: Hate Crime Against Asian Indians in Jersey City, New Jersey," *Middle States Geographer* (1996): 30–38.
53 Baldoz, *The Third Asiatic Invasion*, 141.
54 Misir, "The Murder of Navroze Mody," 502.
55 Douglass Crouse, "Bigots Target Hindu Family," *Bergen Record* (New Jersey), June 1, 2006.
56 PTI, "Indian Man Attacked in Apparent Hate Crime in New Jersey," *Times of India*, July 7, 2015, accessed August 18, 2016, http://timesofindia.indiatimes.com/nri/us-canada-news/Indian-man-attacked-in-apparent-hate-crime-in-New-Jersey/articleshow/47968471.cms.
57 Al Kamen, "After Immigration, an Unexpected Fear," *Washington Post*, November 16, 1992, accessed August 18, 2016, https://www.washingtonpost.com/archive/politics/1992/11/16/after-immigration-an-unexpected-fear/d082d2d2–8918–4609–8ad4–27a492d96ed2/.
58 Ibid.
59 Misir, "The Murder of Navroze Mody," 501.
60 Claire J. Kim, "The Racial Triangulation of Asian Americans," *Politics & Society* 27, no. 1 (1999): 105–138.
61 Nazli Kibria, "Not Asian, Black or White? Reflections on South Asian American Racial Identity," *Amerasia Journal* 22, no. 2 (1996): 77–86.
62 See Lisa Marie Cacho, *Social Death: Racialized Rightlessness and the Criminalization of the Unprotected* (New York: New York University Press, 2012).
63 Kevin Coyne, "Turbans Make Targets, Some Sikhs Find," *New York Times*, June 15, 2008, accessed May 14, 2013, http://www.nytimes.com/2008/06/15/nyregion/nyregionspecia12/15colnj.html.
64 Derald Wing Sue, "Racial Microaggressions in Everyday Life," *Psychology Today*, October 5, 2010, accessed August 18, 2016, https://www.psychologytoday.com/blog/microaggressions-in-everyday-life/201010/racial-microaggressions-in-everyday-life.
65 Coyne, "Turbans Make Targets, Some Sikhs Find."
66 Sandhya Shukla, "Building Diaspora and Nation: The 1991 'Cultural Festival of India,'" *Cultural Studies* 11, no. 2 (1997): 296–315. See also http://www.swaminarayan.org/festivals/1991usa/.
67 Ibid., 302.
68 Monisha Das Gupta, *Unruly Immigrants: Rights, Activism, and Transnational South Asian Politics in the United States* (Durham, NC: Duke University Press, 2006), 77.
69 Vivodh Anand, "Unwelcome in Edison: Report of a Town's Xenophobic Conflation of Race and Religion," in *Democracy and Religion: Free Exercise and Diverse Visions*, ed. David W. Odell-Scott (Kent, OH: Kent State University Press, 2004), 282.
70 Ibid., 287.

71 *Indo-Amer. Cultural Soc. v. Tp. of Edison*, 9758 Lexis Nexus (United States District Court, D. New Jersey July 10, 1996). Also see Andy Newman, "Ruling Favors Hindu Festival," *New York Times*, September 30, 1996, accessed February 18, 2015, http://www.nytimes.com/1996/09/30/nyregion/ruling-favors-hindu-festival.html.
72 Anand, "Unwelcome in Edison," 290.
73 Ibid.
74 Chris Gaetano, "Durham Woods Assault Suspects Arrested," *Sentinel*, October 24, 2007, accessed February 22, 2015, http://em.gmnews.com/news/2007–10–24/front_page/003.html.
75 Brian Amaral, "Organizers of Navratri Celebration in Edison Pledge Quiet Weekend after Noise Complaints," nj.com, October 2, 2014, accessed August 18, 2016, http://www.nj.com/middlesex/index.ssf/2014/10/navratri_festival_edison_noise_complaints.html.
76 Prema A. Kurien, "Multiculturalism and 'American' Religion: The Case of Hindu Indian Americans," *Social Forces* 85, no. 2 (2006): 724.
77 See https://www.irs.gov/charities-non-profits/churches-religious-organizations. Accessed November 19, 2016.
78 Prashad, *The Karma of Brown Folk*, 2.
79 It is also true that adherents of non-Christian monotheistic religions like Judaism feel marginalized in the United States since Christian holidays like Christmas and Easter, for all intents and purposes, are observed by state institutions as well as the private sector. Of course, even though Islam shares common roots with Judaism and Christianity, it is treated with great suspicion.
80 Brent Johnson, "Edison's Angels Fighting to Keep Their Fields," *Star-Ledger*, May 3, 2009, accessed February 18, 2015, http://www.nj.com/news/local/index.ssf/2009/05/edisons_angels_fighting_to_kee.html.
81 Ibid.
82 Borja Majumdar and Sean Brown, "Why Baseball, Why Cricket? Differing Nationalisms, Differing Challenges," *International Journal of the History of Sport* 24, no. 2 (2007): 139.
83 http://sepiamutiny.com/blog/2005/06/09/edison_may_get/. Accessed November 19, 2016.
84 Adam Green, "Jersey Boy," *American Prospect*, January 9, 2006, accessed February 14, 2015, http://prospect.org/article/jersey-boy.
85 Patricia A. Miller and Rochelle Lauren Gerszberg, "Edison at Critical Turning Point, Stephens Says," *Edison Metuchen Sentinel*, October 26, 2005, accessed February 15, 2015, http://www1.gmnews.com/2005/10/26/edison-at-critical-turning-point-stephens-says/.
86 Yung Kim, "Groups Accept Shock Jocks' Apology; NJ 101.5-FM, Coalition Reach 'Understanding,'" *Record* (Bergen County, New Jersey), May 28, 2005, News sec., http://02e1137.netsolhost.com/Villages/Asian/arts_culture_media/pc_jersey_boys_0505.asp.
87 Ibid.
88 http://aaldef.org/press-releases/press-release/aaldef-exit-poll-reveals-trends-in-growing-nj.html. Accessed November 19, 2016.
89 Green, "Jersey Boy."
90 Ibid.

91 Lisa Featherstone, "Wal-Mart's Good (and Bad) Sides," *Nation*, June 10, 2005, accessed August 19, 2016, https://www.thenation.com/article/wal-marts-good-and-bad-sides/. Also see http://www1.gmnews.com/2004/12/21/planning-board-refuses-to-reopen-wal-mart-hearing/, accessed November 4, 2016.

92 Tom Caiazza, Tom. "Developer Sues Township, Mayor over Building Permit," GMNews Archive, May 1, 2007, accessed August 19, 2016, http://www1.gmnews.com/2007/05/02/developer-sues-township-mayor-over-building-permit/.

93 Kristina Nwazota, "Challenging Wal-Mart," *PBS*, August 20, 2004, accessed August 19, 2016, http://www.pbs.org/newshour/updates/business-july-dec04-challenging-08–20/.

94 Cheng, "'Diversity' on Main Street," 132.

95 Ibid.

96 Jonathan Miller, "Edison Works to Cope With Simmering Ethnic Tensions," *New York Times*, October 09, 2006, Accessed August 19, 2016, http://www.nytimes.com/2006/10/10/nyregion/10edison.html?_r=0; also see Diane C. Walsh, "Edison Police Sued over Immigration Arrest of Protester," nj.com, July 2, 2008, accessed August 19, 2016, http://www.nj.com/news/index.ssf/2008/07/edison_police_sued_over_immigr.html.

97 See http://www.passtheroti.com/posts/139; accessed November 19, 2016. Also see, Suleman Din, "Asian Indians Face Off with Police Allies," *Star-Ledger*, August 3, 2006.

98 Ibid.

99 Asian American Legal Defense and Education Fund, "Press Release: Indian Immigrant Sues Edison Township, NJ Police for Brutality and Violation of First Amendment Rights—AALDEF," July 2, 2008, accessed August 19, 2016, http://aaldef.org/press-releases/press-release/indian-immigrant-sues-edison-township-nj-police-for-brutality-and-violation-of-first-amendment-right.html.

100 Sofya Aptekar, "Organizational Life and Political Incorporation of Two Asian Immigrant Groups: A Case Study," *Ethnic and Racial Studies* 32, no. 9 (2009): 1528.

101 Douglass Crouse, "Bigots Target Hindu Family," *Bergen Record* (New Jersey), June 1, 2006.

102 Justine Leigh Abrams, "Big Box Retailer: Harmless Chain or Community Pain?" (undergraduate thesis, Rutgers University, 2011).

103 http://www.nj.com/news/local/index.ssf/2009/06/edison_councilwoman_antonia_ri.html.

104 http://www.nj.com/middlesex/index.ssf/2013/09/racist_graffiti_hits_indian-american_mayoral_candidates_campaign_signs_in_edison.html.

105 D. W., "Karaoke Crackdown Stirs Ethnic Anger in Palisades Park," *New York Times*, September 8, 1996, http://search.proquest.com/docview/109650121?accountid=14505.

106 Ibid.

107 http://aapaonline.org/2013/03/29/asian-american-stereotypes/.

108 R. Hanley, "New Jersey Towns Tell Asian-Owned Stores: Advertise in English, Too," *New York Times*, April 9, 1996, http://search.proquest.com/docview/430551732?accountid=14505.

109 http://www.nj.com/news/index.ssf/2015/11/10_most_spoken_languages_in_nj_other_than_english.html.

110 The Asian ethnoburb of Fort Lee, New Jersey, is the focus of study by Noriko Matsumoto, "Constructing Multiethnic Space: East Asian Immigration in Fort Lee, New Jersey" (PhD diss., City University of New York Graduate Center, 2012). Matsumoto suggests that "fluid social and spatial relations" exist in Fort Lee. She finds that that the presence of Asian (specifically Korean American) entrepreneurs, while met with some tension, has not necessarily led to outright conflicts and has in fact been welcomed in many ways. Indeed, this is a place where local notions of "American" have become more inclusive of Korean Americans. Although it is beyond the scope of this study, it would be important to examine how various Asian groups may be differently racialized in the New Jersey context. To what extent are Indians, as brown Asians, racialized differently from East Asians? And even among East Asians, might religion and history or diplomatic relations shape how Koreans are racialized versus, for example, the Japanese or Chinese?

111 http://www.nj.com/news/local/index.ssf/2009/06/edison_councilwoman_antonia ri.html.

112 http://www.nj.com/news/index.ssf/2011/03/nj_commission_factors_in_fast-.html. It should be noted that the election of a second-generation immigrant in the ethnoburb of Prospect Park was also met with an aggressive backlash from whites. Prospect Park is located about fifteen miles west of Palisades Park (and therefore just a bit farther from New York City), and 31 percent of its population is foreign-born. More than half of the borough's population is Latino and another 20 percent is African American. When Syria-born Mohamed T. Kairullah first ran for mayor, after serving several terms as a council member, fliers around town demanded that he not run in "our clean town"; moreover, they claimed that his victory would "poison our thoughts" about America. Presumably because he is both Syrian and Muslim, he poses some kind of threat. Indeed, insinuations were made that he had terrorist connections. Nevertheless, his colleagues on the council picked him for the slot. He continues to serve as Prospect Park's mayor. Unlike Choi, Kairullah has gotten and continues to get the backing of key Democratic Party players. It is beyond the scope of this chapter to fully analyze and understand what made a mayoral candidate accused of being a terrorist (Kairullah) in one town more successful than a mayoral candidate accused of serving special (racial) interests (Choi) in another town. However, my own sense about him was that his demeanor probably appealed to whites on some level. When we met for an interview, Kairullah donned a volunteer firefighter jacket. His affect felt very "blue collar." Although he wasn't born in the United States, Kairullah spent much of his growing up in Prospect Park and seems, perhaps because of his working-class demeanor, to have been accepted as a genuine hometown boy. Whatever the explanation may be, it is clear that the politics of race and immigration continue to be front and center in American's ethnoburbs. Mayor Khairullah's successful bid for the office of mayor in his ethnoburb, though not necessarily an Asian suburb, may point to new possibilities and openings for immigrants of color in different places in the state of New Jersey. Despite the fact that Khairullah is Muslim and was born in Syria and indeed that his town is in slightly closer proximity to New York than Morristown, where post-9/11 national security fears have shaped local political discourse in significant ways, he is now in leadership. I can't answer the question of why or how that happened, but that it did is worth paying attention to.

Chapter 4 Being the Problem: Perspectives from Immigrant New Jerseyans

1 W. E. B. Du Bois, *The Souls of Black Folk: Essays and Sketches* (1903; reprint Greenwich, CT: Fawcett Publications, 1961).
2 Moustafa Bayoumi, *How Does It Feel to Be a Problem?: Being Young and Arab in America* (New York: Penguin Press, 2008), 6.
3 I do not mean to conflate the racialized experiences of different peoples of color. However, I draw inspiration from Du Bois as well as Bayoumi for their scholar-activism and for the ways they foreground their own experiences in these particular texts. Their racialization experiences are ultimately what drive them to do the work that they do. This is true for me too.
4 This is certainly true when you do a search on of the terms "immigrant terrorist" on Google. Of course, many white Americans may fear that anyone with links to Islam and the Arab world, regardless of their garb, is potentially a sleeper-cell, terrorist.
5 http://thehill.com/blogs/ballot-box/presidential-races/251239-trump-shares-ideas-for-real-immigration-reform.
6 http://www.wsj.com/articles/trump-saying-illegal-immigrants-have-to-go-targets-obama-orders-1439738967.
7 http://www.wsj.com/articles/donald-trump-calls-for-ban-on-muslim-entry-into-u-s-1449526104.
8 Du Bois, *Souls of Black Folk*, 13.
9 Sunaina Maira, *Missing: Youth, Citizenship, and Empire after 9/11* (Durham, NC: Duke University Press, 2009), 26 (emphasis in the original).
10 Cecilia Menjívar and Leisy J. Abrego, "Legal Violence: Immigration Law and the Lives of Central American Immigrants," *American Journal of Sociology* 117, no. 5 (2012): 1383.
11 Danny Breslauer, "Travel Coach Canham Finds a Global Village on H.P. Turf," *Mirror* (Highland Park, NJ), December 9, 2010, 11.
12 David L. Andrews, Robert Pitter, Detlev Zwick, and Darren Ambrose, "Soccer, Race, and Suburban Space," in *Sporting Dystopias: The Making and Meaning of Urban Sport Cultures*, ed. Ralph C. Wilcox (Albany: State University of New York Press, 2003), 197.
13 Jennifer H. Cunningham, "Program Takes Aim at School Bullying; Curriculum Emphasizes Inclusion, Civility," *Record* (Bergen County, New Jersey), February 24, 2006, Passaic edition.
14 Rene D. Flores, "Taking the Law into Their Own Hands: Do Local Anti-Immigrant Ordinances Increase Gun Sales?" *Social Problems* 62 (2015): 363–390.
15 The Hazelton case, though not entirely different from the cases I discuss in New Jersey, has been a topic of focus for many immigration scholars and advocates. I think much of this attention has to do with its litigious nature. It was taken all the way to the Supreme Court.
16 Janet Post, "Three Arrested in Beating Death of Immigrant in Pennsylvania," *Militant*, August 4, 2008.
17 https://www.splcenter.org/fighting-hate/intelligence-report/2011/immigrant%E2%80%99s-beating-death-police-cover-shake-pennsylvania-community.
18 Flores, "Taking the Law Into Their Own Hands," 376.
19 Ibid., 381.

20 Andre Jacobs, "An Immigrant Segment by Radio's 'Jersey Guys' Draws Fire," *New York Times*, March 22, 2007, accessed February 9, 2015, http://www.nytimes.com/2007/03/23/nyregion/23jersey.html?ref=nyregion.

21 Roxanne Lynn Doty, *The Law into Their Own Hands: Immigration and the Politics of Exceptionalism* (Tucson: University of Arizona Press, 2009), 72.

22 Christopher A. Bail, "The Fringe Effect: Civil Society Organizations and the Evolution of Media Discourse about Islam since the September 11th Attacks." *American Sociological Review* 77, no. 6 (2012): 855–79. doi:10.1177/0003122412465743, 870.

23 http://www.splcenter.org/get-informed/case-docket.

24 Maria Luisa Tucker, "A Neo-Nazi Field Trip to the Met," *Village Voice*, June 5, 2007, accessed August 17, 2016, http://www.villagevoice.com/2007-06-05/news/a-neo-nazi-field-trip-to-the-met/.

25 See http://www.nj.com/mercer/index.ssf/2011/04/neo-nazi_demonstration_at_nj_s.html, accessed November 5, 2016.

26 See http://www.njhomelandsecurity.gov/analysis/whitesupremacists, accessed November 5, 2016. Also see, http://www.nj.com/south/index.ssf/2015/03/new_jersey_has_fourth_highest_number_of_hate_group.html, accessed November 5, 2016.

27 Elizabeth Llorente, "Group Targets Illegal Immigration; Palisades Park Protest Small but Ardent in Message," *Record* (Bergen County, New Jersey), January 8, 2006.

28 Ralph Ellison, *Invisible Man* (New York: Vintage International, 1995).

29 http://www.nytimes.com/2004/01/07/nyregion/clinton-apologizes-for-gandhi-remark.html?_r=0.

30 Tiffany Yip, Gilbert C. Gee, and David T. Takeuchi, "Racial Discrimination and Psychological Distress: The Impact of Ethnic Identity and Age among Immigrant and United States–born Asian Adults," *Developmental Psychology* 44, no. 3 (2008): 789.

31 For a study of Latino immigrants, see Lorraine Moya Salas, Cecilia Ayón, and Maria Gurrola, "Estamos Traumados: The Effect of Anti-Immigrant Sentiment and Policies on the Mental Health of Mexican Immigrant Families," *Journal of Community Psychology* 41, no. 8 (2013): 1005–1020. For a study of Indian immigrants, see Muninder K. Ahluwalia and Laura Pelletticre, "Sikh Men Post-9/11: Misidentification, Discrimination, and Coping," *Asian American Journal of Psychology* 1, no. 4 (2010): 303–314.

32 Quoted inTram Nguyen, *We Are All Suspects Now: Untold Stories from Immigrant Communities after 9/11* (Boston: Beacon Press, 2005), 19.

33 See my discussion of "misrecognition" in chapter 3.

34 Jasbir Puar and Amit Rai, "Perverse Projectiles Under the Specter of (Counter) terrorism: The Remaking of a Model Minority," *Social Text* (2004): 82.

35 For research that documents the psychological impact of post-9/11 racial misidentification and profiling on Sikh men, see Ahluwalia and Pellettiere, "Sikh Men Post-9/11," 303–314.

36 Amnesty as such has not been granted to undocumented immigrants since the Reagan administration in the 1980s. The Obama administration offered some relief for the children of undocumented parents through the Deferred Action for

Childhood Arrivals (DACA) policy, but it is not a categorical "amnesty" program for undocumented immigrants.

37 Cacho, *Racialized Rightlessness*, 17.

38 The most recent attempt at introducing a driver's license to undocumented immigrants was in 2015. See, http://www.northjersey.com/news/n-j-senate-bill-granting-driver-s-licenses-to-unauthorized-immigrants-getting-reworked-1.1464980, accessed November 5, 2016.

39 In Atlantic City, 8,000 people were reported to have lost their jobs in 2014 with the closure of four casinos. It is unclear whether casinos in New Jersey are still a draw for low-skilled immigrants with limited English skills. See http://www.pressofatlanticcity.com/business/immigrants-reconsider-futures-as-casinos-shut/article_c8ab458a-78f8–11e4–879f-7bc43d4dcb75.html, accessed November 5, 2016. Interestingly, despite the casino closures, immigrants kept Atlantic City from suffering a major population loss. New immigrants settled in the community to join their families and friends, even though many had lost their jobs. See http://www.pressofatlanticcity.com/news/immigrants-lessen-atlantic-county-population-loss/article_18b67326-f29f-11e5-a4d9-dbf9c60f7803.html, accessed November 5, 2016.

40 Thierry Devos and Hafsa Mohamed, "Shades of American Identity: Implicit Relations between Ethnic and National Identities," *Social and Personal Psychology Compass* 8, no. 12 (2014): 739–754.

41 Ibid.

42 Matthew Frye Jacobson, *Whiteness of a Different Color: European Immigrants and the Alchemy of Race* (Cambridge, MA: Harvard University Press, 1998), 4.

43 Sherry B. Ortner, *New Jersey Dreaming: Capital, Culture, and the Class of '58* (Durham, NC: Duke University Press, 2003), 51.

44 http://www.nytimes.com/2007/06/28/washington/28cnd-immig.html, accessed November 5, 2016.

45 See http://www.trentonian.com/article/TT/20011119/TMP02/311199999, accessed November 5, 2016. Jersey City has been the site of anti-terror investigation since before 9/11 as the terrorists associated with the 1993 bombing of the World Trade Center, see http://edition.cnn.com/2001/US/09/26/inv.newjersey.cities/, accessed November 5, 2016.

46 Suleman Din, "Terror City," *Colorlines* 7, no. 3 (Spring 2004).

47 Amnesty International, "USA: Jailed Without Justice," Amnesty International USA, March 25, 2009, accessed August 20, 2016, http://www.amnestyusa.org/research/reports/usa-jailed-without-justice.

48 Jamie Duffy, "New Jersey Pro-immigration Leaders Call for a Halt to 287(g) on the Steps of Town Hall," nj.com, October 8, 2009.

49 Linda Greenhouse, "Supreme Court Limits Detention in Cases of Deportable Immigrants," *New York Times*, June 28, 2001, accessed August 20, 2016, http://www.nytimes.com/2001/06/29/us/supreme-court-issue-confinement-supreme-court-limits-detention-cases-deportable.html?_r=0.

50 Tanya Maria Golash-Boza, *Immigration Nation: Raids, Detentions, and Deportations in Post-9/11 America* (Boulder, CO: Paradigm Publishers, 2012) 64.

51 Ibid.

52 Amnesty International, "USA: Jailed Without Justice."

53 See https://www.ice.gov/detention-facilities#, accessed November 5, 2016.

54 See the ACLU-New Jersey's 2007 report on immigrant detention in the state, https://www.aclu-nj.org/files/9613/1540/4573/051507DetentionReport.pdf, accessed November 5, 2016.
55 Mark Dow, *American Gulag: Inside U.S. Immigration Prisons* (Berkeley: University of California Press, 2004), 8. The ACLU-New Jersey's 2007 report on immigrant detention in New Jersey provides further details on the revenues county jails have generated by renting space to the DHS for housing immigrant detainees, see https://www.aclu-nj.org/files/9613/1540/4573/051507DetentionReport.pdf, accessed November 5, 2016. A 2014 report indicates that county jails can even generate revenue from charging exorbitant rates to immigrant detainees for their telephone use. See, https://www.thenation.com/article/dialing-dollars-how-county-jails-profit-immigrant-detainees/, accessed November 5, 2016.
56 Dow, *American Gulag*, 46.
57 New Jersey Civil Rights Defense Committee, *Voices of the Disappeared: An Investigative Report on New Jersey Immigrant Detention* (New Jersey Civil Rights Defense Committee, 2008).
58 Ibid.
59 Nina Bernstein, "Immigrant Detainee Dies, and a Life Is Buried, Too," *New York Times*, April 2, 2009, accessed August 20, 2016, http://www.nytimes.com/2009/04/03/nyregion/03detain.html?_r=0.
60 The United States does not deport people back to Cuba, but it also cannot hold them in detention indefinitely, as determined by the Supreme Court decision in *Clark et al. v. Martinez*. If the Supreme Court had made a different decision, this immigrant could very well still be in detention.
61 Correspondence to the NJCRDC.
62 Jonathan Miller, "Calling Off the Dogs," *NYTimes.com*, December 5, 2004, accessed August 20, 2016, http://query.nytimes.com/gst/fullpage.html?res=9E06E4D81F3EF936A35751C1A9629C8B63&pagewanted=all. Also see Daniel Zwerdling, "U.S. Detainee Abuse Cases Fall Through the Cracks," NPR, November 18, 2004, accessed August 20, 2016, http://www.npr.org/2004/11/18/4173701/u-s-detainee-abuse-cases-fall-through-the-cracks.
63 Ann-Marie Cusac, "Ill-Treatment on Our Shores," *Progressive*, February 28, 2002, accessed August 20, 2016, http://www.progressive.org/mag_cusacmarch02.

Chapter 5 Fighting on the Home Front

1 "McMansion" is a derogatory term used to describe some large new suburban homes. Evoking the fast-food chain McDonald's, McMansions are thought to be mass-produced, poorly made, unremarkable, stock suburban houses that nevertheless attempt to project wealth and affluence.
2 City of Bridgeton, "History of Bridgeton, New Jersey," accessed March 1, 2016, http://www.cityofbridgeton.com/history.php.
3 http://www.census.gov/quickfacts/table/PST045215/3407600. Accessed August 19, 2016.
4 City of Bridgeton, "History of Bridgeton, New Jersey."
5 Though not necessarily reflected in the official history, it is true that Bridgeton, and Cumberland County more broadly, draws Mexican immigrants because of demands for agricultural labor beyond nurseries or ornamental plant farms since the 1980s.

See https://www.census.gov/srd/papers/pdf/ex95–22.pdf, accessed November 5, 2016, for a discussion of the transition from Puerto Rican farm workers to Mexican farmworkers. According to this report, there has been a shift from sending regions within Mexico as more indigenous, Mixtec- and Zapotec-speaking Mexicans have replaced mestizo Mexicans. Also see, http://www.nytimes.com/2006/04/30/nyregion/nyregionspecial2/30njCOVER.html, accessed November 5, 2016, for explanations for late-1990s to mid-2000s immigration from Mexico. Some experts suggest that Mexico immigration into the Cumberland County region is actually a secondary migration as many immigrants began living and working in California then relocated to New Jersey in response to concerns about anti-immigrant policies like Proposition 187 being passed by the California electorate.

6 Dianne Harris, "Race, Space, and the Destabilization of Practice," *Landscape Journal* 26, no. 1 (2007): 2.

7 I share legal scholar Linda Bosniak's skepticism (and indeed the skepticism of many critical scholars) about citizenship. It's why I'm hesitant to name the kinds of activisms I see as about practices of or aspirations for citizenship. Bosniak argues, "Citizenship is commonly portrayed as the most desired of conditions, as the highest fulfillment of democratic and egalitarian aspiration. But this, I believe, reflects a habit of citizenship romanticism that tends to obscure the deeper challenges that the concept poses. These challenges derive from citizenship's basic ethical ambiguity. The idea of citizenship is commonly invoked to convey a state of democratic belonging or inclusion, yet this inclusion is usually premised on a conception of community that is bounded and exclusive." See Linda Bosniak, *The Citizen and the Alien: Dilemmas of Contemporary Membership* (Princeton, NJ: Princeton University Press, 2006), 1. By now, it should be clear that American citizenship is fundamentally premised on racialized, gendered, classed, and sexualized exclusions.

8 Genevieve Carpio, Clara Irazábal, and Laura Pulido, "Right to the Suburb? Rethinking Lefebvre and Immigrant Activism," *Journal of Urban Affairs* 33, no. 2 (2011): 187.

9 Ibid., 188.

10 Steve Pile, "Where Is the Subject? Geographical Imaginations and Spatializing Subjectivity," *Subjectivity* 23, no. 1 (2008): 210.

11 Irene Bloemraad, Kim Voss, and Taeku Lee, "The Protests of 2006: What They Were, How Do We Understand Them, Where Do We Go?," in *Rallying for Immigrant Rights: The Fight for Inclusion in 21st Century America*, ed. Kim Voss and Irene Bloemraad (Berkeley: University of California Press, 2011), 3–18.

12 Shannon Gleason, "Activism and Advocacy," in *Hidden Lies and Human Rights in the United States: Understanding the Controversies and Tragedies of Undocumented Immigration*, vol. 3, ed. Lois Ann Lorentzen (Santa Barbara, CA: Praeger, 2014), 208.

13 "Thousands Rally in Trenton for New Immigration Rights," News 12 New Jersey, March 20, 2006, accessed August 20, 2016, http://newjersey.news12.com/news/thousands-rally-in-trenton-for-new-immigration-rights-1.8246346?pts=297068.

14 Brian Williams, "Immigrant Rights Rallies Persist in U.S.," *Militant*, May 8, 2006, accessed August 20, 2016, http://www.themilitant.com/2006/7018/701803.html.

15 Carlos Avila, "Bipartisan Interest Increases in Immigration Issues in Election Year," *Trentonian*, February 24, 2013, accessed March 1, 2016, http://www.trentonian.com/article/TT/20130224/NEWS01/130229774.

16 Christopher Robbins, "Freehold Immigration Reform March Draws Activists from across N.J.," nj.com, October 5, 2013, accessed August 20, 2016, http://www.nj.com/monmouth/index.ssf/2013/10/freehold_immigration_reform_march_draws_activists_from_across_nj.html.

17 Selena Hill, "New Jersey Activists Protest Federal Deportation Raids, Demand Local Immigrant's Release," Latin Post RSS, February 2, 2016, accessed August 20, 2016, http://www.latinpost.com/articles/112837/20160202/new-jersey-activists-protest-federal-deportation-raids-demand-local-immigrants-release.htm.

18 Tom Baldwin, "Hispanic Leaders Urge Licenses Reconsidered," *Home News Tribune* (East Brunswick, New Jersey), May 21, 2005.

19 Kelly Flynn, "Immigration Reform Rally Seeks a New Jersey for All," philly.com, March 27, 2015, accessed August 20, 2016, http://articles.philly.com/2015-03-27/news/60520965_1_undocumented-drivers-undocumented-immigrants-police-officers.

20 Brent Johnson, "Lawmakers Push Bill to Give Unauthorized Immigrants N.J. Driver's Licenses," nj.com, November 16, 2015, accessed March 1, 2016, http://www.nj.com/politics/index.ssf/2015/11/bill_would_give_unauthorized_immigrants_nj_drivers.html.

21 Claude Brodesser-Akner, "Christie *Says He'll 'Never' Approve Giving Driver's Licenses to Undocumented N.J. Residents," nj.com*, April 28, 2015, accessed March 1, 2016, http://www.nj.com/politics/index.ssf/2015/04/christie_says_hell_never_approve_giving_drivers_li.html; Tom Haydon, "Union County Is First to Back Driver's Licenses for Unauthorized Immigrants," nj.com, May 29, 2015, accessed March 1, 2016, http://www.nj.com/union/index.ssf/2015/05/union_county_backs_drivers_licenses_for_immigrants.html.

22 Gleason, "Activism and Advocacy," 220.

23 Increased national visibility around Asian undocumented immigration can be attributed in part to the "coming out" of former *Washington Post* writer Jose Antonio Vargas. See Jose Antonio Vargas, "My Life as an Undocumented Immigrant," *New York Times*, June 25, 2011, accessed August 20, 2016, http://www.nytimes.com/2011/06/26/magazine/my-life-as-an-undocumented-immigrant.html. Undocumented Asian Americans have been formally organizing themselves around the country in groups such as ASPIRE (Asian Students Promoting Immigration Rights through Education) and RAISE (Revolutionizing Asian American Immigrant Stories in the East Coast). See Deepa Iyer, *We Too Sing America: South Asian, Arab, Muslim, and Sikh Immigrants Shape Our Multiracial Future* (New York: New Press, 2015), 120–140.

24 For an overview of the legislative struggle for the passage of the DREAM Act both nationally and on the state-level, see Michael Olivas, "The Political Economy of the Dream Act and the Legislative Process: A Case-Study of Comprehensive Immigration Reform," *Wayne Law Review* 55 (2009): 1757–1810.

25 Susan Donaldson James, "For Illegal Immigrants, a Harsh Lesson," *New York Times*, June 19, 2005; Miguel Perez and Elizabeth Llorente, "Tests Illegals Can't Pass; Legal, Financial Hurdles Block Colleges for Many Aliens," *Record* (Bergen County, New Jersey), August 28, 2005. Some scholars attribute the relative success

of the DREAM movement nationally to the support of faith-based organizations. See Marie T. Friedmann Marquardt and Manuel A. Vasquez, "'To Persevere in Our Struggles': Religion among Unauthorized Latino/a Immigrants in the United States," in *Hidden Lives and Human Rights in the United States: Understanding the Controversies and Tragedies of Undocumented Immigration*, ed. Lois Ann Lorentzen, vol. 3 (Santa Barbara, CA: Praeger, 2014), 303–323.

26 Colleen Roache, "Students Share Stories of Tuition Burdens," *Daily Targum* [Rutgers University, New Brunswick], November 16, 2010.

27 Jenna Portnoy, "Chris Christie Trumpets Signing of Dream Act in Union City," *Star-Ledger*, January 2014, accessed March 3, 2016, http://www.nj.com/politics/index.ssf/2014/01/chris_christie_trumpets_signing_of_dream_act_in_union_city.html.

28 For primary documents on the trade union movement's participation in efforts to exclude Asians from immigrating to the United States, see http://www.oac.cdlib.org/findaid/ark:/13030/c89k4c1p/entire_text/. There is a wealth of scholarship on the American labor movement's racism that I cannot comprehensively cite here, but for an account of unions' racism towards blacks, see Herbert Hill, "The Problem of Race in American Labor History." *Reviews in American History* 24, no. 2 (1996): 189–208. doi:10.1353/rah.1996.0037. Juan Perea examines the racist origins of the National Labor Relations Act, which was supported by the trade union movement. See Juan F. Perea, "The Echoes of Slavery: Recognizing the Racist Origins of the Agricultural and Domestic Worker Exclusion from the National Labor Relations Act," *SSRN Electronic Journal*. doi:10.2139/ssrn.1646496. For a discussion of the labor movement's efforts in recent decades to organize Latino workers, see Ruth Milkman, "Undocumented Immigrant Workers and the Labor Movement," in *Hidden Lives and Human Rights in the United States: Understanding the Controversies and Tragedies of Undocumented Immigration*, ed. Lois Ann Lorentzen, vol. 3 (Santa Barbara, CA: Praeger, 2014), 36.

29 Ruth Milkman, "Immigrant Workers, Precarious Work, and the US Labor Movement," *Globalizations* 8, no. 3 (2011): 361–372.

30 Bloemraad, Voss, and Lee, "The Protests of 2006," 5.

31 Anita Hamilton, "A Day without Immigrants: Making a Statement," *Time*, May 1, 2006, accessed August 20, 2016, http://content.time.com/time/nation/article/0,8599,1189899,00.html.

32 Chris Remington, "The Significance of May Day," PBS, May 2, 2013, accessed August 20, 2016, http://www.pbs.org/wnet/need-to-know/immigration-3/the-importance-of-may-day-across-communities/16881/.

33 Milkman, "Immigrant Workers, Precarious Work," 363.

34 See http://www.cbsnews.com/news/may-day-marches-held-across-the-us-seattle-los-angeles-san-francisco-portland/, and http://www.mercurynews.com/2013/04/30/immigration-reform-drawing-may-day-marches-rallies/ accessed November 5, 2016.

35 NPR staff, "Nation Sees Effects of 'Day without Immigrants," NPR, May 1, 2006, accessed August 20, 2016, http://www.npr.org/templates/story/story.php?storyId=5373661.

36 Taken from a flyer distributed at a March 3, 2007 meeting of the New Jersey May First Coalition. Information about the national conference can also be found at

http://www.iacenter.org/archive-2007/conf_02032007.htm. The International Action Center based in New York City called for the national conference.

37 Amy Goodman, "Mass Immigrant Rights Rally Planned for May Day 2007 One Year after Record Day of Protest," *Democracy Now!*, April 19, 2007, accessed March 8, 2016, http://www.democracynow.org/2007/4/19/mass_immigrant_rights_rally_planned_for.

38 Chris Kutalik, "As Immigrants Strike, Truckers Shut Down Nation's Largest Port," *Labor Notes*, September 28, 2006, accessed August 20, 2016, http://labornotes.org/2006/09/immigrants-strike-truckers-shut-down-nation%E2%80%99s-largest-port.

39 Robinson, William I. "'Aqui Estamos Y No Nos Vamos!' Global Capital and Immigrant Rights," *Race & Class* 48, no. 2 (2006): 77–91. doi:10.1177/0306396806069525.

40 Nazli Kibria, Cara Bowman, and Megan O'Leary, *Race and Immigration* (Malden, MA: Polity Press, 2014), 9.

41 Laura Pulido, "A Day without Immigrants: The Racial and Class Politics of Immigrant Exclusion," *Antipode* 39, no. 1 (2007): 2.

42 http://llanj.info/history/.

43 Elizabeth Llorente, "Immigrants Need Office That's on Their Side," *Record* [Bergen County], January 19, 2006.

44 http://www.njslom.org/immigration_task_force.html; also see http://politickernj.com/2007/08/governor-corzine-creates-blue-ribbon-panel-on-immigrant-policy/.

45 Elizabeth Llorente, "Corzine Forms Immigrant Commission," NorthJersey.com, January 13, 2010, accessed August 20, 2016, http://www.northjersey.com/news/panel-to-aid-transition-for-immigrants-1.973736; see http://www.nj.com/politics/index.ssf/2013/12/chris_christie_signs_bill_granting_in-state_tuition_to_nj_immigrants.html, accessed November 5, 2016, for Governor Chris Christie's signing of the New Jersey "Dream Act."

46 Ken Belson and Jill P. Capuzzo, "Towns Rethink Laws Against Illegal Immigrants," *New York Times*, September 26, 2007, accessed February 23 2015, http://www.nytimes.com/2007/09/26/nyregion/26riverside.html?oref=slogin&_r=0.

47 David Holthouse, "How Illegal Immigration Is Dividing a Town's Business Owners," CNN Money, April 18, 2008, accessed February 23, 2015, http://money.cnn.com/2008/04/17/smbusiness/illegal_immigration_dividing.fsb/.

48 Received through "New Jersey Immigration" Google groups listserv, August 30, 2006.

49 Richard Pearsall, "Latinos Praise Election Results in Riverside," *Courier Post* [Camden, New Jersey], November 15, 2006.

50 MaryAnn Spoto, "Town Settles Suit on Latino Laborers: Freehold Must Pay $278,000 in Fees and Respect Rights of Migrants," *Star-Ledger*, November 15, 2006.

51 Ibid.

52 Elizabeth Llorente and Miguel Perez, "Border 'Minutemen' Get Cold Shoulder in N.J.; Group Fighting Illegal Immigration Is Denied Meeting Place," *Record* (Bergen County, NJ), April 14, 2005, News sec.

53 See correspondence between Morristown and ICE, https://www.ice.gov/doclib/foia/memorandumsofAgreementUnderstanding/287gmorristownnj.pdf. Accessed March 11, 2016.

54 Minhaj Hassan, "Morristown Deputizing Plan Stirs up Outcry: Advocates Oppose Town Cops Serving as Immigration Agents," *Daily Record* [Hanover, New Jersey], March 27, 2007.

55 Jamie Duffy, "New Jersey's Latino Leadership Asks Obama to Rescind Morristown's 287(g) Status," nj.com, July 20, 2009, accessed August 20, 2016, http://www.nj.com/morristown/jamieduffy/index.ssf/2009/07/new_jerseys_latino_leadership.html.

56 Jamie Duffy, "Wind of the Spirit Immigration Forum Brings Out Experts on 287(g) in Morristown," nj.com, May 2, 2009, accessed August 20, 2016, http://www.nj.com/morristown/jamieduffy/index.ssf/2009/05/wind_of_the_spirit_forum_bring.html.

57 Michael Rispoli, "Morristown Police, Monmouth County Sheriffs Deputized as Immigration Officials," nj.com, July 10, 2009, accessed August 20, 2016, http://www.nj.com/news/index.ssf/2009/07/morristown_police_monmouth_cou.html.

58 See www.nj-civilrights.org, accessed September 11, 2007.

59 Ibid.

60 See NJ Immigrant and Workers Rights Coalition, "Press Statement by Maria Da Silva on Her Effort to Launch a Class-action Lawsuit against the Unconstitutional US Immigration System," News release, Newark, NJ, 2011. NJWIRC.

61 For an overview of the role of church-based groups in the sanctuary movement, see Lane Van Ham, "Sanctuary Revisited: Central American Refugee Assistance in the History of Church-based Immigrant Advocacy," *Political Theology* 10, no. 4 (2009): 621–645. For a discussion of how the movement was taken up by other sets of actors, see Stephen Nathan Haymes and Maria Vidal De Haymes, "Immigrant Sanctuary: Historical and Contemporary Movements," in *Hidden Lives and Human Rights in the United States: Understanding the Controversies and Tragedies of Undocumented Immigration*, ed. Lois Ann Lorentzen, vol. 3 (Santa Barbara, CA: Praeger, 2014), 257–274.

62 Hiroshi Motomura, "Immigration Outside the Law," *Columbia Law Review* 108 (2008): 2077.

63 Llorente and Perez, "Policing Illegal Immigration."

64 Editorial, "Cooler Heads in Hightstown," *New York Times*, May 13, 2007, accessed March 11, 2016, http://query.nytimes.com/gst/fullpage.html?res=9406E1DA1431F930A25756C0A9619C8B.

65 NOW, "Immigration on Main Street," PBS, October 19, 2007, accessed August 20, 2016, http://www.pbs.org/now/shows/342/.

66 Anthony Faiola. "Looking the Other Way on Immigrants," *Washington Post*, April 10, 2007, accessed August 21, 2016, http://www.washingtonpost.com/wp-dyn/content/article/2007/04/09/AR2007040901471.html.

67 Susan Donaldson James, "Old KKK Town Embraces Its Immigrants, Legal or Not," ABC News, June 28, 2007, accessed February 25, 2015, http://abcnews.go.com/TheLaw/story?id=3326379.

68 Bridget Clerkin, "Hightstown 'Don't Ask' Policy on Immigration Status Raises Concerns," nj.com, June 21, 2011, accessed August 21, 2016, http://www.nj.com/mercer/index.ssf/2011/06/hightstown_dont_ask_policy_on.html.

69 See http://www.centraljersey.com/news/princeton-mayor-stands-by-town-being-a-sanctuary-city-for/article_e6b0c4ce-29a6–11e5-be8d-33dfbc9bf0af.html, accessed November 5, 2016.

70 Warren Crandall, "Town Council Develops Resolution to Clarify Local Police Non-involvement in Federal Immigration Enforcement," *Daily Princetonian*, September 18, 2013, accessed August 21, 2016, http://dailyprincetonian.com/news/2013/09/town-council-develops-resolution-to-clarify-local-police-non-involvement-in-federal-immigration-enforcement/.

The current administration continues to stand firm with the city's policy. See Philip Sean Curran, "Princeton: Mayor Stands by Town Being a Sanctuary City for Illegal Immigrants," *CentralJersey.com*, July 14, 2015, accessed August 21, 2016, http://www.centraljersey.com/news/princeton-mayor-stands-by-town-being-a-sanctuary-city-for/article_e6b0c4ce-29a6–11e5-be8d-33dfbc9bf0af.html.

71 Fausto Giovanny Pinto, "Dover Passes Municipal I.D. Card Program, Third Municipality in State to Do so," nj.com, December 23, 2015, accessed August 17, 2016, http://www.nj.com/morris/index.ssf/2015/12/dover_passes_municipal_id_card_program.html.

72 POP Central Jersey, *Your Neighbors' Homes Were Invaded Last Week by Armed Men From the INS*, Avenel, NJ: POP Central Jersey.

73 This is taken from flyers and e-mail I received while doing organizing work with the NJCRDC and the NJMFC.

74 See http://www.counterpunch.org/2006/01/14/victory-at-passaic-county-jail/, accessed November 5, 2016.

75 Nicholas De Genova, "Conflicts of Mobility, and the Mobility of Conflict: Rightlessness, Presence, Subjectivity, Freedom," *Subjectivity* 29, no. S1 (2009): 445–466.

76 Ibid., 451.

77 Ned Kaufman, *Place, Race, and Story: Essays on the Past and Future of Historic Preservation* (New York: Routledge, 2009), 2.

78 http://www.historicbuildingarts.org/HistoricBuildingArts/HomeFronts_files/Guias%20lg%20newsletter.pdf, accessed November 5, 2016.

79 David Rivera, "Redefining Historic Sustainability in the Largest Historic District in the State," Address, *Celebrating Past, Present and Future: 2014 NJ History and Historic Preservation Conference*, Lincroft, NJ, June 5, 2014.

80 See http://www.historicbuildingarts.org/HistoricBuildingArts/HomeFronts.html, accessed November 5, 2016.

81 For more information see http://www.historicbuildingarts.org/HistoricBuildingArts/HOME.html, accessed November 5, 2016.

82 Flavia Alaya, "Redefining Historic Sustainability in the Largest Historic District in the State," Address, *Celebrating Past, Present and Future: 2014 NJ History and Historic Preservation Conference*, Lincroft, NJ, June 5, 2014.

83 See http://www.historicbuildingarts.org/HistoricBuildingArts/Ferracute_%26_Oberlin_Smith.html, accessed November 5, 2016.

84 Patrick W. Conahey, "Fairfield Township History—Gouldtown," nj.com, October 13, 2009, accessed August 21, 2016, http://www.nj.com/cumberland/voices/index.ssf/2009/10/fairfield_township_history_gou.html.

85 Becky M. Nicolaides and James Zarsadiaz, "Design Assimilation in Suburbia Asian Americans, Built Landscapes, and Suburban Advantage in Los Angeles's San Gabriel Valley since 1970," *Journal of Urban History* (2015): 1–40.

86 Kaufman, *Place, Race, and Story*, 52.

87 Henry C. Jackson, "Postville Immigration Raid Largest Ever in U.S.," TimesRepublican.com, May 14, 2008, accessed August 21, 2016, http://www.timesrepublican.com/page/content.detail/id/506160/Postville-immigration-raid-largest-ever-in-U-S-.html?nav=5005.

88 See https://www.hrw.org/reports/2007/us0707/un_bustamante_report.pdf.

Chapter 6 Conclusion

1 See Felix Frankfurter, "The Case of Sacco and Vanzetti," *The Atlantic*, March 1927, accessed August 18, 2016, http://www.theatlantic.com/magazine/archive/1927/03/the-case-of-sacco-and-vanzetti/306625/. Sacco and Vanzetti were Italian Americans who were executed after being convicted of robbery and murder. Many believe that the judge and jury were prejudiced against them for their political beliefs: they were known anarchists.

2 Kevin J. Mumford, *Newark: A History of Race, Rights, and Riots in America* (New York: New York University Press, 2007), 3.

3 "An Age of Transformation," *Economist*, May 31, 2008, 33. Also see Ali Modarres and Andrew Kirby, "The Suburban Question: Notes for a Research Program," *Cities* 27, no. 2 (2010): 114.

4 Lizabeth Cohen, *A Consumers' Republic: The Politics of Mass Consumption in Postwar America* (New York: Knopf, 2003), 197. See also Wendell Cox, "New Jersey: Still Suburbanizing," *Newgeography.com*, March 9, 2011, accessed August 17, 2016, http://www.newgeography.com/content/002101-new-jersey-still-suburbanizing.

There are some indications that there has been a reversal of suburbanization processes in some areas as well. See James W. Hughes and Joseph J. Seneca, "Opinion: The New Urban Sensibility," NorthJersey.com, November 23, 2014, accessed August 17, 2016, http://www.northjersey.com/opinion/opinion-guest-writers/the-new-urban-sensibility-1.1139872?page=1. However, I contend that suburban living is still at the core of how the American Dream and therefore how American neoliberal citizenship is defined.

5 Erika Lee, *At America's Gates: Chinese Immigration during the Exclusion Era, 1882–1943* (Chapel Hill: University of North Carolina Press, 2003).

6 Danika Medak-Saltzman and Antonio T. Tiongson Jr., "Racial Comparativism Reconsidered," *Critical Ethnic Studies* 1, no. 2 (2015).

7 Grace Kyungwon Hong and Roderick A. Ferguson, *Strange Affinities: The Gender and Sexual Politics of Comparative Racialization* (Durham, NC: Duke University Press, 2011).

8 Mumford, *Newark*, 3–4. Also, Carolina Alonso's dissertation, yet to be completed in the Department of Women and Gender Studies at Rutgers University, New Brunswick, offers an even deeper excavation of racial formations in Freehold.

9 Loïc Wacquant, "Crafting the Neoliberal State: Workfare, Prisonfare, and Social Insecurity," *Sociological Forum* 25, no. 2 (2010): 202.

10 Robert A. Beauregard, *When America Became Suburban* (Minneapolis: University of Minnesota Press, 2006), 144.

11 Saskia Sassen, *Expulsions: Brutality and Complexity in the Global Economy* (Cambridge, MA: Harvard University Press, 2014), 1.

12 Luis Guarnizo, "The Fluid, Multi-Scalar and Contradictory Construction of Citizenship," *Comparative Urban and Community Research* 10 (2012): 20.

13 Jodi Melamed, "The Spirit of Neoliberalism: From Racial Liberalism to Neoliberal Multiculturalism," *Social Text* 24, no. 4 (2006): 1.

14 Ibid., 2.

15 The struggle for truly just and humane immigration policy, however, will take far, far more than the kinds of local struggles I focus on in this book. In fact, struggling for immigration reform, as many critical migration scholars and migrant activists have long argued, can never be enough. The forces that fuel migration to begin with are forces rooted in the contemporary neoliberal, racial capitalist global order and require multi-scalar struggles that are beyond the scope of this book to address. I will leave it to activists like the ones I've worked with in the International Migrants Alliance to do that sort of analysis and organizing. See https://wearemigrants.net/.

16 Eduardo Bonilla-Silva, "The Essential Social Fact of Race," *American Sociological Review* 64, no. 6 (1999): 899.

Selected Bibliography

Adams, James Truslow. *The Epic of America*. Boston: Little, Brown, 1931.

Adler, Rachel H. "'But They Claimed to Be Police, Not La Migra': The Interaction of Residency Status, Class, and Ethnicity in a (Post–Patriot Act) New Jersey Neighborhood." *American Behavioral Scientist* 50, no. 1 (2006): 48–69.

Ahluwalia, Muninder K., and Laura Pellettiere. "Sikh Men Post-9/11: Misidentification, Discrimination, and Coping." *Asian American Journal of Psychology* 1, no. 4 (2010): 303–314.

Ahmad, Muneer. "Homeland Insecurities: Racial Violence the Day after September 11." *Social Text* 20, no. 3(2002): 101–115.

Alba, Richard D., Nancy A. Denton, Shu-Yin J. Leung, and John R. Logan. "Neighborhood Change under Conditions of Mass Immigration: The New York City Region, 1970–1990." *International Migration Review* 29, no. 3 (1995): 625. doi:10.2307/2547497.

Alba, Richard D., John R. Logan, and Brian J. Stults. "The Changing Neighborhood Contexts of the Immigrant Metropolis." *Social Forces* 79, no. 2 (2000): 587–621. doi:10.2307/2675510.

Alexander, Michelle. *The New Jim Crow: Mass Incarceration in the Age of Colorblindness*. New York: New Press, 2012.

Anand, Vivodh. "Unwelcome in Edison: Report of a Town's Xenophobic Conflation of Race and Religion." In *Democracy and Religion: Free Exercise and Diverse Visions*, edited by David W. Odell-Scott, 282. Kent, OH: Kent State University Press, 2004.

Ancheta, Angelo N. *Race, Rights, and the Asian American Experience*. New Brunswick, NJ: Rutgers University Press, 2006.

Anderson, Elijah. "'The White Space.'" *Sociology of Race and Ethnicity* 1, no. 1 (2015): 10–21.

Andrews, David L., Robert Pitter, Detlev Zwick, and Darren Ambrose. "Soccer, Race, and Suburban Space." In *Sporting Dystopias: The Making and Meaning of Urban Sport Cultures*, edited by Ralph C. Wilcox, 197. Albany: State University of New York Press, 2003.

Aptekar, Sofya. "Organizational Life and Political Incorporation of Two Asian Immigrant Groups: A Case Study." *Ethnic and Racial Studies* 32, no. 9 (2009): 1511–1533.

Bald, Vivek. *Bengali Harlem and the Lost Histories of South Asian America.* Cambridge, MA: Harvard University Press, 2013.

Baldoz, Rick. *The Third Asiatic Invasion: Empire and Migration in Filipino America, 1898–1946.* New York: New York University Press, 2011.

Barlow, Andrew L. *Between Fear and Hope: Globalization and Race in the United States.* Lanham, MD: Rowman & Littlefield, 2003.

Bayoumi, Moustafa. *How Does It Feel to Be a Problem?: Being Young and Arab in America.* New York: Penguin Press, 2008.

Beauregard, Robert A *When America Became Suburban.* Minneapolis: University of Minnesota Press, 2006.

Behdad, Ali. *A Forgetful Nation: On Immigration and Cultural Identity in the United States.* Durham, NC: Duke University Press, 2005).

Bloemraad, Irene, Anna Korteweg, and Gökçe Yurdakul. "Citizenship and Immigration: Multiculturalism, Assimilation, and Challenges to the Nation-State." *Annual Review of Sociology* 34, no. 1 (2008): 153–179.

Bloodsworth-Lugo, Mary K., and Carmen R. Lugo-Lugo. "Citizenship and the Browning of Terror." *Peace Review* 20, no. 3 (2008): 273–282.

Bonilla-Silva, Eduardo. "The Essential Social Fact of Race." *American Sociological Review* 64, no. 6 (1999): 899. doi:10.2307/2657410.

Bosniak, Linda. *The Citizen and the Alien: Dilemmas of Contemporary Membership.* Princeton, NJ: Princeton University Press, 2006.

Boustan, Leah Platt. "Was Postwar Suburbanization 'White Flight'? Evidence from the Black Migration." *Quarterly Journal of Economics* (2010): 417–443.

Brettell, Caroline B., and Faith G. Nibbs. "Immigrant Suburban Settlement and the 'Threat' to Middle Class Status and Identity: The Case of Farmers Branch." *International Migration* 49, no. 1 (2011): 1–30.

Cacho, Lisa Marie. *Social Death: Racialized Rightlessness and the Criminalization of the Unprotected.* New York: New York University Press, 2012.

Cainkar, Louise. "Post 9/11 Domestic Policies Affecting U.S. Arabs and Muslims: A Brief Review." *Comparative Studies of South Asia, Africa, and the Middle East* 24, no. 1 (2004): 247–251.

Capetillo-Ponce, Jorge. "Framing the Debate on Taxes and Undocumented Workers: A Critical Review of Texts Supporting Proenforcement Politics and Practices." In *Keeping Out the Other: A Critical Introduction to Immigration Enforcement Today*, edited by David Brotherton and Philip Kretsedemas, 314–333. New York: Columbia University Press, 2008.

Carpio, Genevieve, Clara Irazábal, and Laura Pulido. "Right to the Suburb? Rethinking Lefebvre and Immigrant Activism." *Journal of Urban Affairs* 33, no. 2 (2011): 185–208.

Chan, Sucheng. *Asian Americans: An Interpretive History.* Boston: Twayne, 1991.

Chatterjee, Boishampayan. "Did Suburbanization Cause Residential Segregation? Evidence from U.S. Metropolitan Areas." *Review of Applied Socio-Economic Research* 9, no. 1 (2015): 25–36.

Chavez, Leo R. "Latina Sexuality, Reproduction, and Fertility as Threats to the Nation." In *The Latino Threat: Constructing Immigrants, Citizens, and the Nation*, by Leo R. Chavez, 70–95. Stanford, CA: Stanford University Press, 2008.

———. *The Latino Threat: Constructing Immigrants, Citizens, and the Nation.* Stanford, CA: Stanford University Press, 2008.

Cheng, Wendy. *The Changs Next Door to the Diazes: Remapping Race in Suburban California.* Minneapolis: University of Minnesota Press, 2013.

———. "“Diversity” on Main Street? Branding Race and Place in the New ‘Majority-Minority’ Suburbs." *Identities* 17, no. 5 (2010): 458–486.

Choy, Catherine Ceniza. *Empire of Care: Nursing and Migration in Filipino American History.* Durham, NC: Duke University Press, 2003.

Cohen, Lizabeth. *A Consumers' Republic: The Politics of Mass Consumption in Postwar America.* New York: Knopf, 2003.

Coleman, Mathew. "Between Public Policy and Foreign Policy: U.S. Immigration Law Reform and the Undocumented Migrant." *Urban Geography* 29, no. 1 (2008): 4–28.

———. "What Counts as the Politics and Practice of Security, and Where? Devolution and Immigrant Insecurity after 9/11." *Annals of the Association of American Geographers* 99, no. 5 (2009): 904–913. doi:10.1080/00045600903245888.

Das Gupta, Monisha. *Unruly Immigrants: Rights, Activism, and Transnational South Asian Politics in the United States.* Durham, NC: Duke University Press, 2006.

Davies, Carole Boyce. "Deportable Subjects: U.S. Immigration Laws and the Criminalizing of Communism." *South Atlantic Quarterly* 100, no. 4 (2001): 949–966.

Davis, Mike. *Prisoners of the American Dream: Politics and Economy in the History of the US Working Class.* London: Verso, 1999.

De Genova, Nicholas. "Conflicts of Mobility, and the Mobility of Conflict: Rightlessness, Presence, Subjectivity, Freedom." *Subjectivity* 29, no. S1 (2009): 445–466. doi:10.1057/sub.2009.22.

———. "The Production of Culprits: From Deportability to Detainability in the Aftermath of 'Homeland Security.'" *Citizenship Studies* 11, no. 5 (2007): 421–448.

Del Carmen, Alejandro. "Profiling, Racial: Historical and Contemporary Perspectives." In *Encyclopedia of Race and Crime*, compiled by Helen Taylor Greene and Shaun L. Gabbidon, 666–668. Los Angeles: Sage, 2009.

"Delegation of Immigration Authority Section 287(g) Immigration and Nationality Act." Accessed February 2, 2015. http://www.ice.gov/factsheets/287g.

Denton, Stacy. "The Rural Past-in-Present and Postwar Sub/urban Progress." *American Studies* 53, no. 2 (2014): 119–140. doi:10.1353/ams.2014.0090.

Desforges, Luke, and Joanne Maddern. "Front Doors to Freedom, Portal to the Past: History at the Ellis Island Immigration Museum, New York." *Social & Cultural Geography* 5, no. 3 (2004): 437–457.

Dhingra, Pawan. *Life behind the Lobby: Indian American Motel Owners and the American Dream.* Stanford, CA: Stanford University Press, 2012.

Dinzey-Flores, Zaire Zenit. *Locked In, Locked Out: Gated Communities in a Puerto Rican City.* Philadelphia: University of Pennsylvania Press, 2013.

Doty, Roxanne Lynn. *The Law into Their Own Hands: Immigration and the Politics of Exceptionalism.* Tucson: University of Arizona Press, 2009.

Dow, Mark. *American Gulag: Inside U.S. Immigration Prisons.* Berkeley: University of California Press, 2004.

Dowling, Julie A., and Jonathan Xavier Inda. "Governing Migrant Illegality." Introduction to *Governing Immigration through Crime: A Reader*, edited by Julie A. Dowling and Jonathan Xavier Inda, 1–39. Stanford, CA: Stanford University Press, 2013.

Du Bois W. E. B. *The Souls of Black Folk: Essays and Sketches.* 1903. Reprint. Greenwich, CT: Fawcett Publications, 1961.

Ellis, Mark. "Unsettling Immigrant Geographies: US Immigration and the Politics of Scale." *Tijdschrift voor Economische en Sociale Geografie* 97, no. 1 (2006): 49–58.

Ellison, Ralph. *Invisible Man.* New York: Vintage International, 1995.

Esbenshade, Jill, and Barbara Obzurt. "Local Immigration Regulation: A Problematic Trend in Public Policy." *Harvard Journal of Hispanic Policy* 20 (2007–2008): 33–47.
Espiritu, Yen Le. *Asian American Women and Men: Labor, Laws, and Love.* Thousand Oaks, CA: Sage, 1997.
Faist, Thomas. "'Extension du Domiane de la Lutte': International Migration and Security Before and After September 11, 2001." *International Migration Review* 36 (2002): 7–14.
Foner, Nancy. *From Ellis Island to JFK: New York's Two Great Waves of Immigration.* New Haven, CT: Yale University Press, 2000.
Frey, William H. *Melting Pot Suburbs: A Census 2000 Study of Suburban Diversity.* Report. Washington DC: Brookings Institution Press, 2001.
Fujiwara, Lynn. *Mothers without Citizenship: Asian Immigrant Families and the Consequences of Welfare Reform.* Minneapolis: University of Minnesota Press, 2008.
Fussell, Elizabeth. "Warmth of the Welcome: Attitudes Toward Immigrants and Immigration Policy in the United States." *Annual Review of Sociology* 40, no. 1 (2014): 479–498. doi:10.1146/annurev-soc-071913-043325.
García, Carlos Sandoval. *Shattering Myths on Immigration and Emigration in Costa Rica.* Lanham, MD: Lexington Books, 2011.
Gemmell, Jon. *The Politics of South African Cricket.* New York: Routledge, 2004.
Gilbert, Liette. "Immigration as Local Politics: Re-bordering Immigration and Multiculturalism through Deterrence and Incapacitation." *International Journal of Urban and Regional Research* 33, no. 1 (2009): 26–42.
Gilmore, Ruth Wilson. "Fatal Couplings of Power and Difference: Notes on Racism and Geography." *Professional Geographer* 54, no. 1 (2002): 15–24.
Golash-Boza, Tanya Maria. *Immigration Nation: Raids, Detentions, and Deportations in Post-9/11 America.* Boulder, CO: Paradigm Publishers, 2012.
———. "Targeting Latino Men: Mass Deportation from the USA, 1998–2012." *Ethnic and Racial Studies* 38, no. 8 (2014): 1221–1228.
Gonzales, Alfonso. *Reform without Justice: Latino Migrant Politics and the Homeland Security State.* New York: Oxford University Press, 2014.
Greason, Walter. *Suburban Erasure: How the Suburbs Ended the Civil Rights Movement in New Jersey.* Madison, NJ: Fairleigh Dickinson University Press, 2013.
Grosfoguel, Ramón. *Colonial Subjects: Puerto Ricans in a Global Perspective.* Berkeley: University of California Press, 2003.
Guarnizo, Luis. "The Fluid, Multi-Scalar, and Contradictory Construction of Citizenship." *Comparative Urban and Community Research* 10 (2012): 11–37.
Gutierrez, Elizabeth. "The 'Dotbuster' Attacks: Hate Crime against Asian Indians in Jersey City, New Jersey." *Middle States Geographer* (1996): 30–38.
Hancock, Ange-Marie. *The Politics of Disgust: The Public Identity of the Welfare Queen.* New York: New York University Press, 2004.
Hanlon, Bernadette. "A Typology of Inner-Ring Suburbs: Class, Race, and Ethnicity in U.S. Suburbia." *City & Community* 8, no. 3 (2009): 221–246.
Hardwick, Susan W. "Toward a Suburban Immigrant Nation." In *Twenty-First-Century Gateways: Immigrant Incorporation in Suburban America,* by Audrey Singer, Susan Wiley Hardwick, and Caroline Brettell, 31–52. Washington, DC: Brookings Institution Press, 2008.
Harris, Dianne. "Race, Space, and the Destabilization of Practice." *Landscape Journal* 26, no. 1 (2007): 1–9.

Harris, Richard. *Building a Market: The Rise of the Home Improvement Industry, 1914–1960.* Chicago: University of Chicago Press, 2012.

Haymes, Stephen Nathan, and Maria Vidal De Haymes. "Immigrant Sanctuary: Historical and Contemporary Movements." In *Hidden Lives and Human Rights in the United States: Understanding the Controversies and Tragedies of Undocumented Immigration,* edited by Lois Ann Lorentzen, vol. 3, 257–274. Santa Barbara, CA: Praeger, 2014.

Hernández, Ramona. *The Mobility of Workers under Advanced Capitalism: Dominican Migration to the United States.* New York: Columbia University Press, 2002.

Hernández-León, Rubén. *Metropolitan Migrants: The Migration of Urban Mexicans to the United States.* Berkeley: University of California Press, 2008.

Hing, Bill Ong. *Making and Remaking Asian America through Immigration Policy, 1850–1990.* Stanford, CA: Stanford University Press, 1993.

HoSang, Daniel. *Racial Propositions: Ballot Initiatives and the Making of Postwar California.* Berkeley: University of California Press, 2010,

Howard, Ebenezer, and Frederic J. Osborn. *Garden Cities of To-morrow.* 1898. Reprint. Cambridge, MA: MIT Press, 1965.

Hsiao, Andrew. "The Hidden History of Asian-American Activism in New York City." *Social Policy* 28, no. 4 (1998): 23–31.

Hughey, Matthew W. "White Backlash in the 'Post-Racial' United States." *Ethnic and Racial Studies* 37, no. 5 (2014): 721–730.

Itzigsohn, José. *Encountering American Faultlines: Race, Class, and the Dominican Experience in Providence.* New York: Russell Sage Foundation, 2009.

Iyer, Deepa. *We Too Sing America: South Asian, Arab, Muslim, and Sikh Immigrants Shape Our Multiracial Future.* New York: New Press, 2015.

Jackson, Kenneth T. *Crabgrass Frontier: The Suburbanization of the United States.* New York: Oxford University Press, 1985.

Jacob, Charles E. "Reaganomics: The Revolution in American Political Economy." *Law and Contemporary Problems* 48, no. 4 (1985): 7.

Jacobson, Robin Dale. *The New Nativism: Proposition 187 and the Debate over Immigration.* Minneapolis: University of Minnesota Press, 2008.

Johnson, Heather Beth. *The American Dream and the Power of Wealth: Choosing Schools and Inheriting Inequality in the Land of Opportunity.* New York: Routledge, 2006.

Jones-Correa, Michael. "The Origins and Diffusion of Racial Restrictive Covenants." *Political Science Quarterly* 115, no. 4 (2001): 541–568.

Kalita, S. Mitra. *Suburban Sahibs: Three Immigrant Families and Their Passage from India to America.* New Brunswick, NJ: Rutgers University Press, 2003.

Kaplan, Amy. "Violent Belongings and the Question of Empire Today: Presidential Address to the American Studies Association, Hartford, Connecticut, October 17, 2003." *American Quarterly* 56, no. 1 (2004): 1–18. doi:10.1353/aq.2004.0010.

Katznelson, Ira. *When Affirmative Action Was White: An Untold History of Racial Inequality in Twentieth-Century America.* New York: W. W. Norton, 2005.

Kaufman, Ned. *Place, Race, and Story: Essays on the Past and Future of Historic Preservation.* New York: Routledge, 2009.

Kibria, Nazli. "Not Asian, Black or White? Reflections on South Asian American Racial Identity." *Amerasia Journal* 22, no. 2 (1996): 77–86. doi:10.17953/amer.22.2.m363851655m22432.

Kibria, Nazli, Cara Bowman, and Megan O'Leary. *Race and Immigration.* Malden, MA: Polity Press, 2014.

Kim, Claire J. "The Racial Triangulation of Asian Americans." *Politics & Society* 27, no. 1 (1999): 105–138. doi:10.1177/0032329299027001005.

Kim, Joon K. "California's Agribusiness and the Farm Labor Question: The Transition from Asian to Mexican Labor, 1919–1939." *Atzlán: A Journal of Chicano Studies* 37, no. 2 (2012): 43–72.

Kirp, David L., John P. Dwyer, and Larry A. Rosenthal. *Our Town: Race, Housing, and the Soul of Suburbia.* New Brunswick, NJ: Rutgers University Press, 1995.

Kurien, P. A. "Multiculturalism and 'American' Religion: The Case of Hindu Indian Americans." *Social Forces* 85, no. 2 (2006): 723–741.

Kushner, David. *Levittown: Two Families, One Tycoon, and the Fight for Civil Rights in America's Legendary Suburb.* New York: Walker and Company, 2009.

LaBrack, Bruce, and Karen Leonard. "Conflict and Compatibility in Punjabi-Mexican Immigrant Families in Rural California, 1915–1965." *Journal of Marriage and Family* 46, no. 3 (1984): 527–537.

Lacayo, Richard. "Suburban Legend: William Levitt." *Time*, July 3, 1950.

Lee, Erika. *At America's Gates: Chinese Immigration during the Exclusion Era, 1882–1943.* Chapel Hill: University of North Carolina Press, 2003.

Levin, Jack, and Jack McDevitt. *Hate Crimes Revisited: America's War against Those Who Are Different.* Boulder, CO: Westview, 2002.

Li, Wei. *Ethnoburb: The New Ethnic Community in Urban America.* Honolulu: University of Hawai'i Press, 2009.

Lipsitz, George. "The Racialization of Space and the Spatialization of Race: Theorizing the Hidden Architecture of Landscape." *Landscape Journal* 26, no. 1 (2007): 10–23.

———. *The Possessive Investment in Whiteness: How White People Profit from Identity Politics.* Philadelphia: Temple University Press, 1998.

Loewen, James W. *Sundown Towns: A Hidden Dimension of American Racism.* New York: New Press, 2005.

Logan, John R., Wenquan Zhang, and Richard D. Alba. "Immigrant Enclaves and Ethnic Communities in New York and Los Angeles." *American Sociological Review* 67, no. 2 (2002): 299.

Londoño, Johana, and Arlene Davila. "Race and the Cultural Spaces of Neoliberalism: Introduction." *Identities* 17, no. 5 (2010): 455–457. doi:10.1080/1070289x.2010.527584.

Low, Setha. "Behind the Gates: Life, Security, and the Pursuit of Happiness in Fortress America." In *The Suburb Reader*, edited by Becky M. Nicolaides and Andrew Wiese, 460–468. New York: Taylor and Francis Group, 2006.

Luibheid, Eithne. "Sexuality, Migration, and the Shifting Line between Legal and Illegal Status." *GLQ: A Journal of Lesbian and Gay Studies* 14, no. 2–3 (2008): 289–315. doi:10.1215/10642684-2007-034.

Maira, Sunaina. *Missing: Youth, Citizenship, and Empire after 9/11.* Durham, NC: Duke University Press, 2009.

Majumdar, Boria, and Sean Brown. "Why Baseball, Why Cricket? Differing Nationalisms, Differing Challenges." *International Journal of the History of Sport* 24, no. 2 (2007): 139–156. doi:10.1080/09523360601045732.

Martos, Sofia D. "Coded Codes: Discriminatory Intent, Modern Political Mobilization, and Local Immigration Ordinances." *NYU Law Review* 85 (2010): 2099–2137.

Matsumoto, Noriko. "Constructing Multiethnic Space: East Asian Immigration in Fort Lee, New Jersey." PhD diss., Graduate Center, City University of New York, 2012.

Mccarthy, Cameron, Alicia P. Rodriguez, Ed Buendia, Shuaib Meacham, Stephen David, Heriberto Godina, K. E. Supriya, and Carrie Wilson-Brown. "Danger in the Safety Zone: Notes on Race, Resentment, and the Discourse of Crime, Violence, and Suburban Security." *Cultural Studies* 11, no. 2 (1997): 274–295. doi:10.1080/09502389700490151.

McGirr, Lisa. *Suburban Warriors: The Origins of the New American Right.* Princeton, NJ: Princeton University Press, 2001.

McKenzie, Evan. "Privatopia: Homeowner Associations and the Rise of Residential Private Government." In *The Suburb Reader*, edited by Becky M. Nicolaides and Andrew Wiese, 455–459. New York: Taylor and Francis Group, 2006.

McKinley, Jesse. "Arizona Law Takes a Toll on Nonresident Students." *New York Times*, January 27, 2008.

Medak-Saltzman, Danika, and Antonio T. Tiongson Jr. "Racial Comparativism Reconsidered." *Critical Ethnic Studies* 1, no. 2 (2015): 1.

Melamed, J. "The Spirit of Neoliberalism: From Racial Liberalism to Neoliberal Multiculturalism." *Social Text* 24, no. 4 (2006): 1–24. doi:10.1215/01642472-2006-009.

Melendy, H. Brett. *Asians in America: Filipinos, Koreans, and East Indians.* Boston: Twayne, 1977.

Menjívar, Cecilia, and Leisy J. Abrego. "Legal Violence: Immigration Law and the Lives of Central American Immigrants 1." *American Journal of Sociology* 117, no. 5 (2012): 1380–1421. doi:10.1086/663575.

Milkman, Ruth. "Undocumented Immigrant Workers and the Labor Movement." In *Hidden Lives and Human Rights in the United States: Understanding the Controversies and Tragedies of Undocumented Immigration*, edited by Lois Ann Lorentzen, vol. 3, 36–53. Santa Barbara, CA: Praeger, 2014.

Misir, Deborah N. "The Murder of Navroze Mody: Race, Violence, and the Search for Order." In *Contemporary Asian America: A Multidisciplinary Reader*, edited by Min Zhou and James V. Gatewood, 501–517. New York: New York University Press, 2000.

Mize, Ronald L., and Alicia C. S. Swords. *Consuming Mexican Labor: From the Bracero Program to NAFTA.* Toronto: University of Toronto Press, 2010.

Modarres, Ali, and Andrew Kirby. "The Suburban Question: Notes for a Research Program." *Cities* 27, no. 2 (2010): 114–121.

Motomura, Hiroshi. "Immigration Outside the Law." *Columbia Law Review* 108 (2008): 2037–097. Accessed February 23, 2015.

Muhammad, Khalil Gibran. *The Condemnation of Blackness: Race, Crime, and the Making of Modern Urban America.* Cambridge, MA: Harvard University Press, 2010.

Mumford, Kevin J. *Newark: A History of Race, Rights, and Riots in America.* New York: New York University Press, 2007.

Newton, Lina. *Illegal, Alien, or Immigrant: The Politics of Immigration Reform.* New York: New York University Press, 2008.

Nicolaides, Becky M., and Andrew Wiese. "Imagining Suburbia: Visions and Plans from the Turn of the Century." In *The Surburb Reader*, edited by Becky M. Nicolaides and Andrew Wiese, 164–165. New York: Routledge, 2006.

Olivas, Michael. "The Political Economy of the Dream Act and the Legislative Process: A Case-Study of Comprehensive Immigration Reform." *Wayne Law Review* 55 (2009): 1757–1810.

Oliveri, Rigel C. "Between a Rock and a Hard Place: Landlords, Latinos, Anti-illegal Immigrant Ordinances, and Housing Discrimination." *Vanderbilt Law Review* 62, no. 55 (2009): 55–125.

Orfield, Gary. "School Desegregation after Two Generations: Race, Schools, and Opportunity in Urban Society." In *Race in America: The Struggle for Equality*, edited by Herbert Hill and James E. Jones, 240–262. Madison: University of Wisconsin Press, 1993.

Ortner, Sherry B. *New Jersey Dreaming: Capital, Culture, and the Class of '58*. Durham, NC: Duke University Press, 2003.

Perea, Juan F. "The Statue of Liberty: Notes from Behind the Gilded Door." In *Immigrants Out!: The New Nativism and the Anti-immigrant Impulse in the United States*, edited by Juan F. Perea, 44–58. New York: New York University Press, 1997.

Perez, Miguel, and Elizabeth Llorente. "Tests Illegals Can't Pass; Legal, Financial Hurdles Block Colleges for Many Aliens." *Record* (Bergen County, New Jersey), August 28, 2005, A01.

Pile, Steve. "Where Is the Subject? Geographical Imaginations and Spatializing Subjectivity." *Subjectivity* 23, no. 1 (2008): 206–218.

Pitter, Robert, Detlev Zwick, and Darren Ambrose. "Soccer, Race, and Suburban Space." In *Sporting Dystopias: The Making and Meanings of Urban Sport Cultures*, edited by David L. Andrews, 197–220. Albany: State University of New York Press, 2003.

Portes, Alejandro, and Rubén G. Rumbaut. *Immigrant America: A Portrait*. Berkeley: University of California Press, 1990.

Prashad, Vijay. *The Karma of Brown Folk*. Minneapolis: University of Minnesota Press, 2000.

Pulido, Laura. "A Day Without Immigrants: The Racial and Class Politics of Immigrant Exclusion." *Antipode* 39, no. 1 (2007): 1–7. doi:10.1111/j.1467–8330.2007.00502.x.

Rahim, Abdur. *Canadian Immigration and South Asian Immigrants*. Xlibris, 2014.

Rajan, Paul R., and Kavita Bindra. "Immigration and Legal Matters K-1 Visas Fiancé of U.S. Citizens." *Tiranga in NJ*, November 30, 2006.

Ramakrishnan, S. Karthick, and Tom (Tak) Wong. "Partisanship, Not Spanish: Explaining Municipal Ordinances Affecting Undocumented Immigrants." In *Taking Local Control: Immigration Policy Activism in U.S. Cities and States*, edited by Monica Varsanyi, 73–92. Stanford, CA: Stanford University Press, 2010.

Rana, Junaid Akram. *Terrifying Muslims: Race and Labor in the South Asian Diaspora*. Durham, NC: Duke University Press, 2011.

Rodriguez, Robyn Magalit. *Migrants for Export: How the Philippine State Brokers Labor to the World*. Minneapolis: University of Minnesota Press, 2010.

Roediger, David R. *Working Toward Whiteness: How America's Immigrants Became White*. New York: Basic Books, 2005.

Saito, Leland T. "From 'Blighted' to 'Historic': Race, Economic Development, and Historic Preservation in San Diego, California." *Urban Affairs Review* 45, no. 166 (Nov. 2009): 166–187.

Salas, Lorraine Moya, Cecilia Ayón, and Maria Gurrola. "Estamos Traumados: The Effect of Anti-Immigrant Sentiment and Policies on the Mental Health of Mexican Immigrant Families." *Journal of Community Psychology* 41, no. 8 (2013): 1005–1020. doi:10.1002/jcop.21589.

Salmore, Barbara G., and Stephen A. Salmore. *New Jersey Politics and Government: The Suburbs Come of Age*. 4th ed. New Brunswick, NJ: Rutgers University Press, 2013.

Sassen, Saskia. *Expulsions: Brutality and Complexity in the Global Economy*. Cambridge, MA: Harvard University Press, 2014.

Sexton, Jared, and Elizabeth Lee. "Figuring the Prison: Prerequisites of Torture at Abu Ghraib." *Antipode* 38, no. 5 (2006): 1005–1022.

Shah, Nayan. *Contagious Divides: Epidemics and Race in San Francisco's Chinatown.* Berkeley: University of California Press, 2001.

Shaw, Douglas V. *Immigration and Ethnicity in New Jersey History.* Trenton: New Jersey Historical Commission, 1994.

Sheikh, Irum. "Racializing, Criminalizing, and Silencing 9/11 Deportees." In *Keeping Out the Other: A Critical Introduction to Immigration Enforcement Today*, edited by David Brotherton and Philip Kretsedemas, 81–107. New York: Columbia University Press, 2008.

Singer, Audrey. "Twenty-First Century Gateways: An Introduction." In *Twenty-First-Century Gateways: Immigrant Incorporation in Suburban America*, by Audrey Singer, Susan Wiley Hardwick, and Caroline Brettell, 3–30. Washington, DC: Brookings Institution Press, 2008.

Taibbi, Matt. *The Divide: American Injustice in the Age of the Wealth Gap.* New York: Spiegel and Grau, 2014.

Teaford, Jon C. *The American Suburb: The Basics.* New York: Routledge, 2008.

Tuan, Mia. *Forever Foreigners or Honorary Whites?: The Asian Ethnic Experience Today.* New Brunswick, NJ: Rutgers University Press, 1998.

Tuttle, Brad R. *How Newark Became Newark: The Rise, Fall, and Rebirth of an American City.* New Brunswick, NJ: Rutgers University Press, 2009.

Van Ham, Lane. "Sanctuary Revisited: Central American Refugee Assistance in the History of Church-based Immigrant Advocacy." *Political Theology* 10, no. 4 (2009): 621–645. doi:10.1558/poth.v10i4.621.

Varsanyi, Monica W. "Immigration Policing Through the Backdoor: City Ordinances, the 'Right to the City,' and the Exclusion of Undocumented Day Laborers." *Urban Geography* 29, no. 1 (2008): 29–52.

———. "Neoliberalism and Nativism: Local Anti-Immigrant Policy Activism and an Emerging Politics of Scale." *International Journal of Urban and Regional Research* (2010).

Vaughan, Jessica M., and James R. Edwards Jr. *The 287(g) Program Protecting Home Towns and Homeland.* Washington DC: Center for Immigration Studies, 2009.

Voss, Kim, Irene Bloemraad, and Taeku Lee. "The Protests of 2006: What They Were, How Do We Understand Them, Where Do We Go?" In *Rallying for Immigrant Rights: The Fight for Inclusion in 21st Century America*, edited by Kim Voss and Irene Bloemraad, 3–18. Berkeley: University of California Press, 2011.

Wacquant, Loïc. "Crafting the Neoliberal State: Workfare, Prisonfare, and Social Insecurity 1." *Sociological Forum* 25, no. 2 (2010): 197–220.

Walker, Kyle E., and Helga Leitner. "The Variegated Landscape of Local Immigration Policies in the United States." *Urban Geography* 32, no. 2 (2011): 156–178.

Wallace, Mike. "Hijacking History: Ronald Reagan and the Statue of Liberty." *Radical History Review*, no. 37 (1987): 119–130.

Walters, William. "Secure Borders, Safe Haven, Domopolitics." *Citizenship Studies* 8, no. 3 (2004): 237–260.

Williams, Brian. "Immigrant Rights Rallies Persist in U.S." *Militant* [New York], May 8, 2006. Accessed 20 Aug. 2016. http://www.themilitant.com/2006/7018/701803.html.

Williams, Jack. *Cricket and Race.* New York: Bloomsbury Academic, 2001.

Wilson, Jill H., Andrey Singer, and Brooke DeRenzis. "Growing Pains: Local Response to Recent Immigrant Settlement in Suburban Washington D.C." In *Taking Local Control: Immigration Policy Activism in U.S. Cities and States*, edited by Monica Varsanyi, 193–215. Stanford, CA: Stanford University Press, 2010.

Wong, Tom K. "287(g) and the Politics of Interior Immigration Control in the United States: Explaining Local Cooperation with Federal Immigration Authorities." *Journal of Ethnic and Migration Studies* 38, no. 5 (2012): 737–756.

Wright, Gwendolyn. *Building the Dream: A Social History of Housing in America.* New York: Pantheon Books, 1981.

Yip, Tiffany, Gilbert C. Gee, and David T. Takeuchi. "Racial Discrimination and Psychological Distress: The Impact of Ethnic Identity and Age among Immigrant and United States–born Asian Adults." *Developmental Psychology* 44, no. 3 (2008): 787–800. doi:10.1037/0012–1649.44.3.787.

Zavella, Patricia. "The Tables Are Turned: Immigration, Poverty, and Social Conflict in California Communities." In *Immigrants Out! The New Nativism and the Anti-Immigrant Impulse in the United States*, edited by Juan F. Perea, 136–161. New York: New York University Press, 1997.

Index

About the Author

ROBYN MAGALIT RODRIGUEZ earned her PhD in sociology at the University of California, Berkeley, and currently serves on the faculty of the Department of Asian American Studies at the University of California, Davis. Previously, she was a faculty member of the Sociology Department at Rutgers University, New Brunswick, New Jersey.

Rodriguez is an Asian migration expert, approaching it from local, national, and transnational perspectives. Her writing has focused significantly on the Philippine labor diaspora. Rodriguez's first book, *Migrants for Export: How the Philippine State Brokers Labor to the World* (2010), received an honorable mention for best social science book by the Association for Asian American Studies. However, Rodriguez has a firm grasp of the broader issues migration from, to, within, and beyond the Asia-Pacific region engenders due to her scholarship and collaborative work as reflected in her coedited anthology (with Ulla Berg) *Transnational Citizenship Across the Americas* (2014). In addition to her books, Rodriguez has published over thirty book chapters, academic articles, and journalistic pieces. The key topics her research explores are the political economy and governance of labor migration, on one hand, and the question of rights and citizenship for migrant workers on the other.

Alongside her scholarly work, Rodriguez has worked as an immigrant rights and antiracism activist. Currently she is working closely with the National Alliance for Filipino Concerns (NAFCON) and Migrante Northern California to support the self-organizing efforts of Filipino migrant workers in the San Francisco Bay Area.